SHADOWMAN

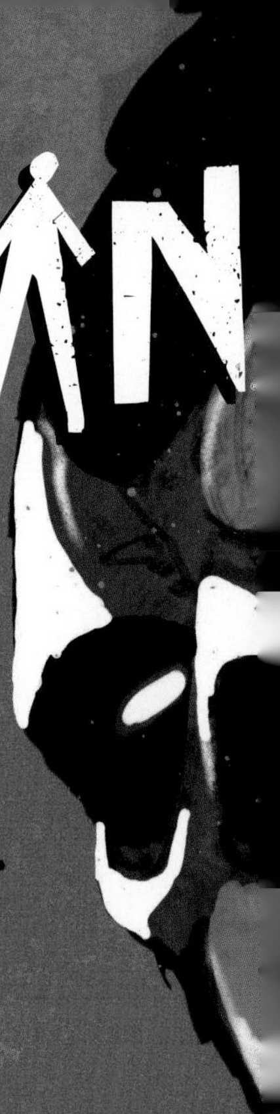

WRITER
CULLEN BUNN

ARTIST
PEDRO ANDREO
(ASSISTANT: ÁLVARO DE MIGUEL, #7-8)

COLORIST
JORDIE BELLAIRE

LETTERER
CLAYTON COWLES

SERIES COVERS
JON DAVIS-HUNT

ASSISTANT EDITOR
AUDREY MEEKER

SENIOR EDITOR
LYSA HAWKINS

GALLERY
PEDRO ANDREO
JONATHAN MARKS BARRAVECCHIA
JORDIE BELLAIRE
DAN BRERETON
ANDREW DALHOUSE
ADAM GORHAM
ADAM POLLINA
MICO SUAYAN
CHRISTIAN WARD

COLLECTION COVER ART
JON DAVIS-HUNT

COLLECTION FRONT ART
CHRISTIAN WARD

COLLECTION BACK COVER ART
PEDRO ANDREO with ANDREW DALHOUSE

COLLECTION EDITOR
IVAN COHEN

COLLECTION DESIGNER
STEVE BLACKWELL

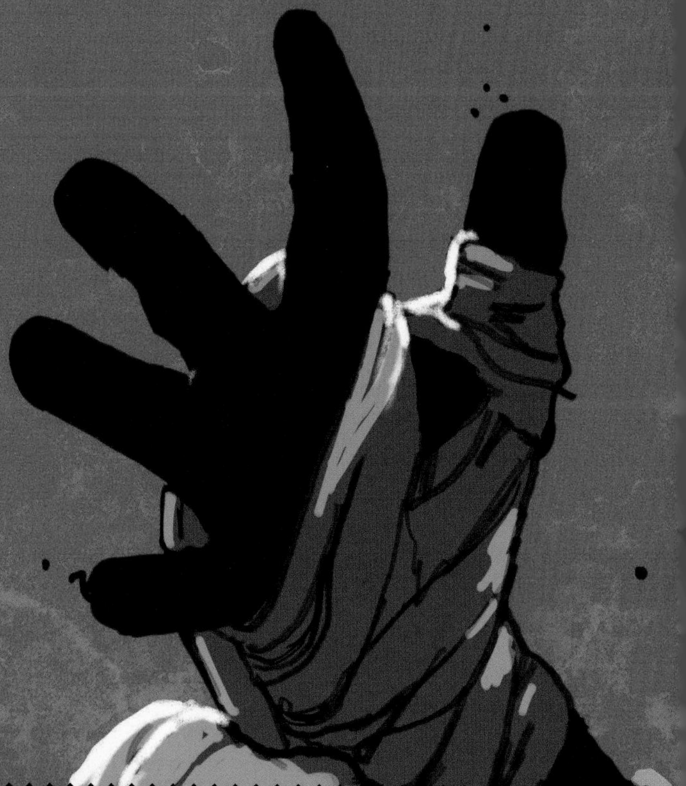

VALIANT

Dan Mintz Chairman **Fred Pierce** Publisher **Walter Black** VP Operations **Gregg Katzman** Director of Marketing, Valiant Publishing
Travis Escarfullery Director of Design & Production **Peter Stern** Director of International Publishing & Merchandising
Rob Levin Executive Editor **Lysa Hawkins** Senior Editor **Audrey Meeker** Assistant Editor **Jeff Walker** Production & Design Manager
John Petrie Senior Manager - Sales & Merchandising **Danielle Ward** Sales Manager **Nic Osborn** Marketing Coordinator
Russ Brown President, Consumer Products, Promotions & Ad Sales

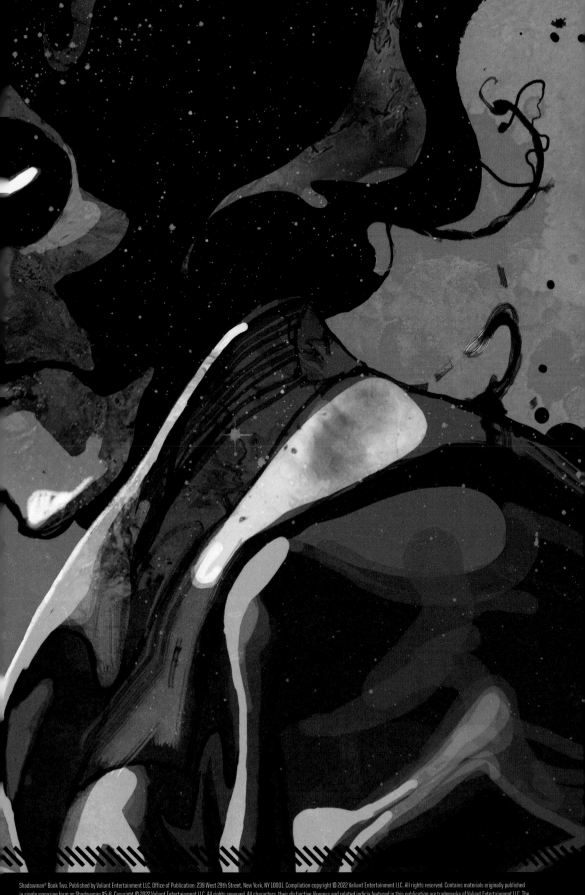

Shadowman® Book Two. Published by Valiant Entertainment LLC. Office of Publication: 239 West 29th Street, New York, NY 10001. Compilation copyright © 2022 Valiant Entertainment LLC. All rights reserved. Contains materials originally published in single magazine form as Shadowman #5-8. Copyright © 2022 Valiant Entertainment LLC. All rights reserved. All characters, their distinctive likeness and related indicia featured in this publication are trademarks of Valiant Entertainment LLC. The stories, characters, and incidents featured in this publication are entirely fictional. Valiant Entertainment does not read or accept unsolicited submissions of ideas, stories, or artwork. Printed in Korea. First Printing. ISBN: 9781682154267

A musician from New Orleans, Jack Boniface is Shadowman. With the help of the shadow loa, Shadowman is one of the few who can protect the earth from the demons of the Deadside. Although the shadow loa has gifted him with incredible supernatural abilities, his powers come with a responsibility that's more than he bargained for...

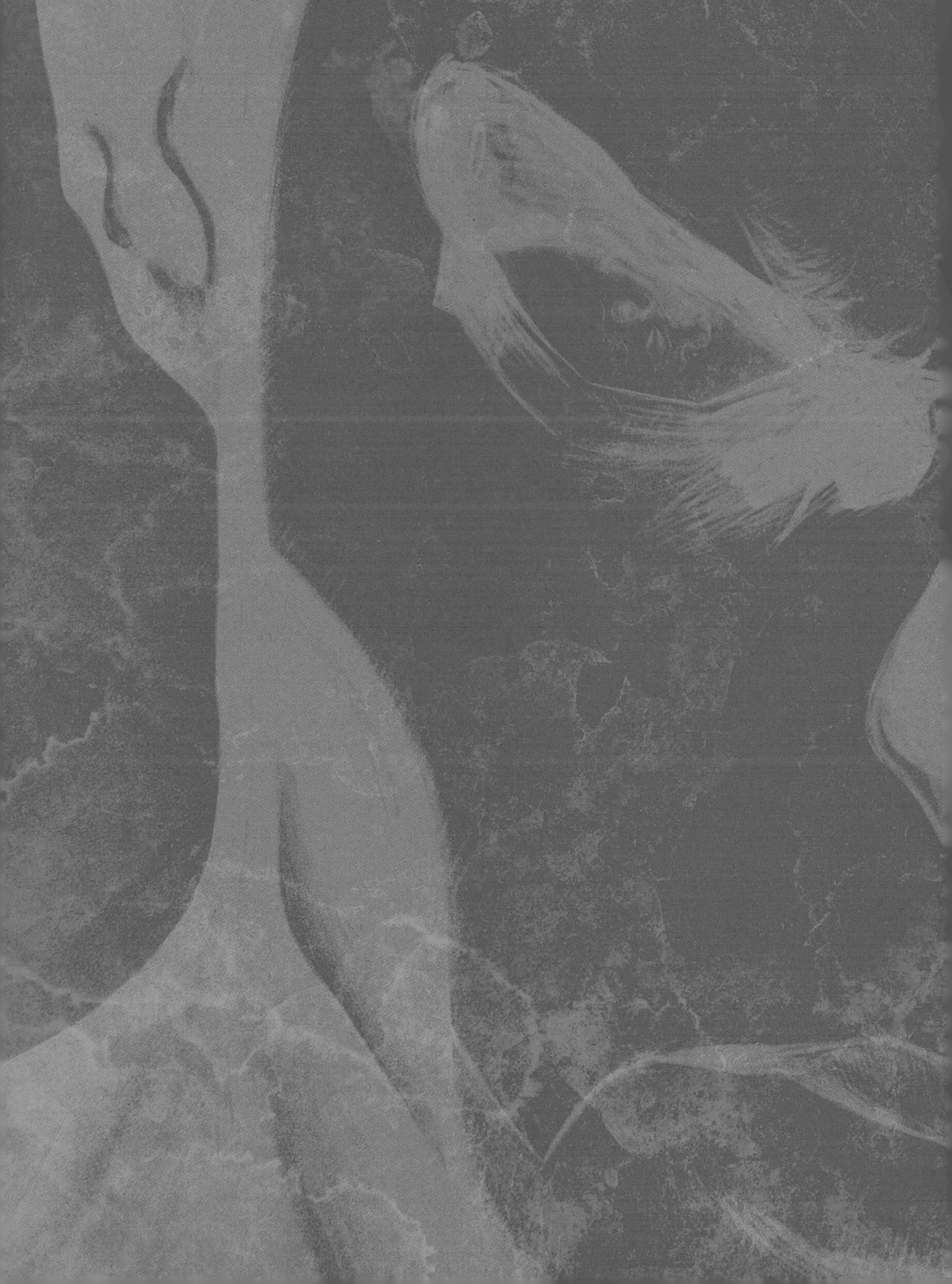

SHADOWMAN®
DEADSIDE WAR PART 1
CULLEN BUNN
PEDRO ANDREO
JORDIE BELLAIRE
CLAYTON COWLES

SHADOWMAN #5
"DEADSIDE WAR: PART 1"

WRITER: Cullen Bunn
ARTIST: Pedro Andreo
COLORIST: Jordie Bellaire
LETTERER: Clayton Cowles
COVER ARTIST: Jon Davis-Hunt
ASSISTANT EDITOR: Audrey Meeker
SENIOR EDITOR: Lysa Hawkins

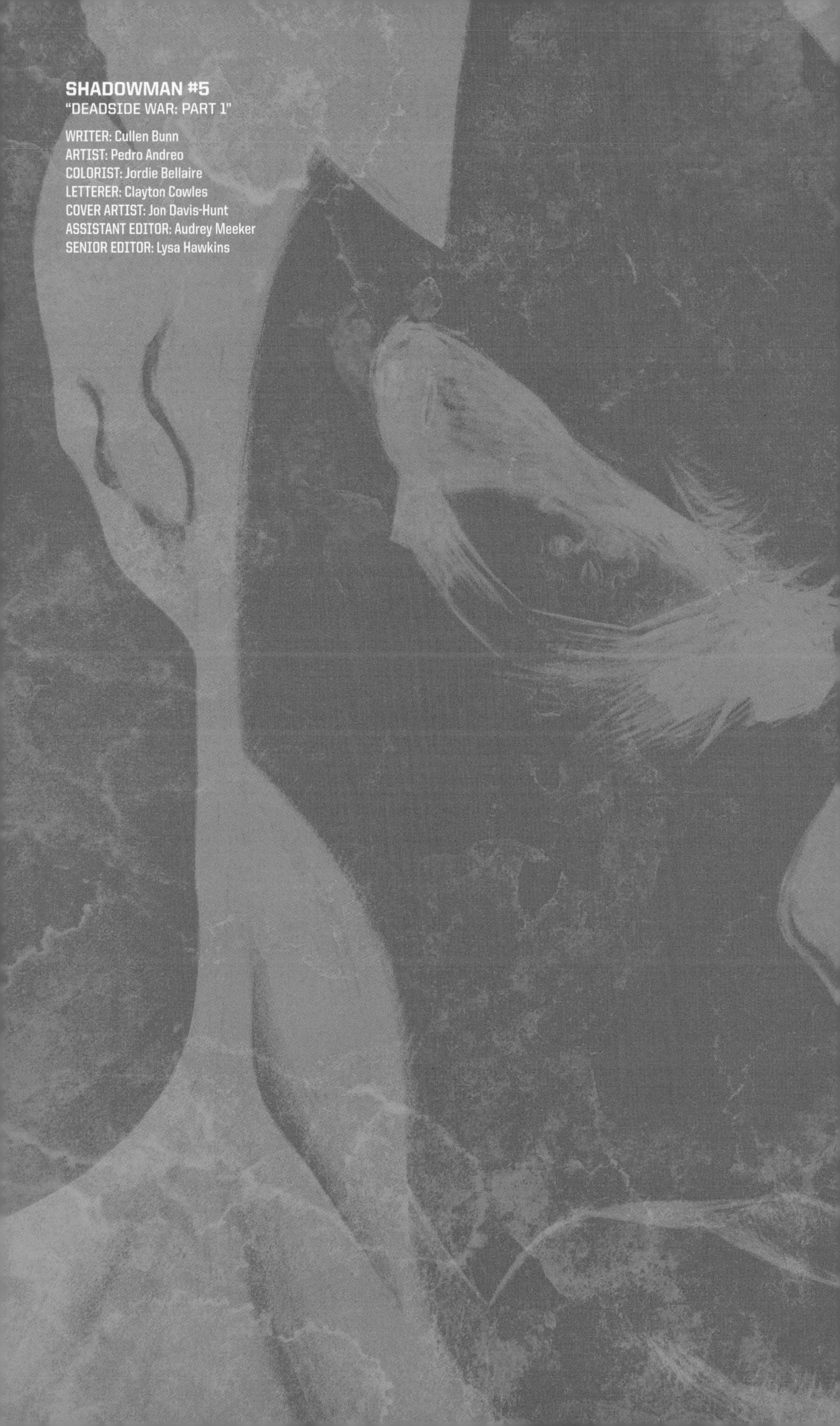

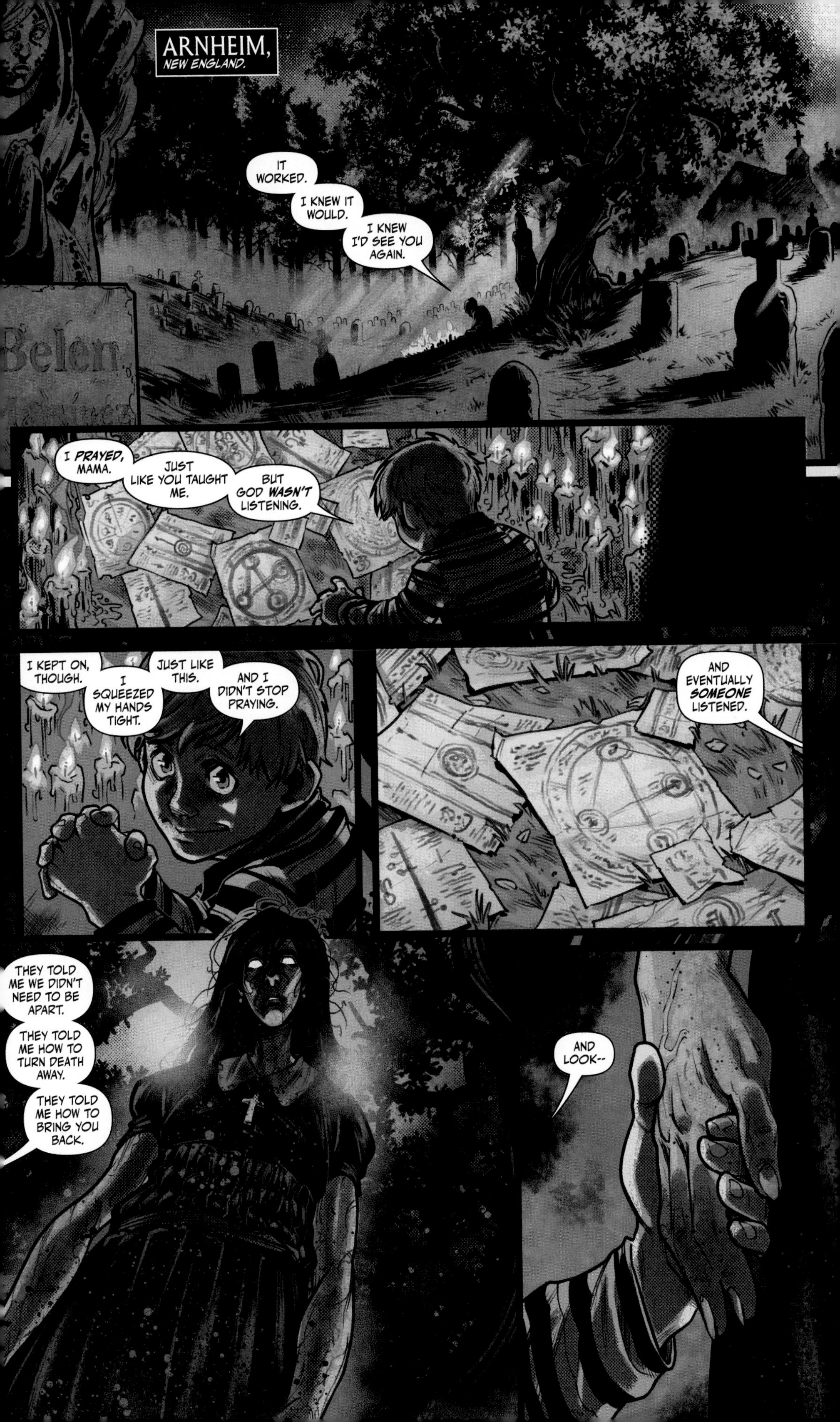
ARNHEIM,
NEW ENGLAND.
IT WORKED.
I KNEW IT WOULD.
I KNEW I'D SEE YOU AGAIN.
Belen
I PRAYED, MAMA.
JUST LIKE YOU TAUGHT ME.
BUT GOD WASN'T LISTENING.
I KEPT ON, THOUGH.
I SQUEEZED MY HANDS TIGHT.
JUST LIKE THIS.
AND I DIDN'T STOP PRAYING.
AND EVENTUALLY SOMEONE LISTENED.
THEY TOLD ME WE DIDN'T NEED TO BE APART.
THEY TOLD ME HOW TO TURN DEATH AWAY.
THEY TOLD ME HOW TO BRING YOU BACK.
AND LOOK--

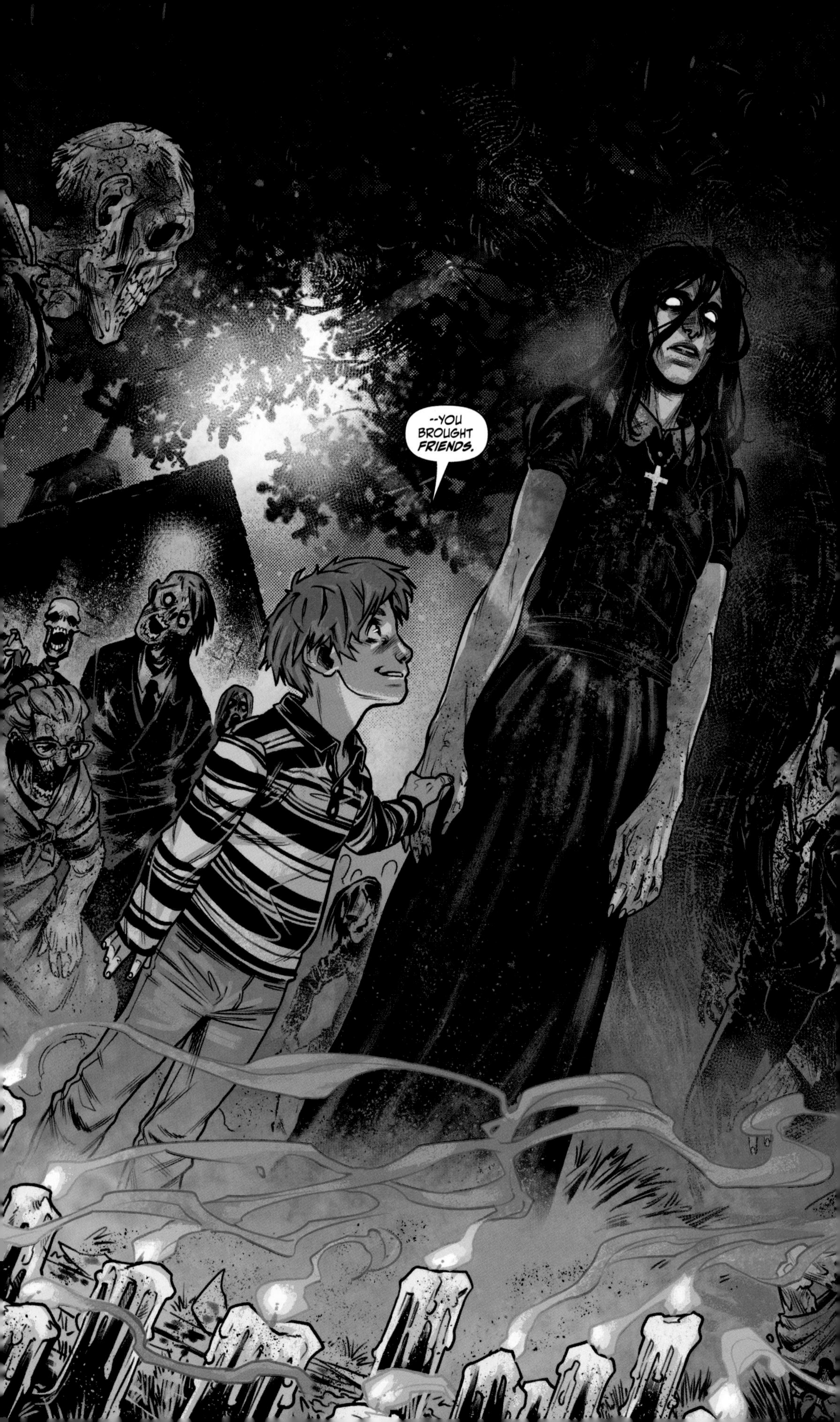
--YOU BROUGHT FRIENDS.

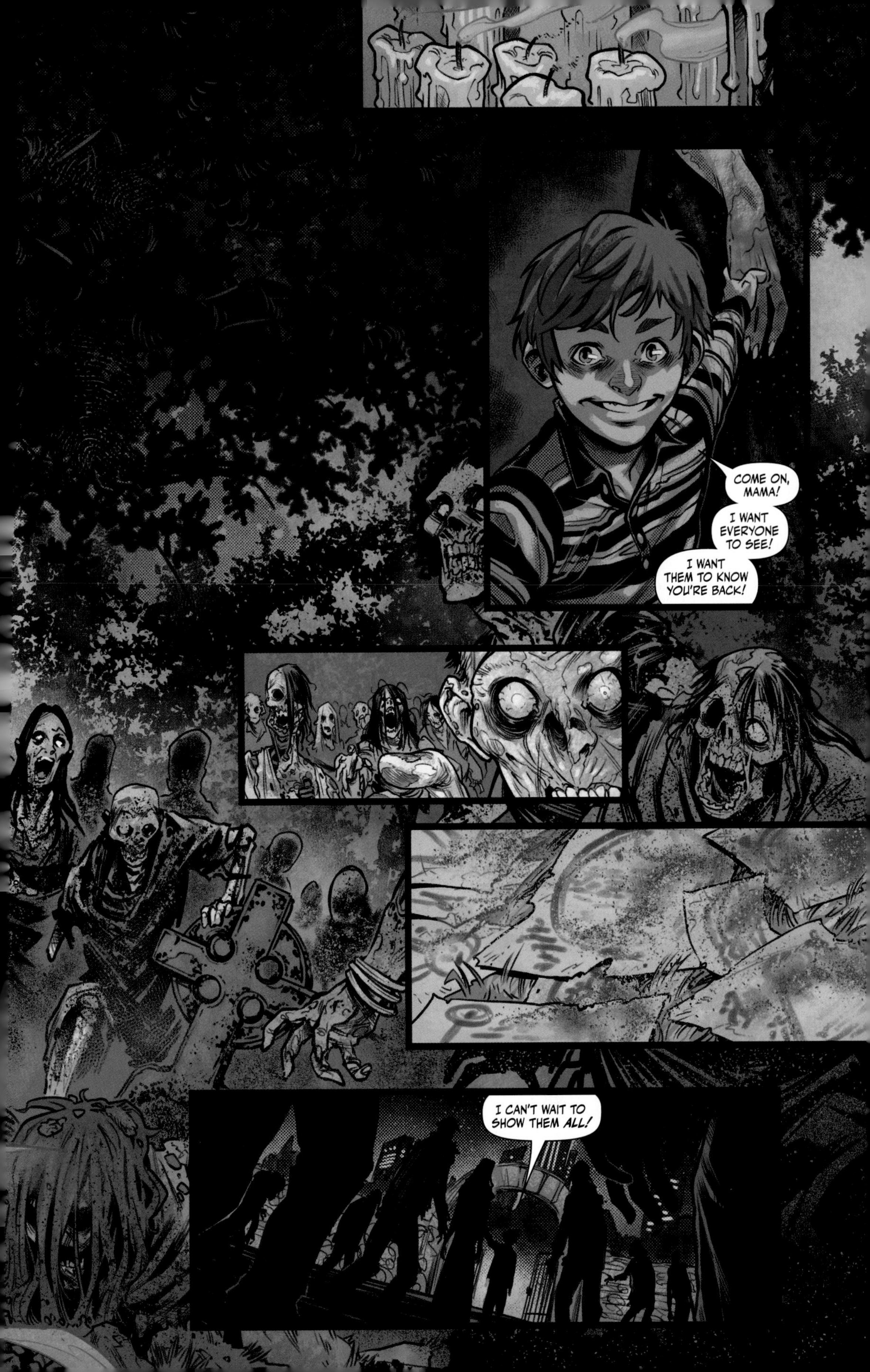
COME ON, MAMA!
I WANT EVERYONE TO SEE!
I WANT THEM TO KNOW YOU'RE BACK!
I CAN'T WAIT TO SHOW THEM ALL!

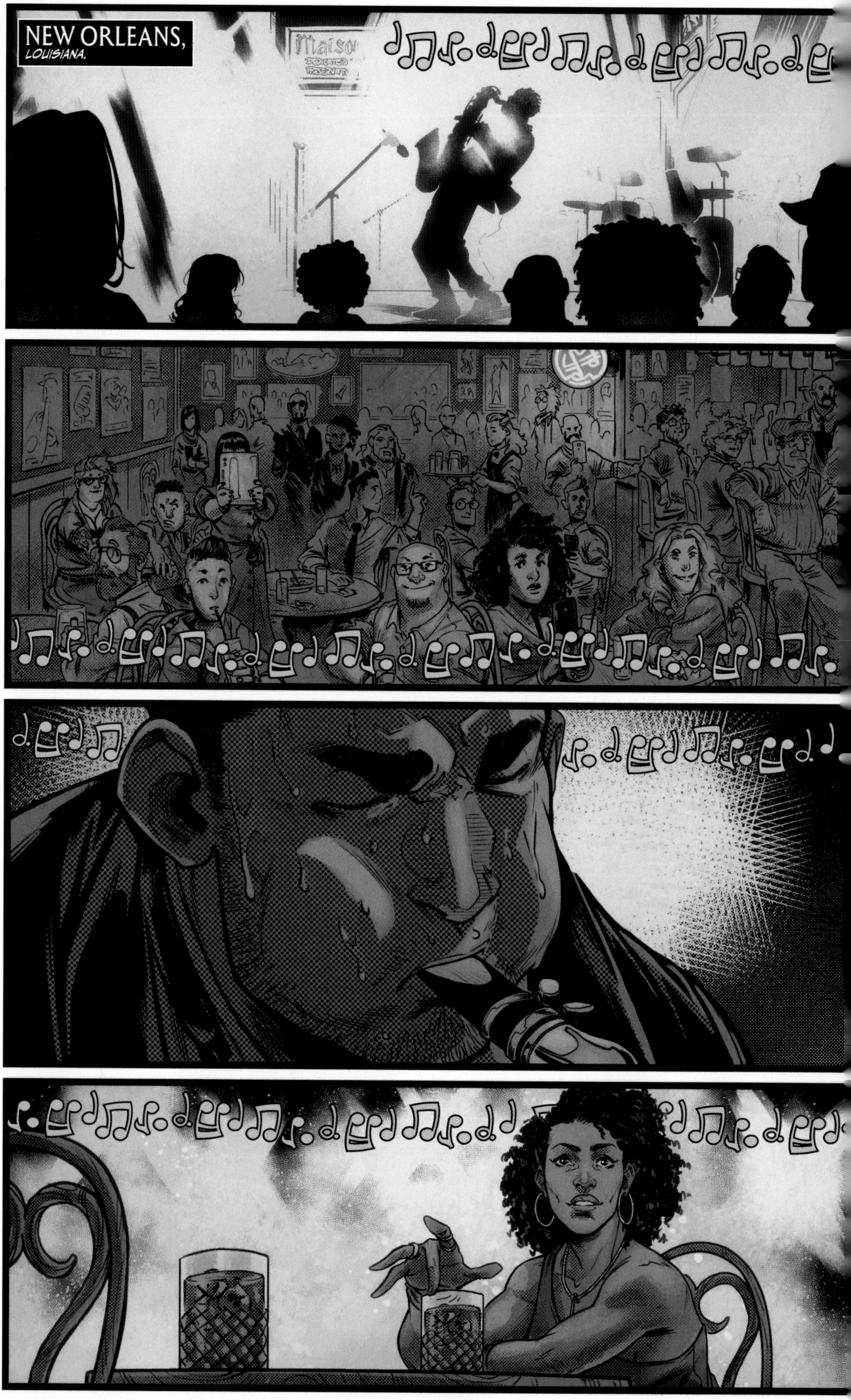
NEW ORLEANS,
LOUISIANA.

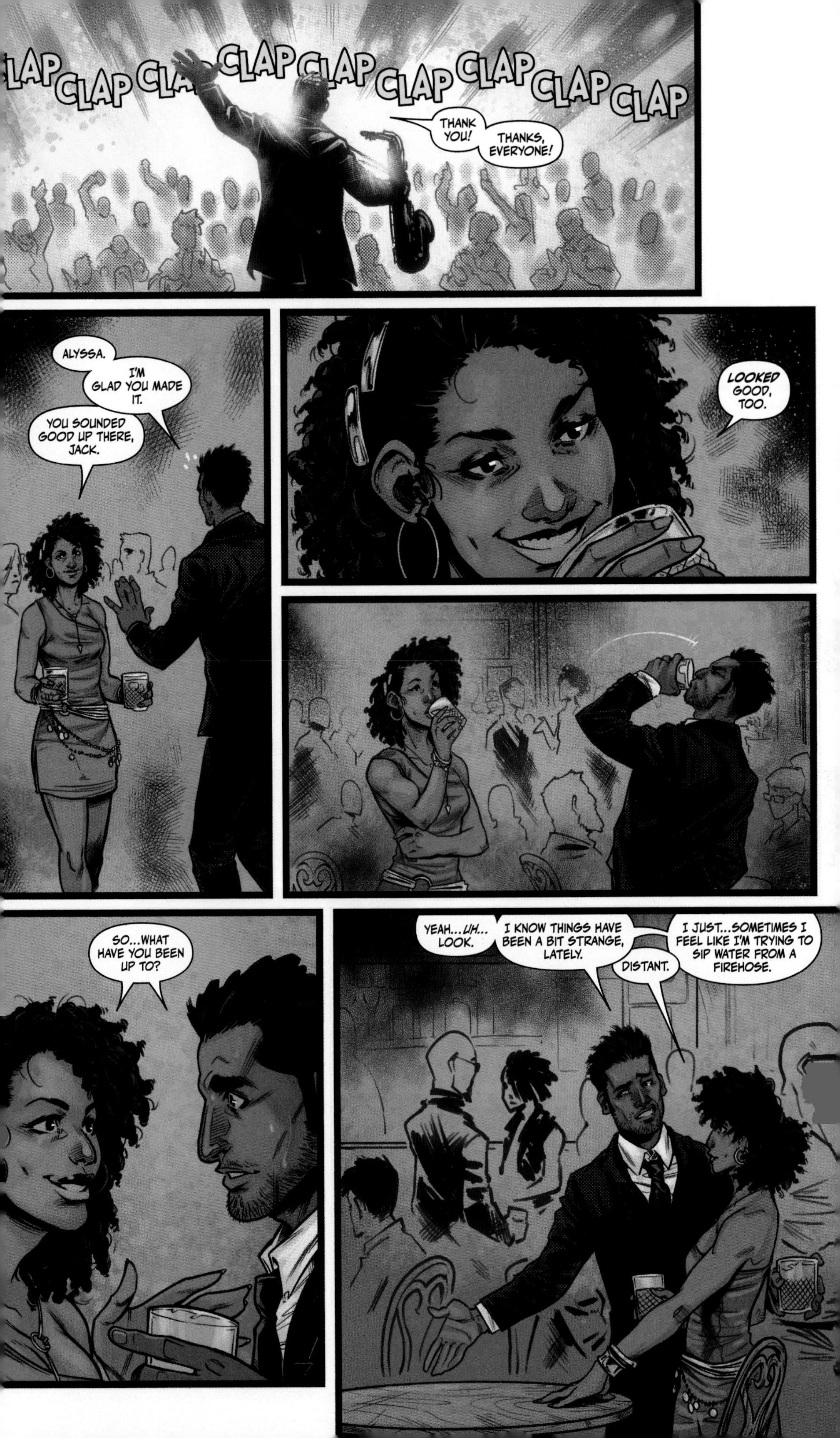
CLAP CLAP CLAP CLAP CLAP CLAP CLAP CLAP CLAP CLAP
THANK YOU!
THANKS, EVERYONE!
YOU SOUNDED GOOD UP THERE, JACK.
ALYSSA.
I'M GLAD YOU MADE IT.
LOOKED GOOD, TOO.
SO...WHAT HAVE YOU BEEN UP TO?
YEAH...UH... LOOK.
I KNOW THINGS HAVE BEEN A BIT STRANGE, LATELY.
DISTANT.
I JUST...SOMETIMES I FEEL LIKE I'M TRYING TO SIP WATER FROM A FIREHOSE.

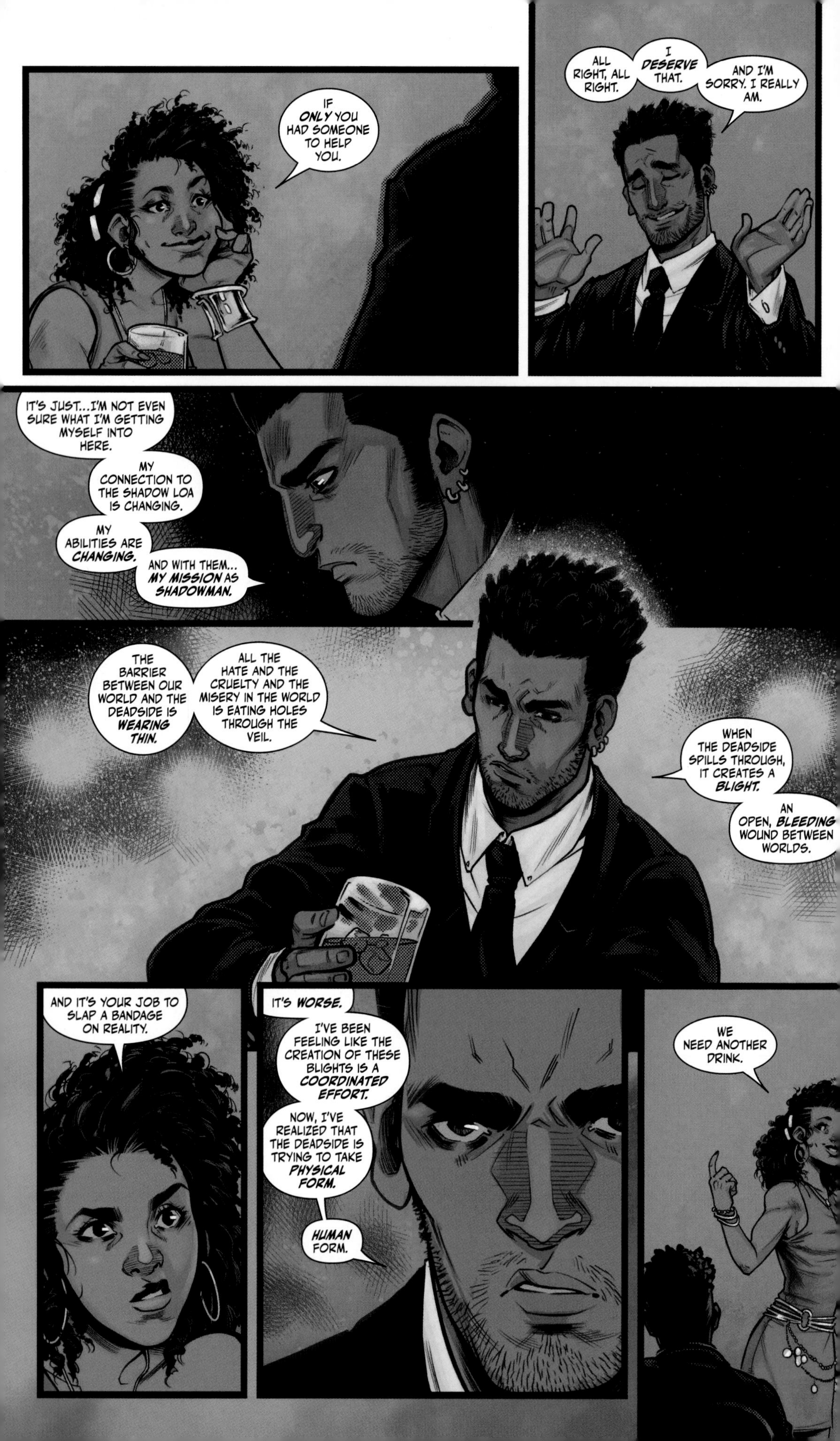
IF ONLY YOU HAD SOMEONE TO HELP YOU.
ALL RIGHT, ALL RIGHT.
I DESERVE THAT.
AND I'M SORRY. I REALLY AM.
IT'S JUST...I'M NOT EVEN SURE WHAT I'M GETTING MYSELF INTO HERE.
MY CONNECTION TO THE SHADOW LOA IS CHANGING.
MY ABILITIES ARE CHANGING.
AND WITH THEM... MY MISSION AS SHADOWMAN.
THE BARRIER BETWEEN OUR WORLD AND THE DEADSIDE IS WEARING THIN.
ALL THE HATE AND THE CRUELTY AND THE MISERY IN THE WORLD IS EATING HOLES THROUGH THE VEIL.
WHEN THE DEADSIDE SPILLS THROUGH, IT CREATES A BLIGHT.
AN OPEN, BLEEDING WOUND BETWEEN WORLDS.
AND IT'S YOUR JOB TO SLAP A BANDAGE ON REALITY.
IT'S WORSE.
I'VE BEEN FEELING LIKE THE CREATION OF THESE BLIGHTS IS A COORDINATED EFFORT.
NOW, I'VE REALIZED THAT THE DEADSIDE IS TRYING TO TAKE PHYSICAL FORM.
HUMAN FORM.
WE NEED ANOTHER DRINK.

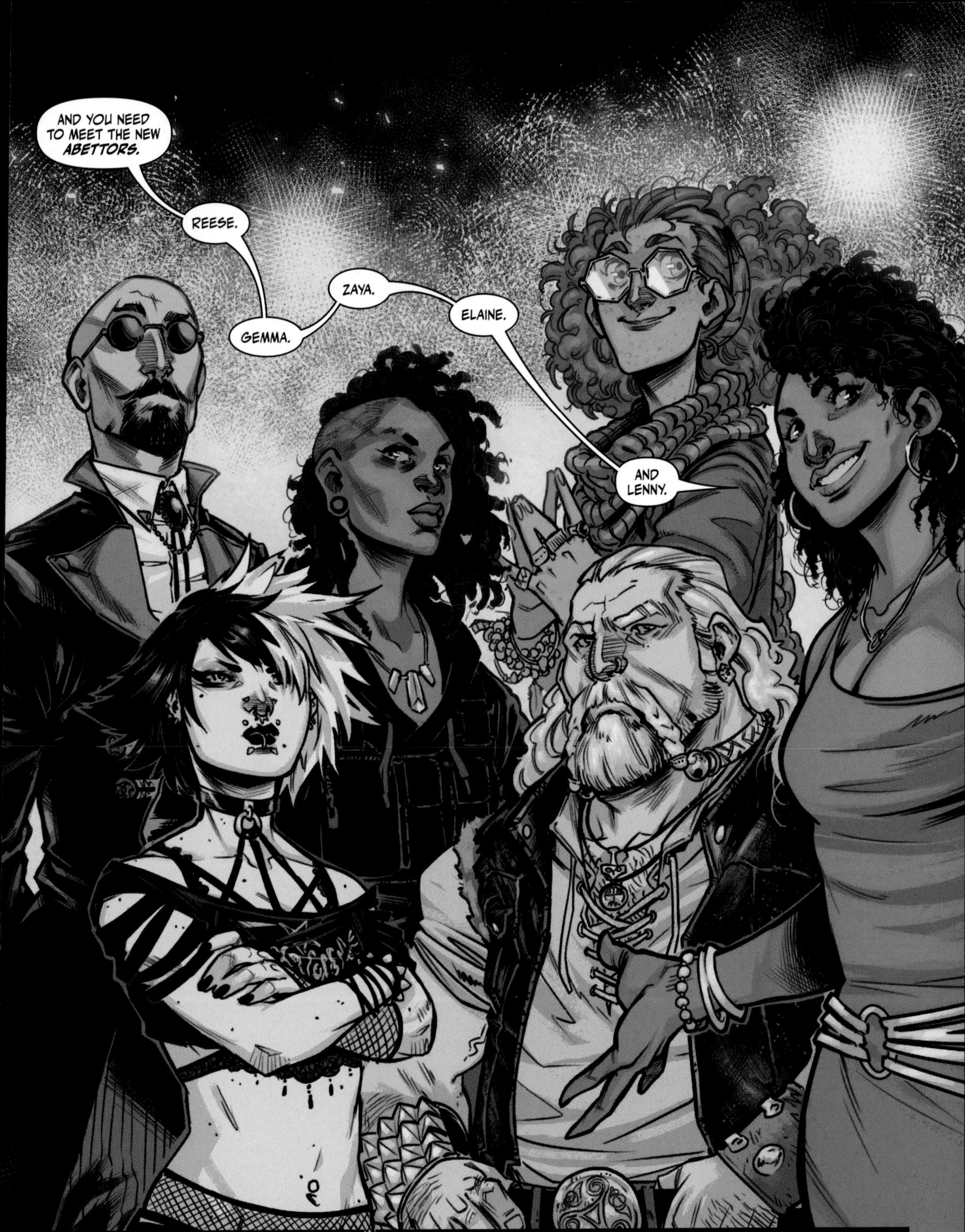
AND YOU NEED TO MEET THE NEW *ABETTORS.*
REESE.
GEMMA.
ZAYA.
ELAINE.
AND LENNY.

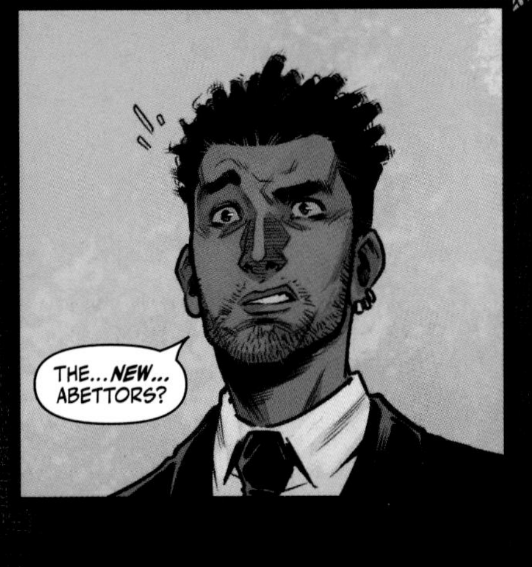
THE... *NEW...* ABETTORS?

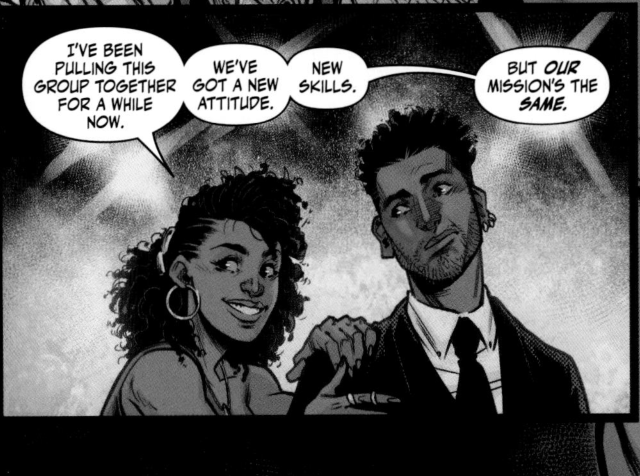
I'VE BEEN PULLING THIS GROUP TOGETHER FOR A WHILE NOW.
WE'VE GOT A NEW ATTITUDE.
NEW SKILLS.
BUT *OUR* MISSION'S THE *SAME.*

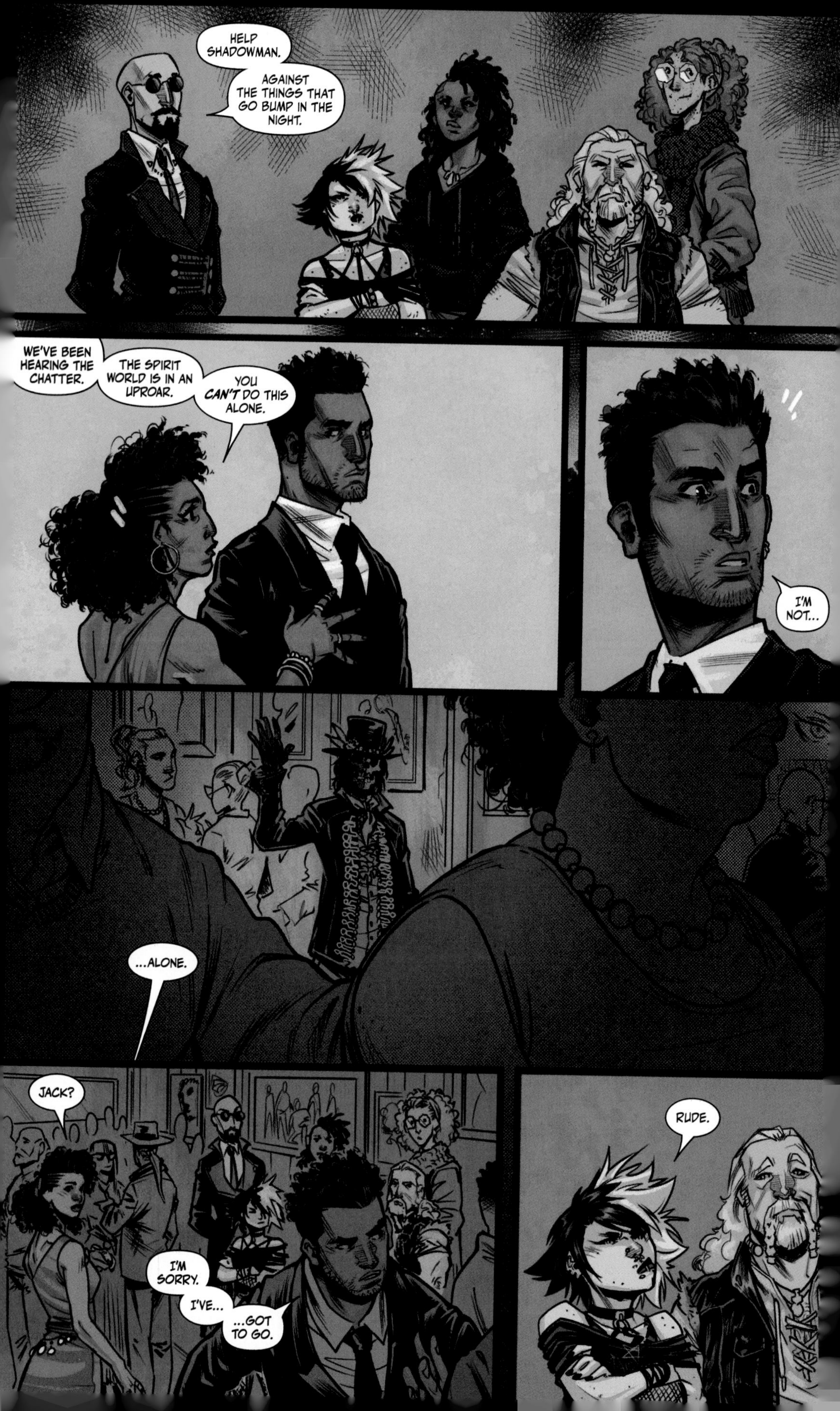
HELP SHADOWMAN.
AGAINST THE THINGS THAT GO BUMP IN THE NIGHT.
WE'VE BEEN HEARING THE CHATTER.
THE SPIRIT WORLD IS IN AN UPROAR.
YOU *CAN'T* DO THIS ALONE.
!!
I'M NOT...
...ALONE.
JACK?
I'M SORRY.
I'VE...
...GOT TO GO.
RUDE.

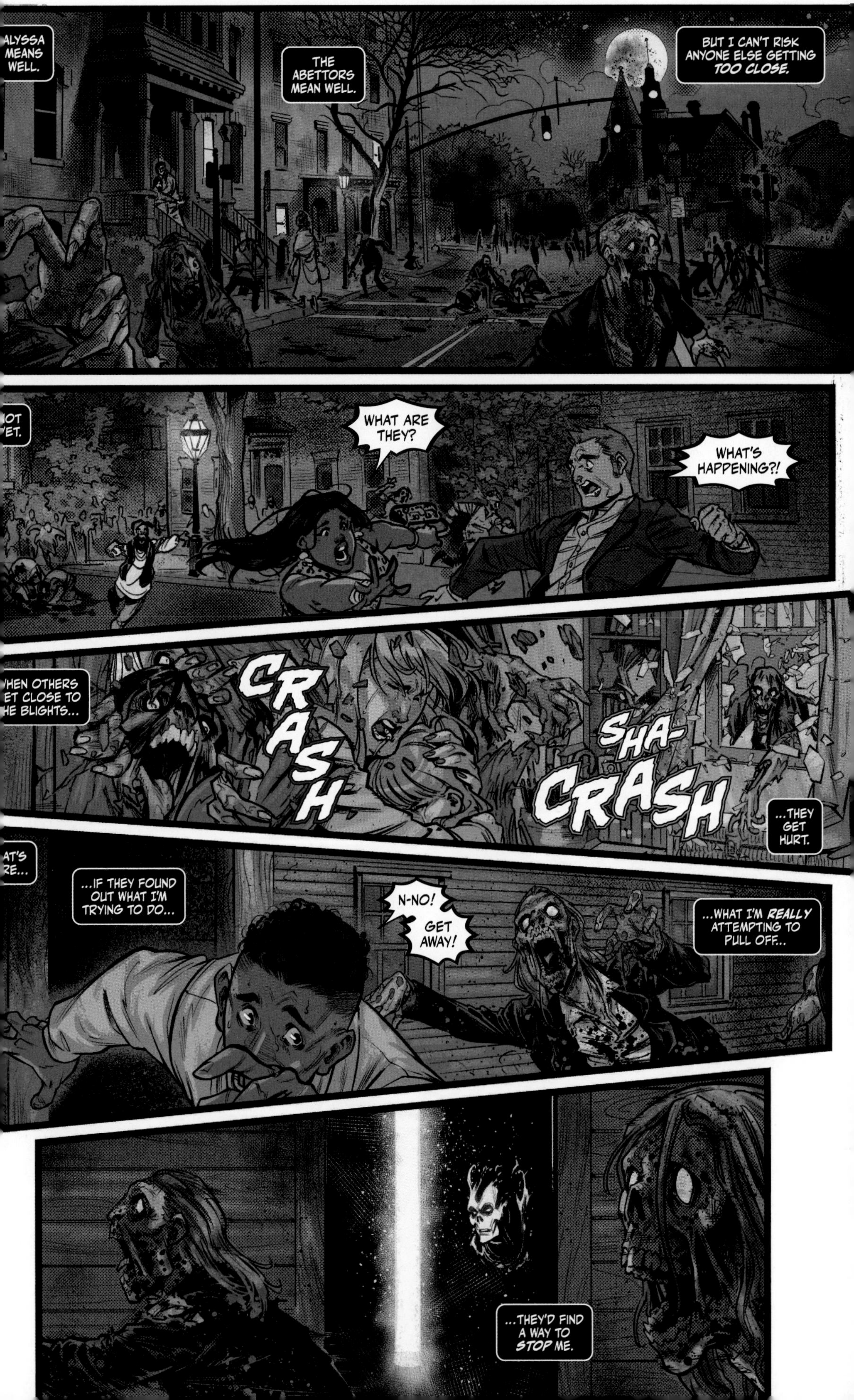

ALYSSA MEANS WELL.
THE ABETTORS MEAN WELL.
BUT I CAN'T RISK ANYONE ELSE GETTING TOO CLOSE.
OT 'ET.
WHAT ARE THEY?
WHAT'S HAPPENING?!
HEN OTHERS ET CLOSE TO HE BLIGHTS...
CRASH
SHA-CRASH
...THEY GET HURT.
AT'S RE...
...IF THEY FOUND OUT WHAT I'M TRYING TO DO...
N-NO!
GET AWAY!
...WHAT I'M REALLY ATTEMPTING TO PULL OFF...
...THEY'D FIND A WAY TO STOP ME.

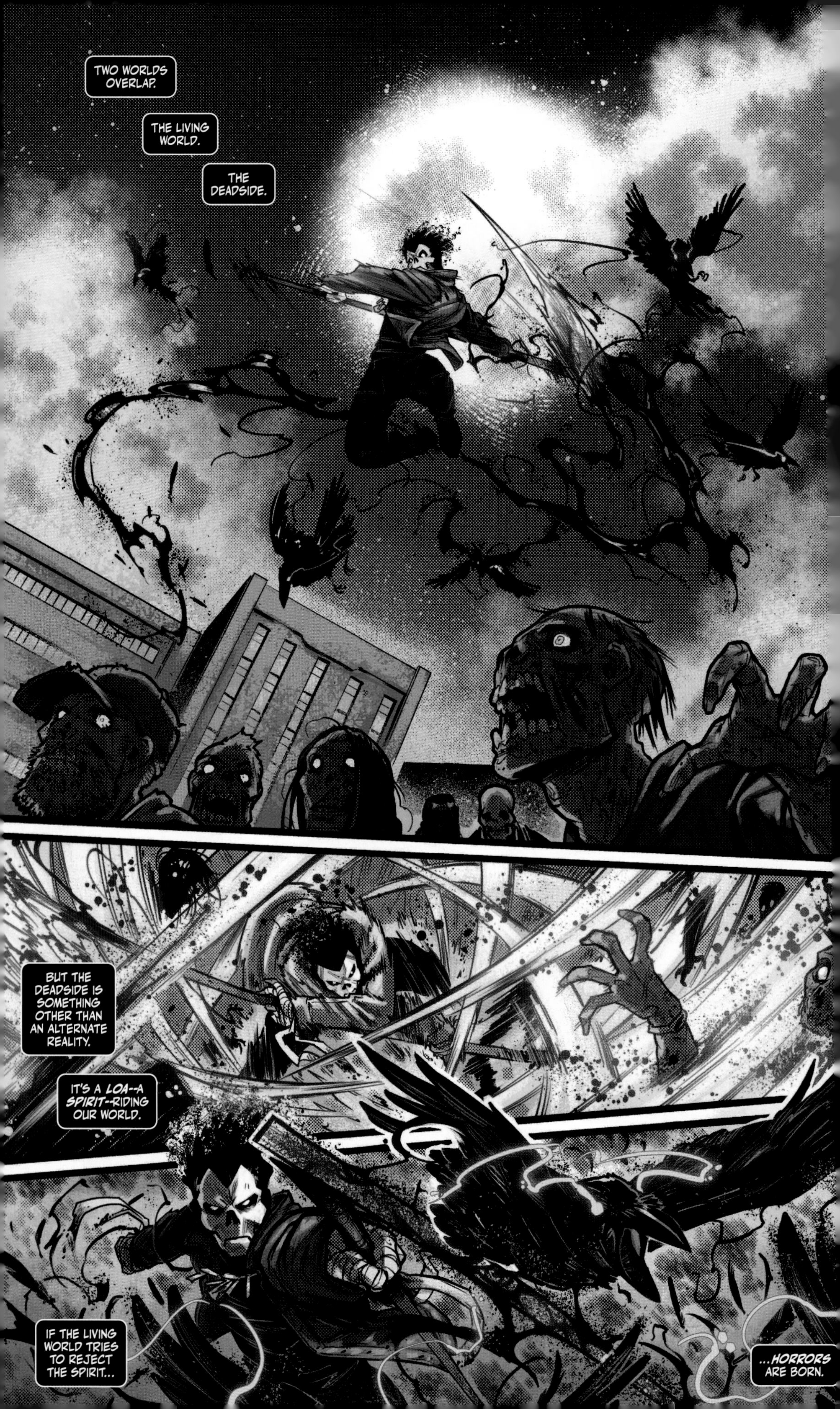
TWO WORLDS OVERLAP.
THE LIVING WORLD.
THE DEADSIDE.
BUT THE DEADSIDE IS SOMETHING OTHER THAN AN ALTERNATE REALITY.
IT'S A *LOA*--A *SPIRIT*--RIDING OUR WORLD.
IF THE LIVING WORLD TRIES TO REJECT THE SPIRIT...
...*HORRORS* ARE BORN.

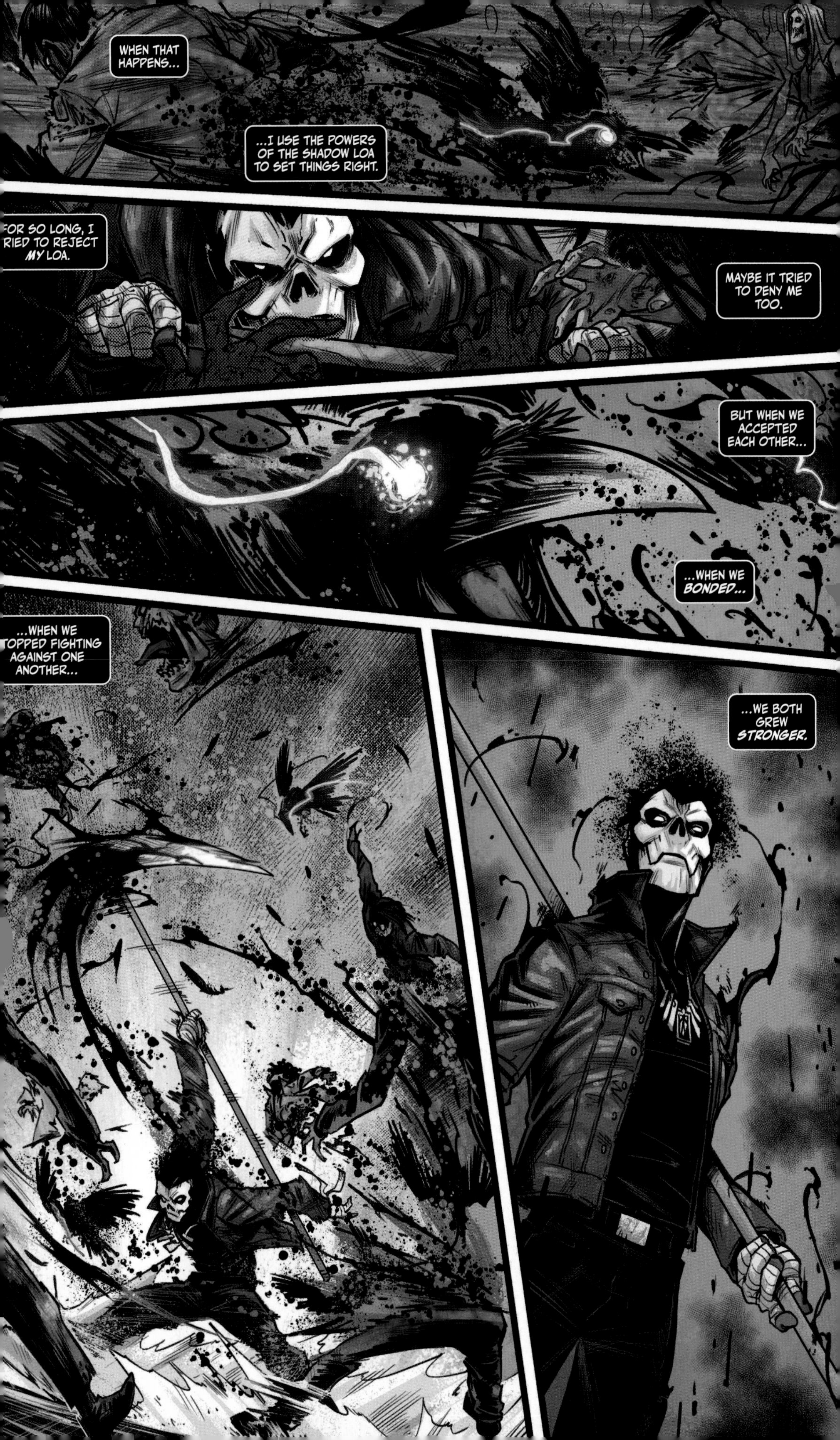
WHEN THAT HAPPENS...
...I USE THE POWERS OF THE SHADOW LOA TO SET THINGS RIGHT.
FOR SO LONG, I TRIED TO REJECT *MY* LOA.
MAYBE IT TRIED TO DENY ME TOO.
BUT WHEN WE ACCEPTED EACH OTHER...
...WHEN WE *BONDED*...
...WHEN WE STOPPED FIGHTING AGAINST ONE ANOTHER...
...WE BOTH GREW *STRONGER.*

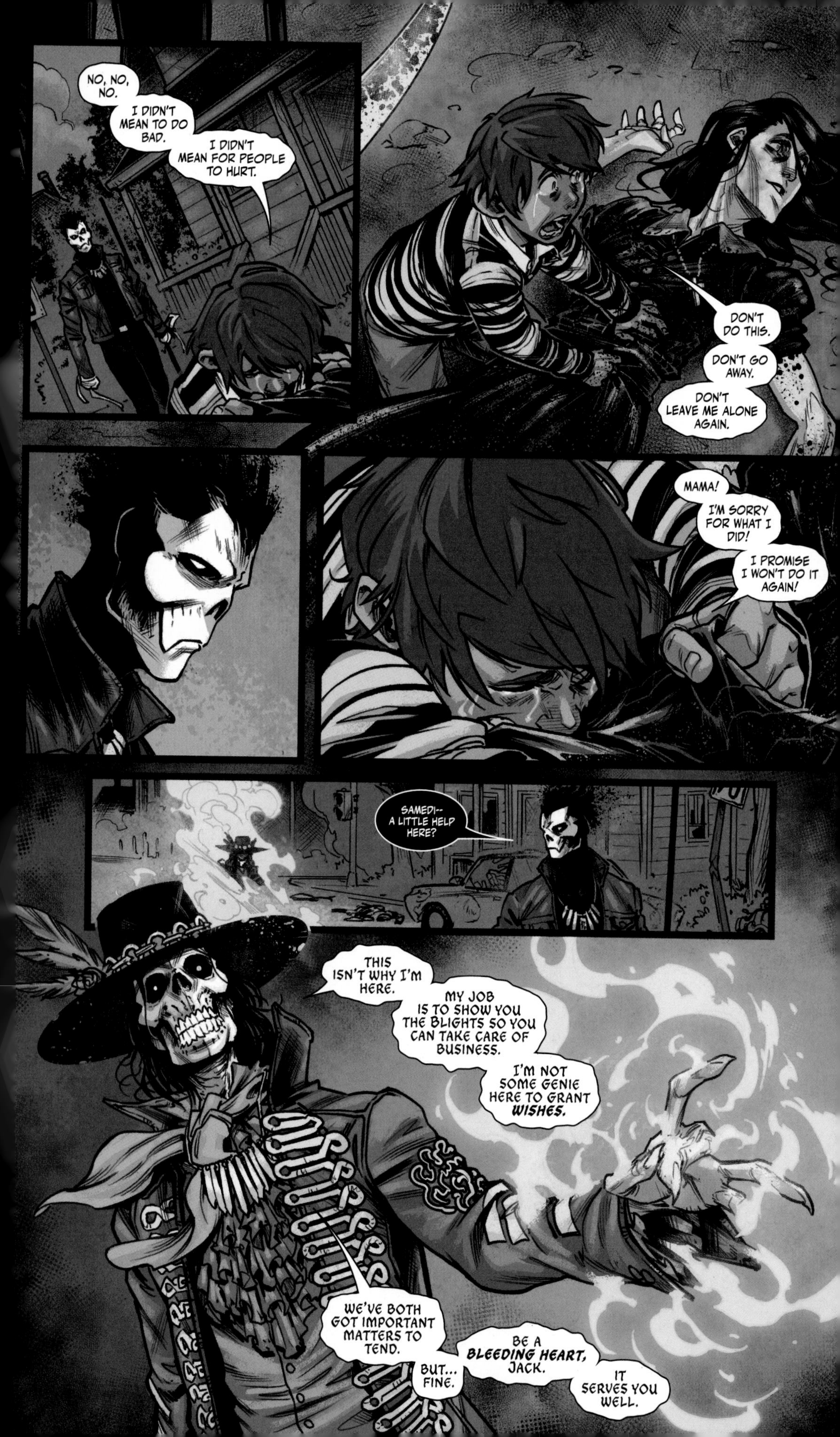
NO, NO, NO.
I DIDN'T MEAN TO DO BAD.
I DIDN'T MEAN FOR PEOPLE TO HURT.
DON'T DO THIS.
DON'T GO AWAY.
DON'T LEAVE ME ALONE AGAIN.
MAMA!
I'M SORRY FOR WHAT I DID!
I PROMISE I WON'T DO IT AGAIN!
SAMEDI-- A LITTLE HELP HERE?
THIS ISN'T WHY I'M HERE.
MY JOB IS TO SHOW YOU THE BLIGHTS SO YOU CAN TAKE CARE OF BUSINESS.
I'M NOT SOME GENIE HERE TO GRANT WISHES.
WE'VE BOTH GOT IMPORTANT MATTERS TO TEND.
BUT... FINE.
BE A BLEEDING HEART, JACK.
IT SERVES YOU WELL.

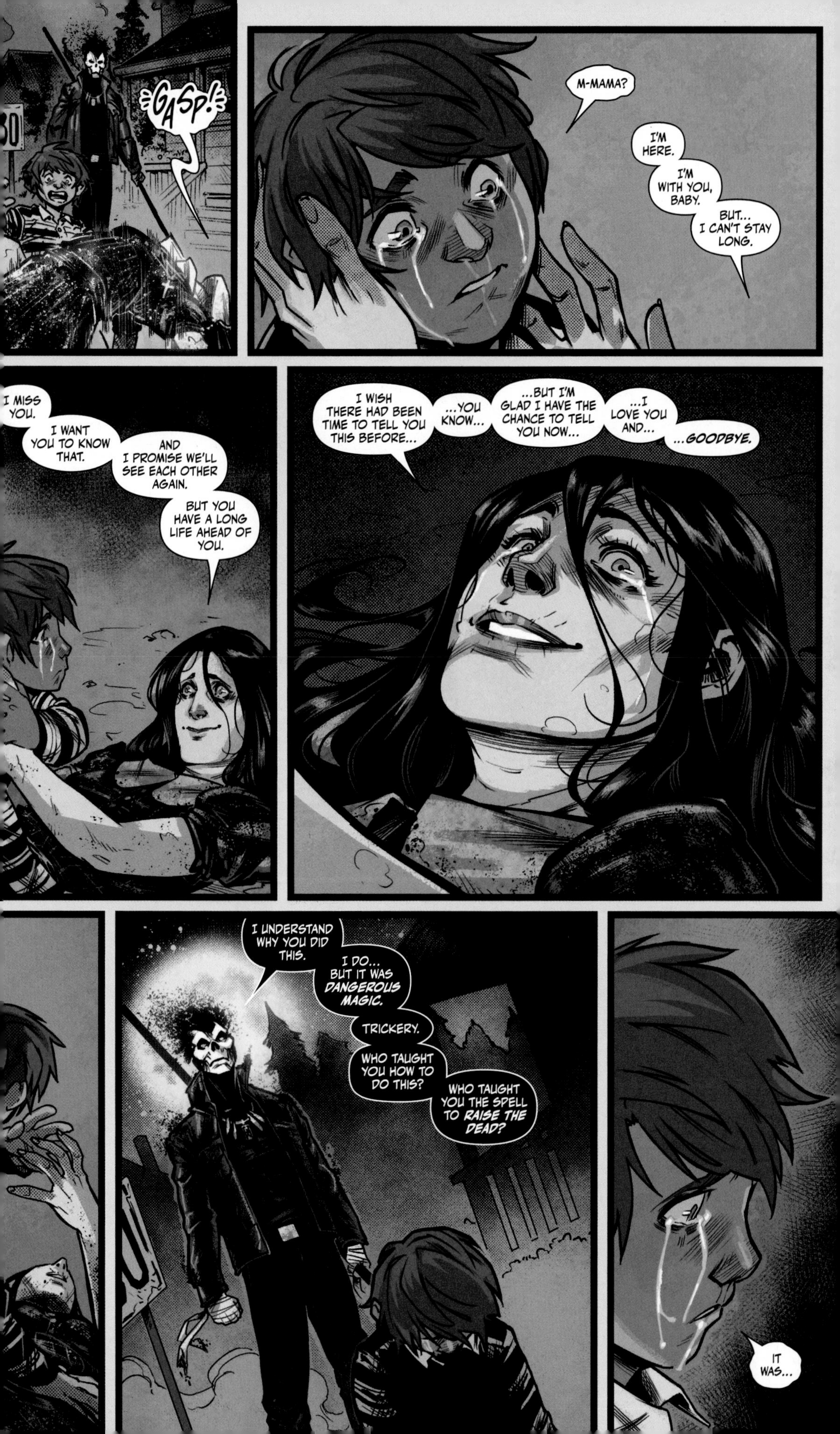

GASP!
M-MAMA?
I'M HERE.
I'M WITH YOU, BABY.
BUT... I CAN'T STAY LONG.
I MISS YOU.
I WANT YOU TO KNOW THAT.
AND I PROMISE WE'LL SEE EACH OTHER AGAIN.
BUT YOU HAVE A LONG LIFE AHEAD OF YOU.
I WISH THERE HAD BEEN TIME TO TELL YOU THIS BEFORE...
...YOU KNOW...
...BUT I'M GLAD I HAVE THE CHANCE TO TELL YOU NOW...
...I LOVE YOU AND...
...GOODBYE.
I UNDERSTAND WHY YOU DID THIS.
I DO... BUT IT WAS DANGEROUS MAGIC.
TRICKERY.
WHO TAUGHT YOU HOW TO DO THIS?
WHO TAUGHT YOU THE SPELL TO RAISE THE DEAD?
IT WAS...

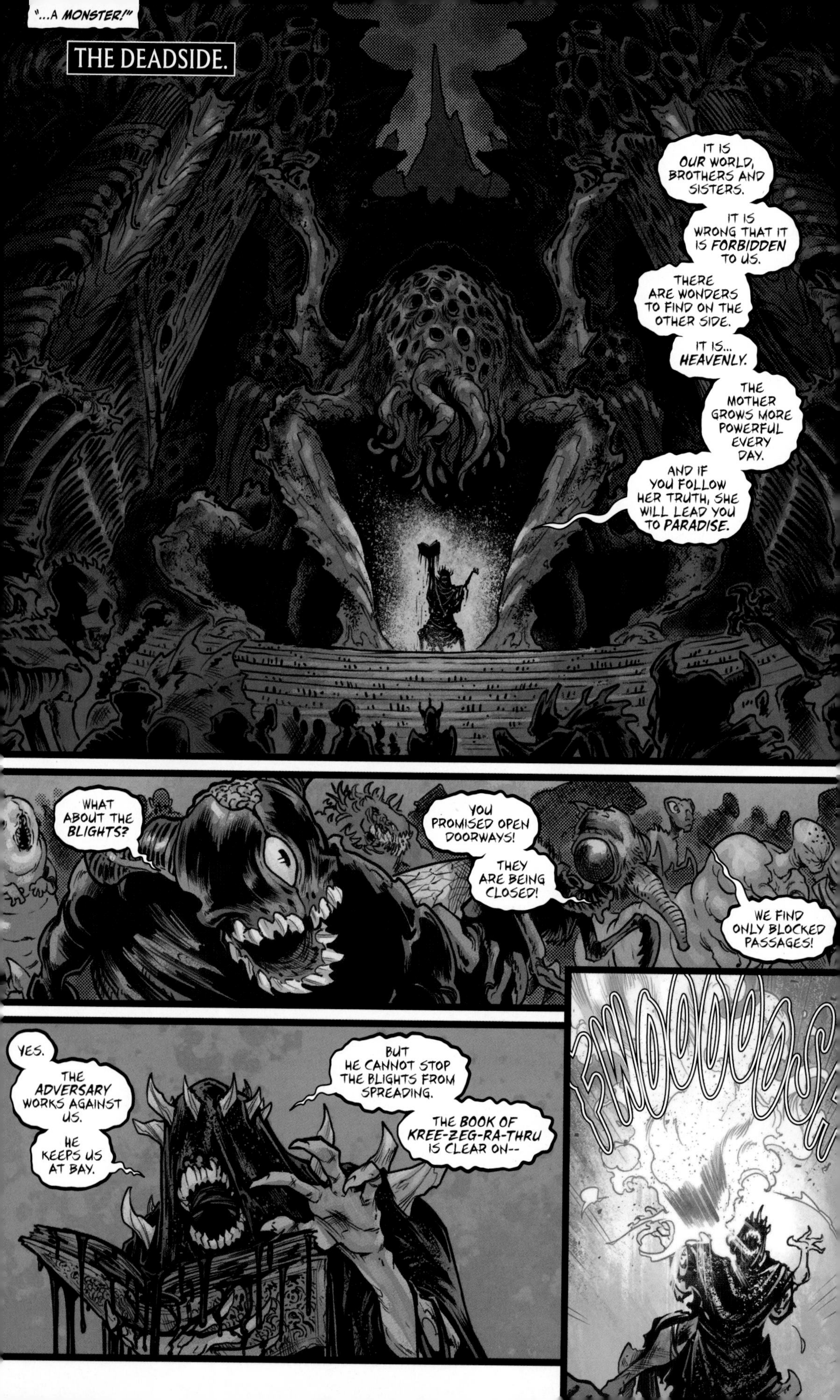
"...A MONSTER!"
THE DEADSIDE.
IT IS OUR WORLD, BROTHERS AND SISTERS.
IT IS WRONG THAT IT IS FORBIDDEN TO US.
THERE ARE WONDERS TO FIND ON THE OTHER SIDE.
IT IS... HEAVENLY.
THE MOTHER GROWS MORE POWERFUL EVERY DAY.
AND IF YOU FOLLOW HER TRUTH, SHE WILL LEAD YOU TO PARADISE.
WHAT ABOUT THE BLIGHTS?
YOU PROMISED OPEN DOORWAYS!
THEY ARE BEING CLOSED!
WE FIND ONLY BLOCKED PASSAGES!
YES.
THE ADVERSARY WORKS AGAINST US.
HE KEEPS US AT BAY.
BUT HE CANNOT STOP THE BLIGHTS FROM SPREADING.
THE BOOK OF KREE-ZEG-RA-THRU IS CLEAR ON--

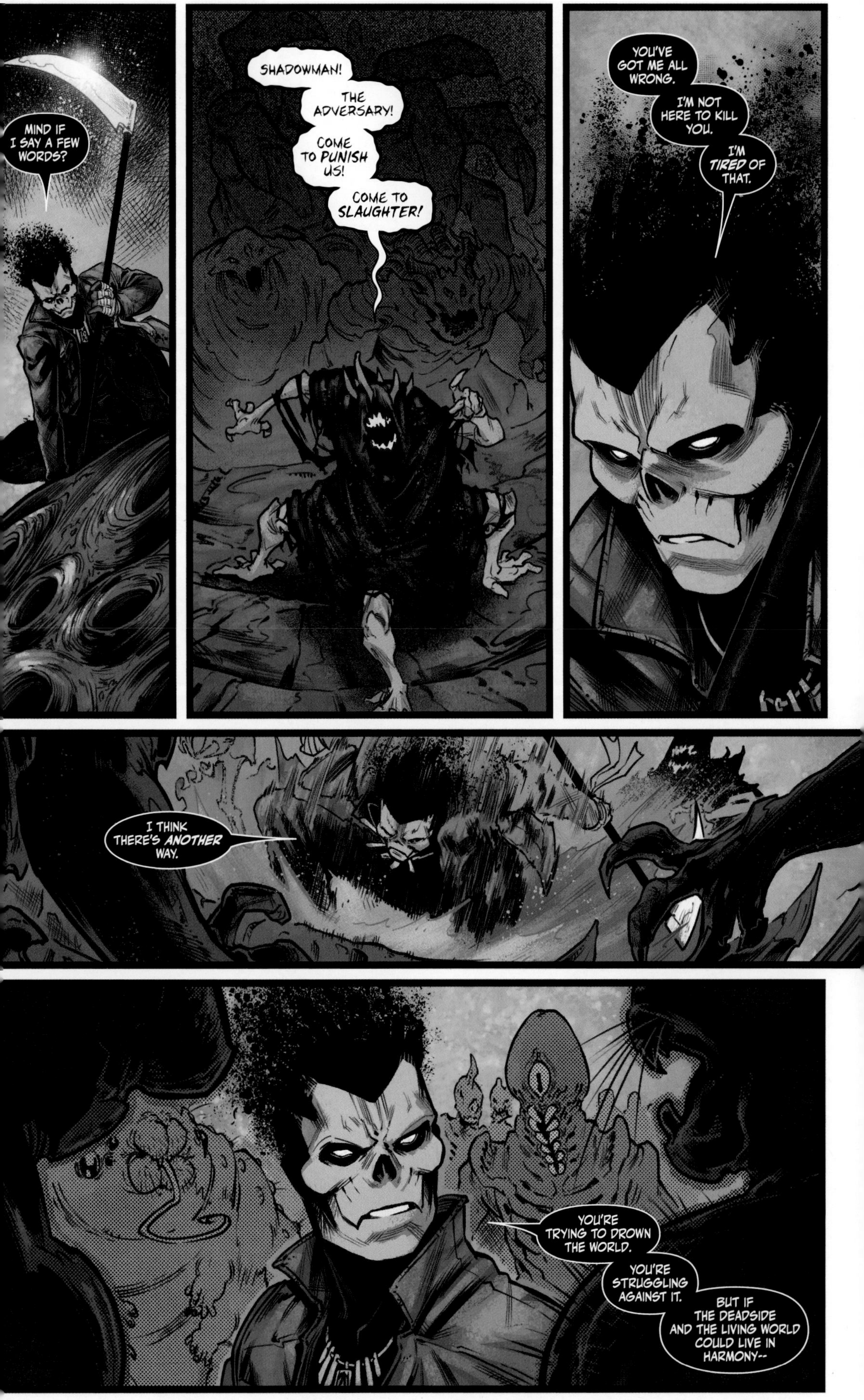
MIND IF I SAY A FEW WORDS?
SHADOWMAN!
THE ADVERSARY!
COME TO PUNISH US!
COME TO SLAUGHTER!
YOU'VE GOT ME ALL WRONG.
I'M NOT HERE TO KILL YOU.
I'M TIRED OF THAT.
I THINK THERE'S ANOTHER WAY.
YOU'RE TRYING TO DROWN THE WORLD.
YOU'RE STRUGGLING AGAINST IT.
BUT IF THE DEADSIDE AND THE LIVING WORLD COULD LIVE IN HARMONY--

NO HARMONY!

IF THERE COULD BE PEACE, WE WOULD NOT BE IMPRISONED HERE!

THE LIVING WORLD SEEKS TO CAST US OUT!

THE MOTHER HAS SPOKEN!

YOU'RE WRONG ABOUT THE WORLD, TOO.

IT'S FAR FROM PERFECT.

IT'S FULL OF SADNESS AND PAIN AND ANGER AND HATE...SOME O' THAT BECAUSE IT IS PULLING AGAINST THE DEADSIDE.

WE WILL NOT BE SWAYED BY YOUR LIES!

THE DEADSIDE WILL SOON BE FLESH AND BLOOD!

SOON, SHE WILL COAX BLIGHTS BY THE THOUSAND!

PARADISE WILL BE DROWNED SO THAT WE MIGHT CLAIM IT!

THEN YOU WILL HAVE A FIGHT ON YOUR HANDS.

IF YOU SWALLOW THE WORLD UP...THEN MY WORLD BECOMES THE DEADSIDE...AND THIS IS ALL YOU'LL EVER KNOW.

BUT IF YOU CAN JUST BE PATIENT...

...IF YOU GIVE ME A CHANCE TO TALK TO THIS QUEEN OF YOURS...

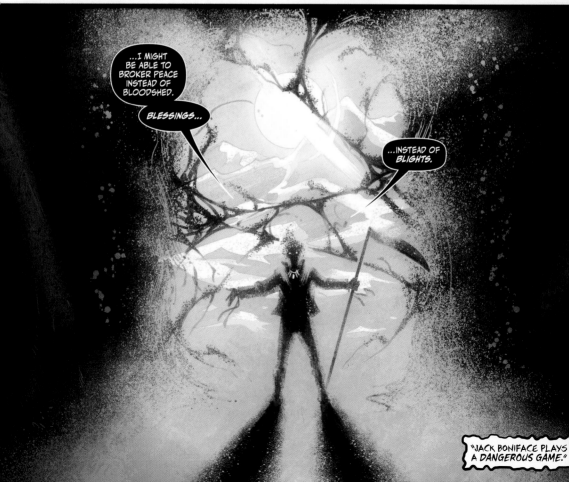

...I MIGHT BE ABLE TO BROKER PEACE INSTEAD OF BLOODSHED.

BLESSINGS...

...INSTEAD OF BLIGHTS.

"JACK BONIFACE PLAYS A DANGEROUS GAME."

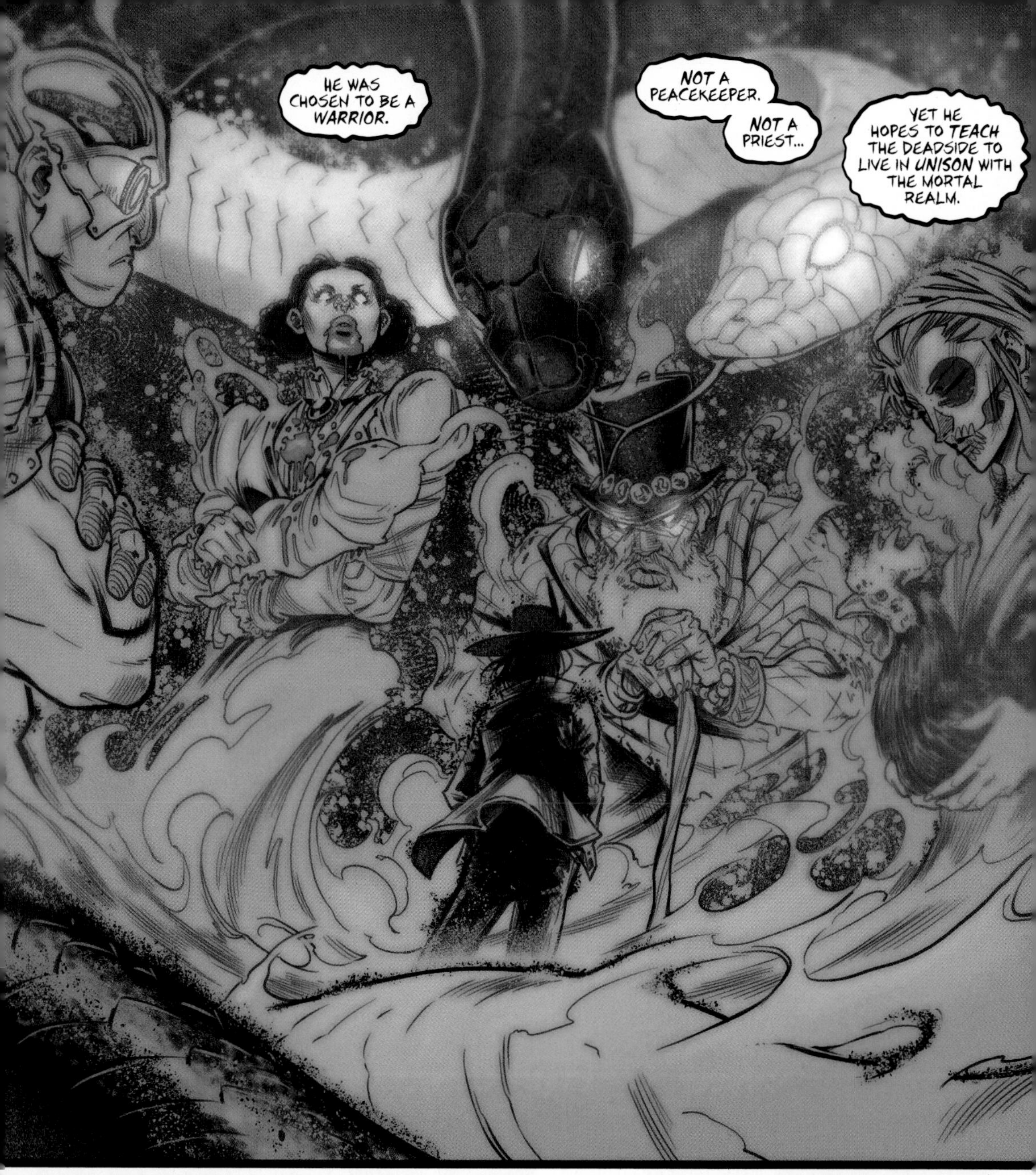
HE WAS CHOSEN TO BE A WARRIOR.
NOT A PEACEKEEPER.
NOT A PRIEST...
YET HE HOPES TO TEACH THE DEADSIDE TO LIVE IN UNISON WITH THE MORTAL REALM.

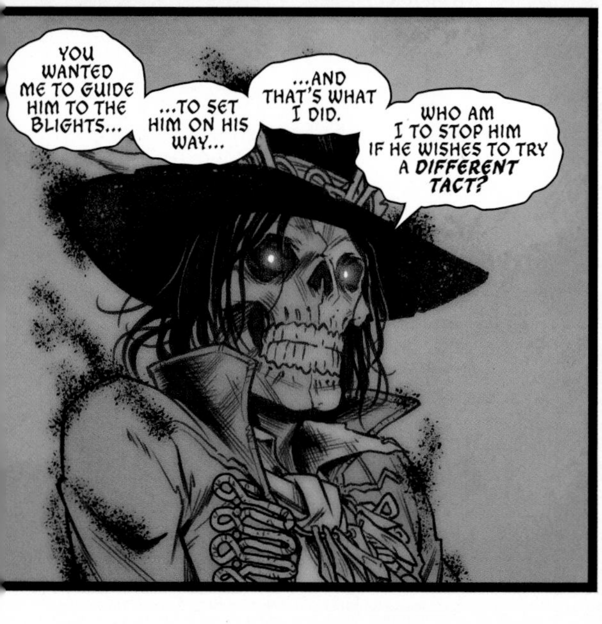
YOU WANTED ME TO GUIDE HIM TO THE BLIGHTS...
...TO SET HIM ON HIS WAY...
...AND THAT'S WHAT I DID.
WHO AM I TO STOP HIM IF HE WISHES TO TRY A DIFFERENT TACT?

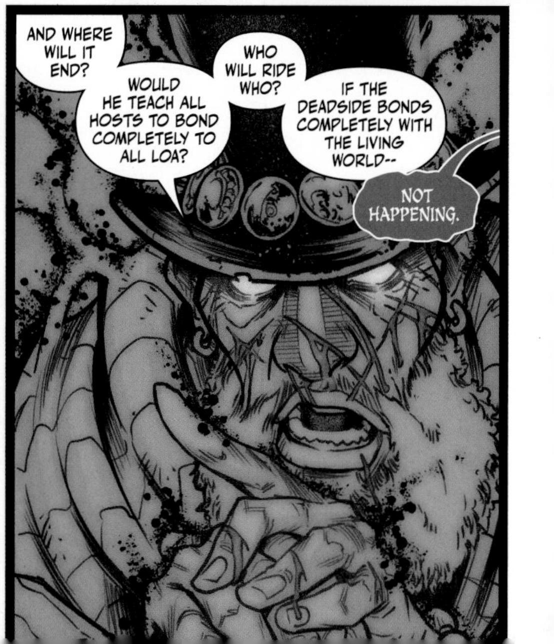
AND WHERE WILL IT END?
WOULD HE TEACH ALL HOSTS TO BOND COMPLETELY TO ALL LOA?
WHO WILL RIDE WHO?
IF THE DEADSIDE BONDS COMPLETELY WITH THE LIVING WORLD--
NOT HAPPENING.

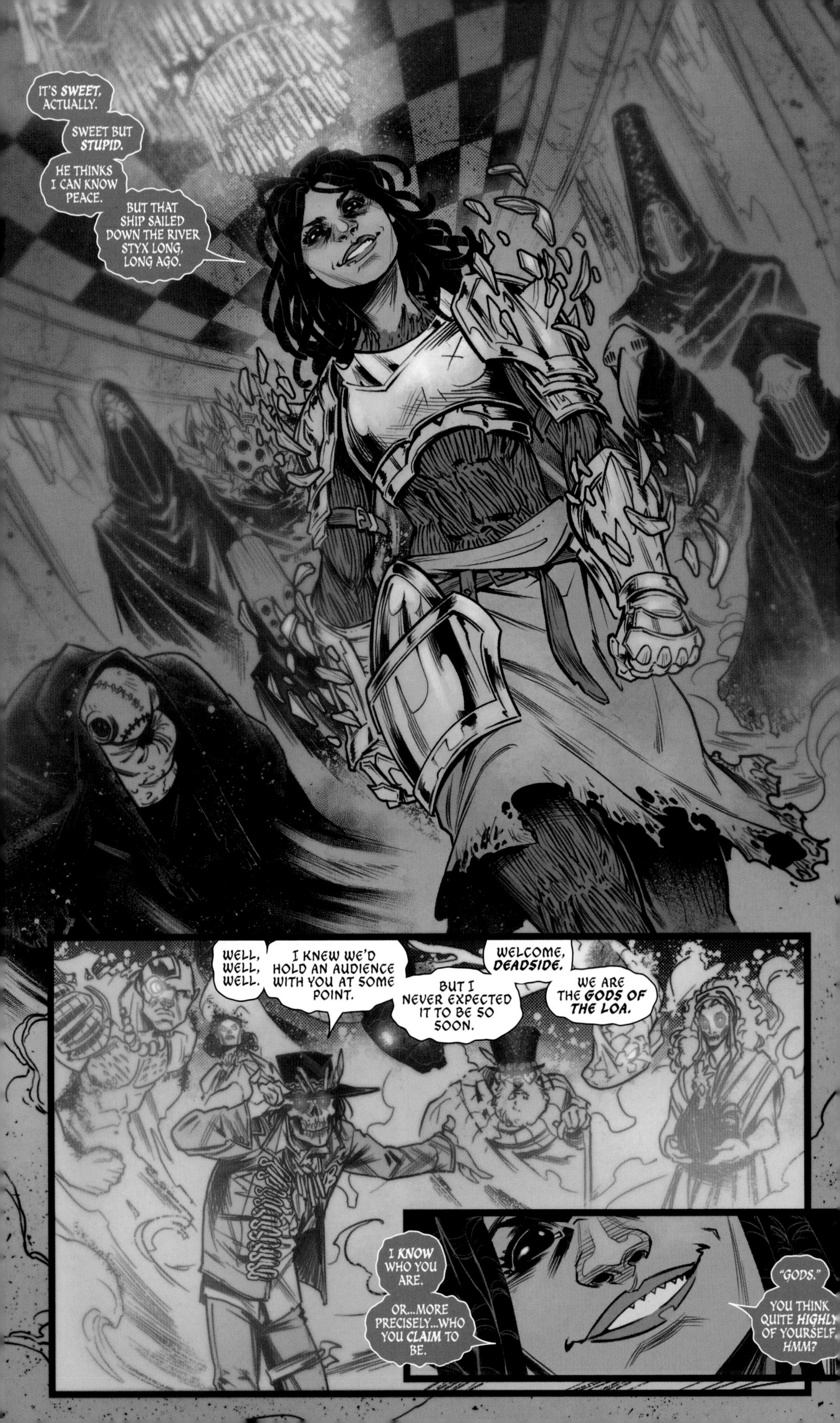
IT'S SWEET, ACTUALLY.
SWEET BUT STUPID.
HE THINKS I CAN KNOW PEACE.
BUT THAT SHIP SAILED DOWN THE RIVER STYX LONG, LONG AGO.
WELL, WELL, WELL.
I KNEW WE'D HOLD AN AUDIENCE WITH YOU AT SOME POINT.
BUT I NEVER EXPECTED IT TO BE SO SOON.
WELCOME, DEADSIDE.
WE ARE THE GODS OF THE LOA.
I KNOW WHO YOU ARE.
OR...MORE PRECISELY...WHO YOU CLAIM TO BE.
"GODS."
YOU THINK QUITE HIGHLY OF YOURSELF, HMM?

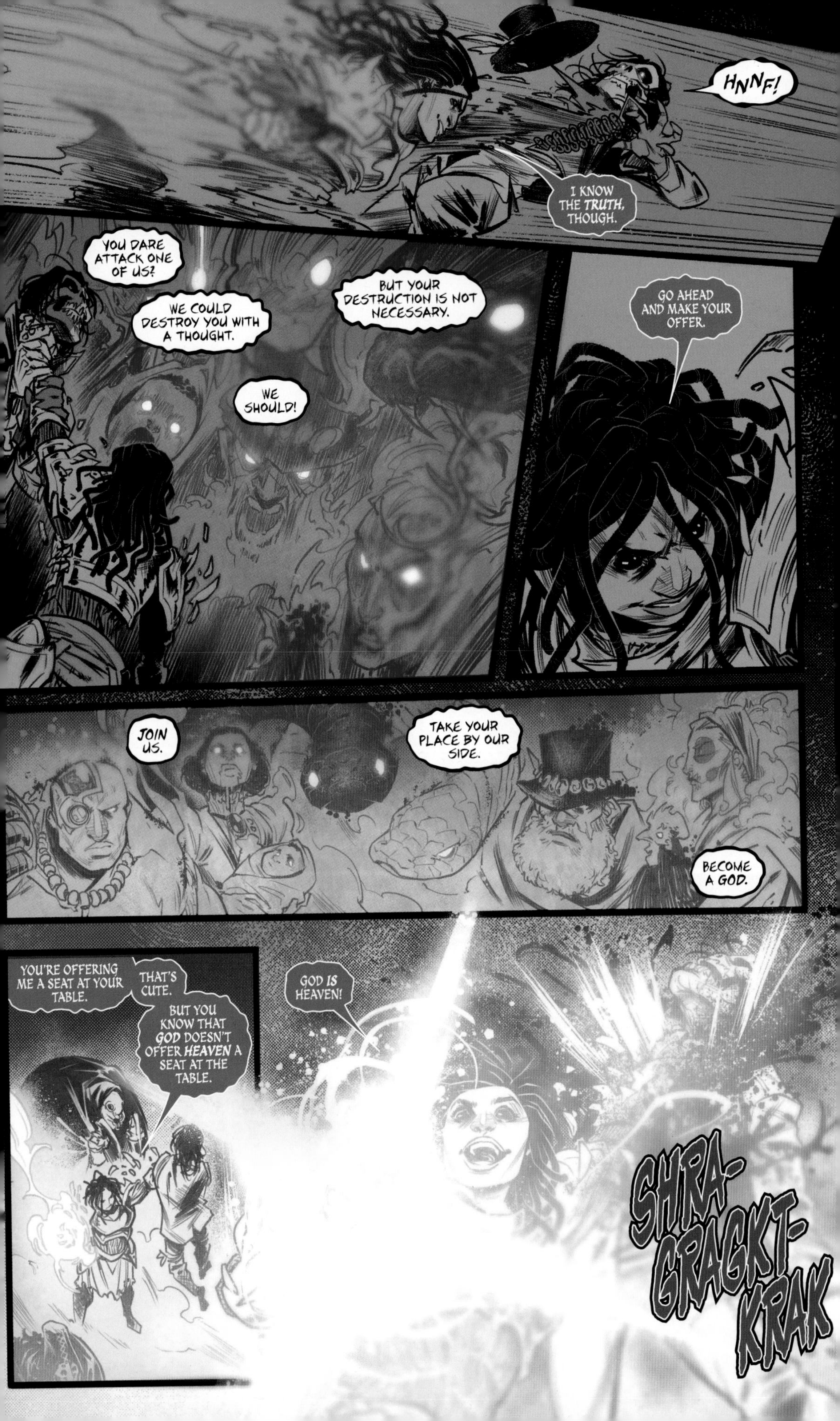
HNNF!
I KNOW THE TRUTH, THOUGH.
YOU DARE ATTACK ONE OF US?
WE COULD DESTROY YOU WITH A THOUGHT.
WE SHOULD!
BUT YOUR DESTRUCTION IS NOT NECESSARY.
GO AHEAD AND MAKE YOUR OFFER.
JOIN US.
TAKE YOUR PLACE BY OUR SIDE.
BECOME A GOD.
YOU'RE OFFERING ME A SEAT AT YOUR TABLE.
THAT'S CUTE.
BUT YOU KNOW THAT GOD DOESN'T OFFER HEAVEN A SEAT AT THE TABLE.
GOD IS HEAVEN!
SHRA-GRAGKT-KRAK

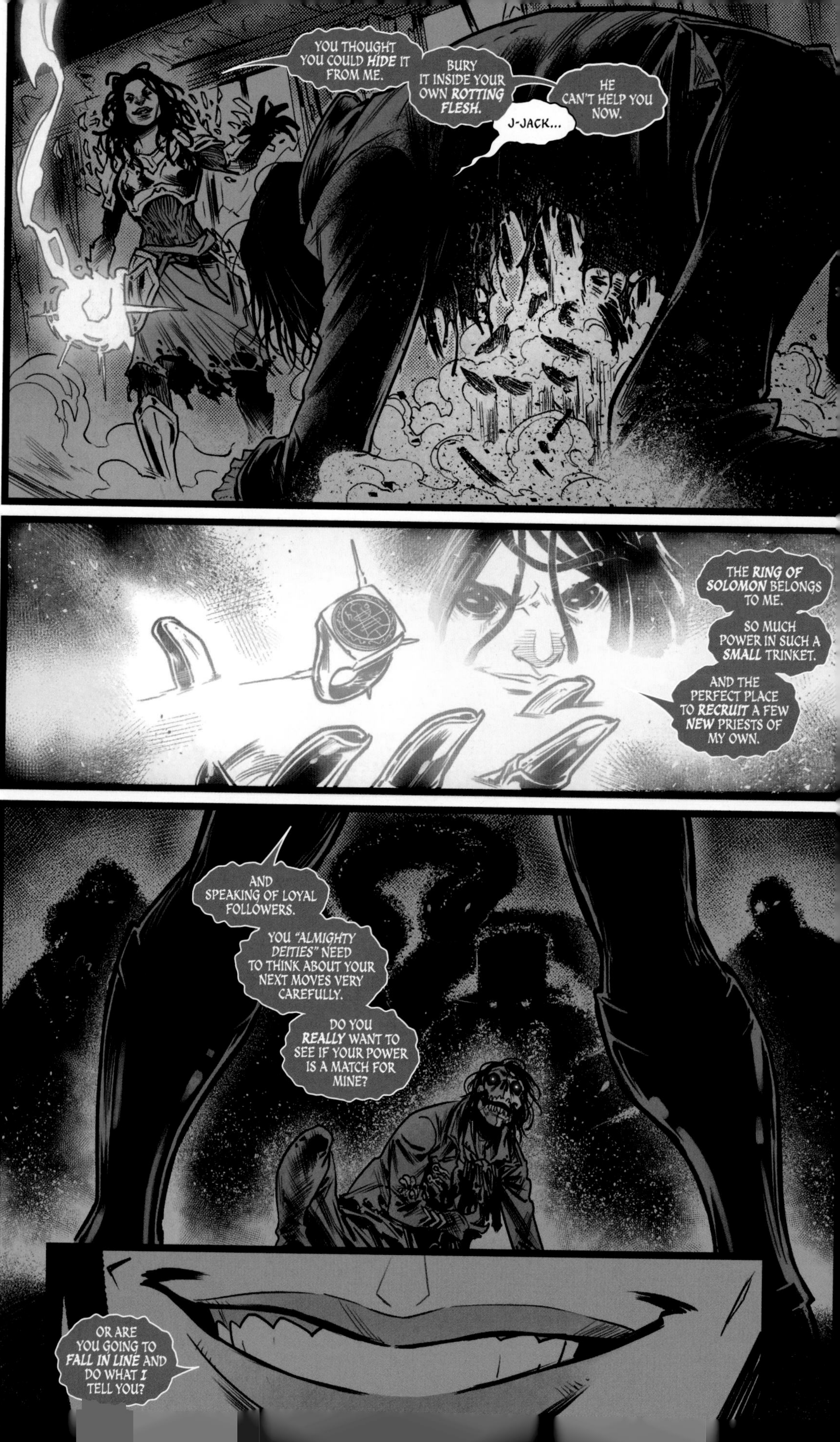
YOU THOUGHT YOU COULD HIDE IT FROM ME.
BURY IT INSIDE YOUR OWN ROTTING FLESH.
J-JACK...
HE CAN'T HELP YOU NOW.
THE RING OF SOLOMON BELONGS TO ME.
SO MUCH POWER IN SUCH A SMALL TRINKET.
AND THE PERFECT PLACE TO RECRUIT A FEW NEW PRIESTS OF MY OWN.
AND SPEAKING OF LOYAL FOLLOWERS.
YOU "ALMIGHTY DEITIES" NEED TO THINK ABOUT YOUR NEXT MOVES VERY CAREFULLY.
DO YOU REALLY WANT TO SEE IF YOUR POWER IS A MATCH FOR MINE?
OR ARE YOU GOING TO FALL IN LINE AND DO WHAT I TELL YOU?

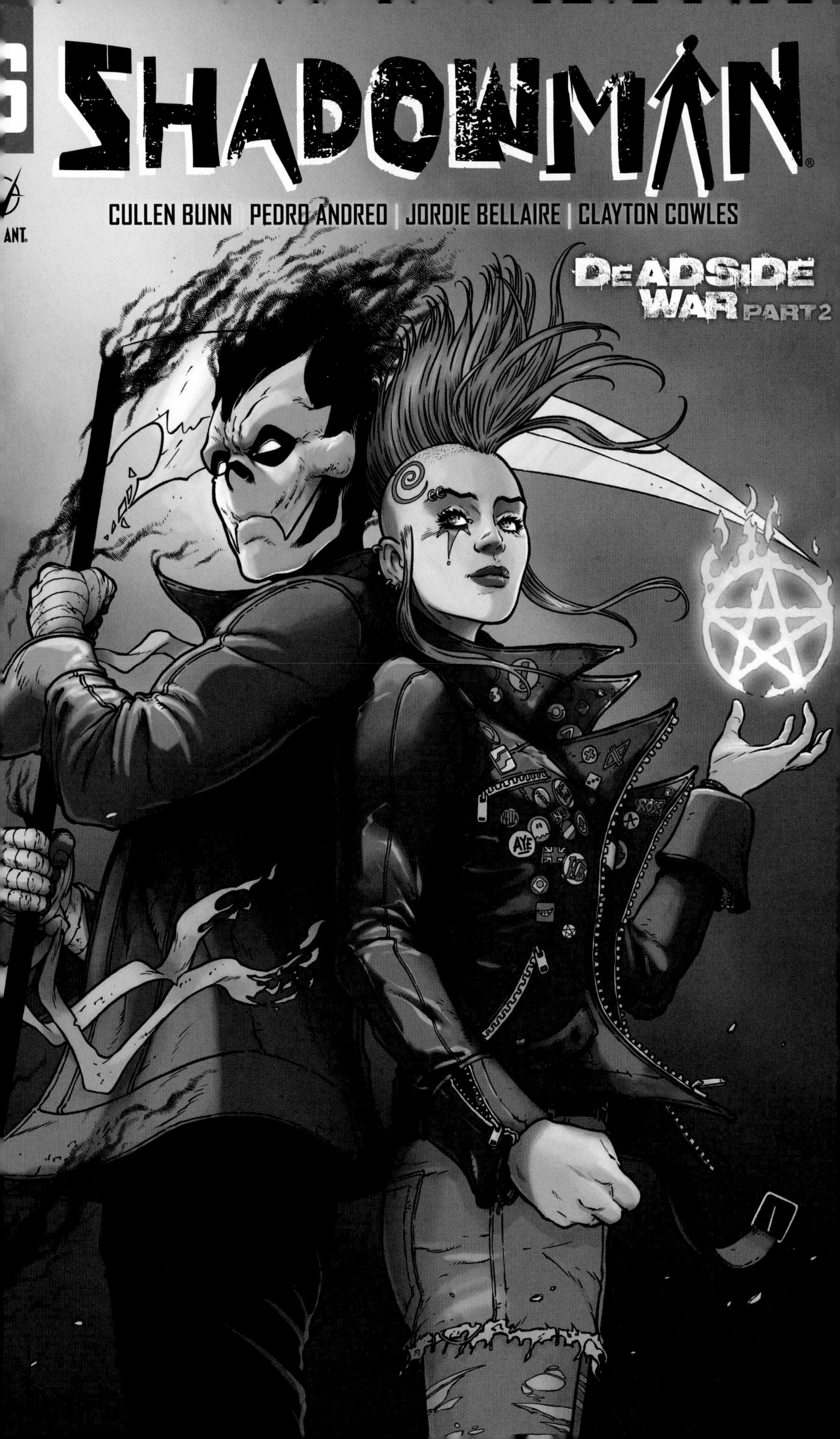

SHADOWMAN
CULLEN BUNN | PEDRO ANDREO | JORDIE BELLAIRE | CLAYTON COWLES
DEADSIDE WAR PART 2

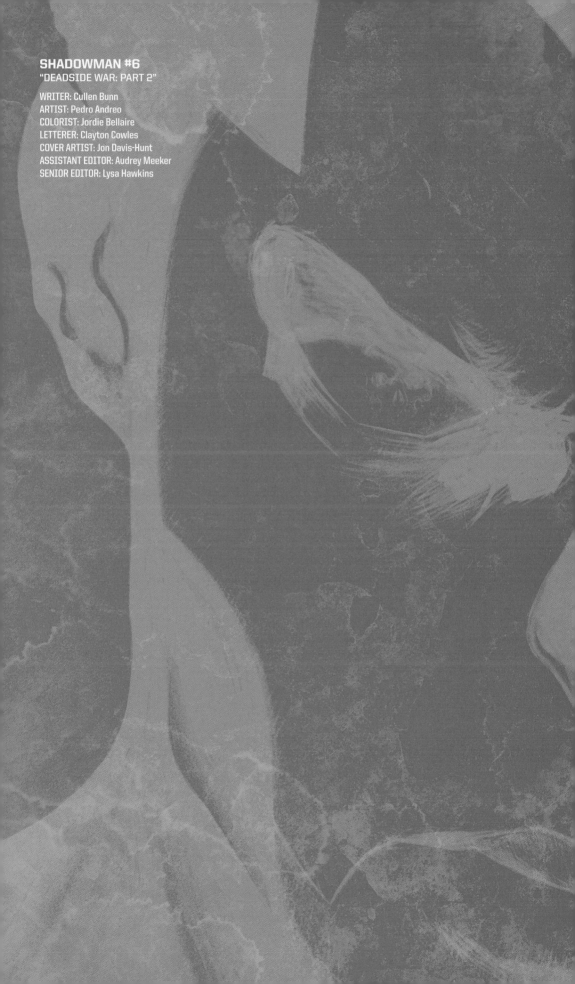

SHADOWMAN #6
"DEADSIDE WAR: PART 2"

WRITER: Cullen Bunn
ARTIST: Pedro Andreo
COLORIST: Jordie Bellaire
LETTERER: Clayton Cowles
COVER ARTIST: Jon Davis-Hunt
ASSISTANT EDITOR: Audrey Meeker
SENIOR EDITOR: Lysa Hawkins

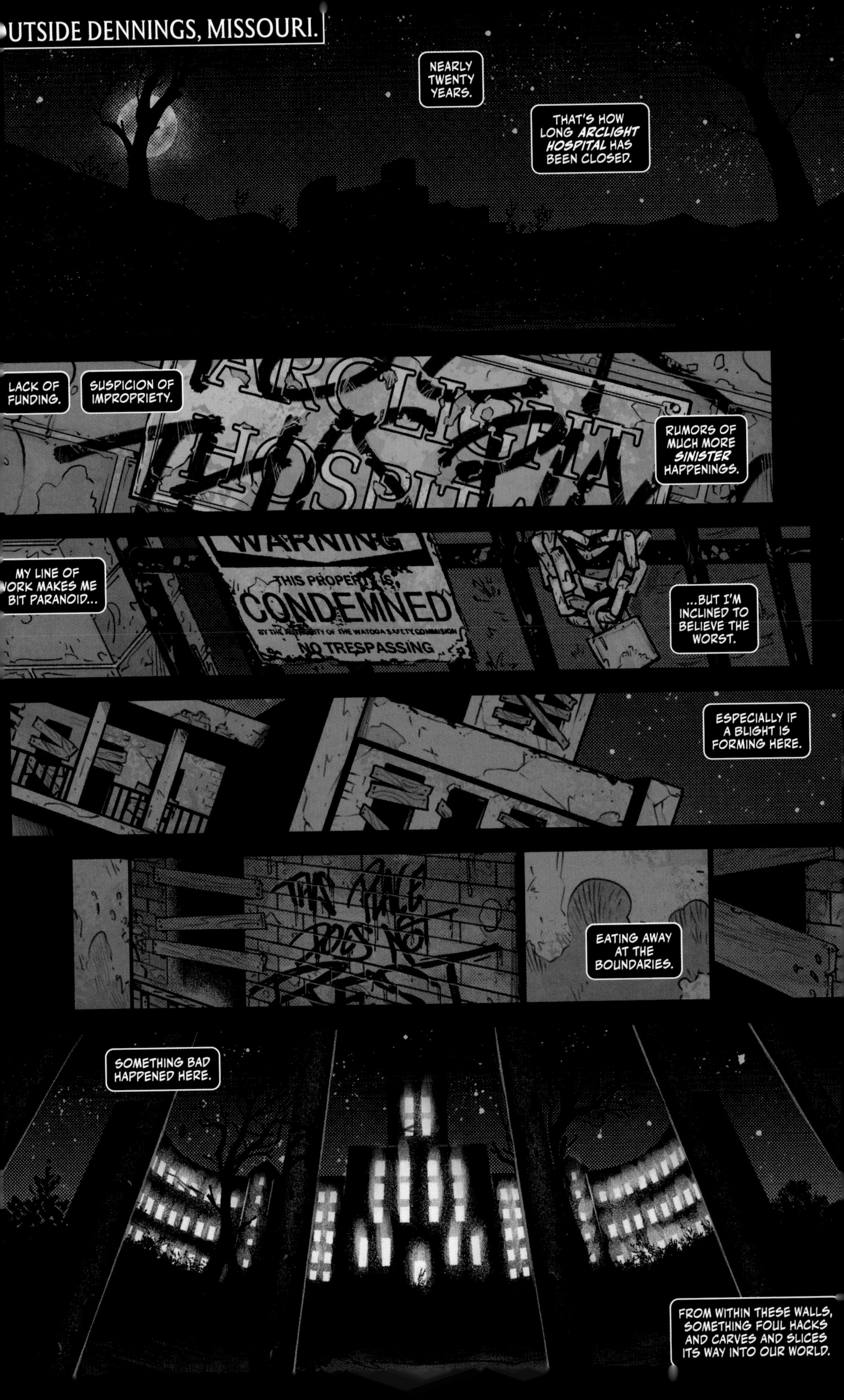
OUTSIDE DENNINGS, MISSOURI.
NEARLY TWENTY YEARS.
THAT'S HOW LONG ARCLIGHT HOSPITAL HAS BEEN CLOSED.
LACK OF FUNDING.
SUSPICION OF IMPROPRIETY.
RUMORS OF MUCH MORE SINISTER HAPPENINGS.
WARNING
CONDEMNED
NO TRESPASSING
MY LINE OF WORK MAKES ME A BIT PARANOID...
...BUT I'M INCLINED TO BELIEVE THE WORST.
ESPECIALLY IF A BLIGHT IS FORMING HERE.
EATING AWAY AT THE BOUNDARIES.
SOMETHING BAD HAPPENED HERE.
FROM WITHIN THESE WALLS, SOMETHING FOUL HACKS AND CARVES AND SLICES ITS WAY INTO OUR WORLD.

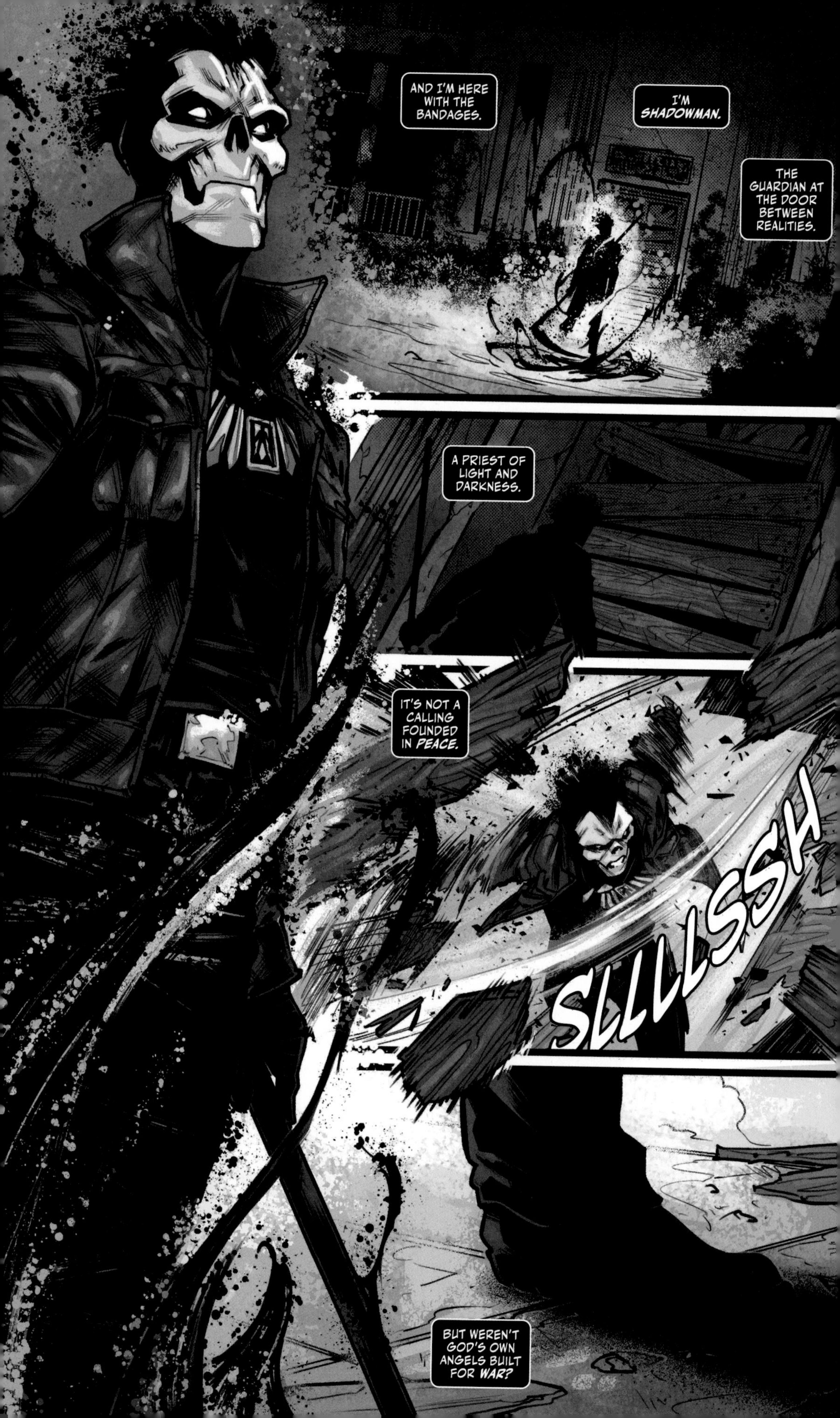
AND I'M HERE WITH THE BANDAGES.
I'M *SHADOWMAN.*
THE GUARDIAN AT THE DOOR BETWEEN REALITIES.
A PRIEST OF LIGHT AND DARKNESS.
IT'S NOT A CALLING FOUNDED IN *PEACE.*
SLLLSSSH
BUT WEREN'T GOD'S OWN ANGELS BUILT FOR *WAR?*

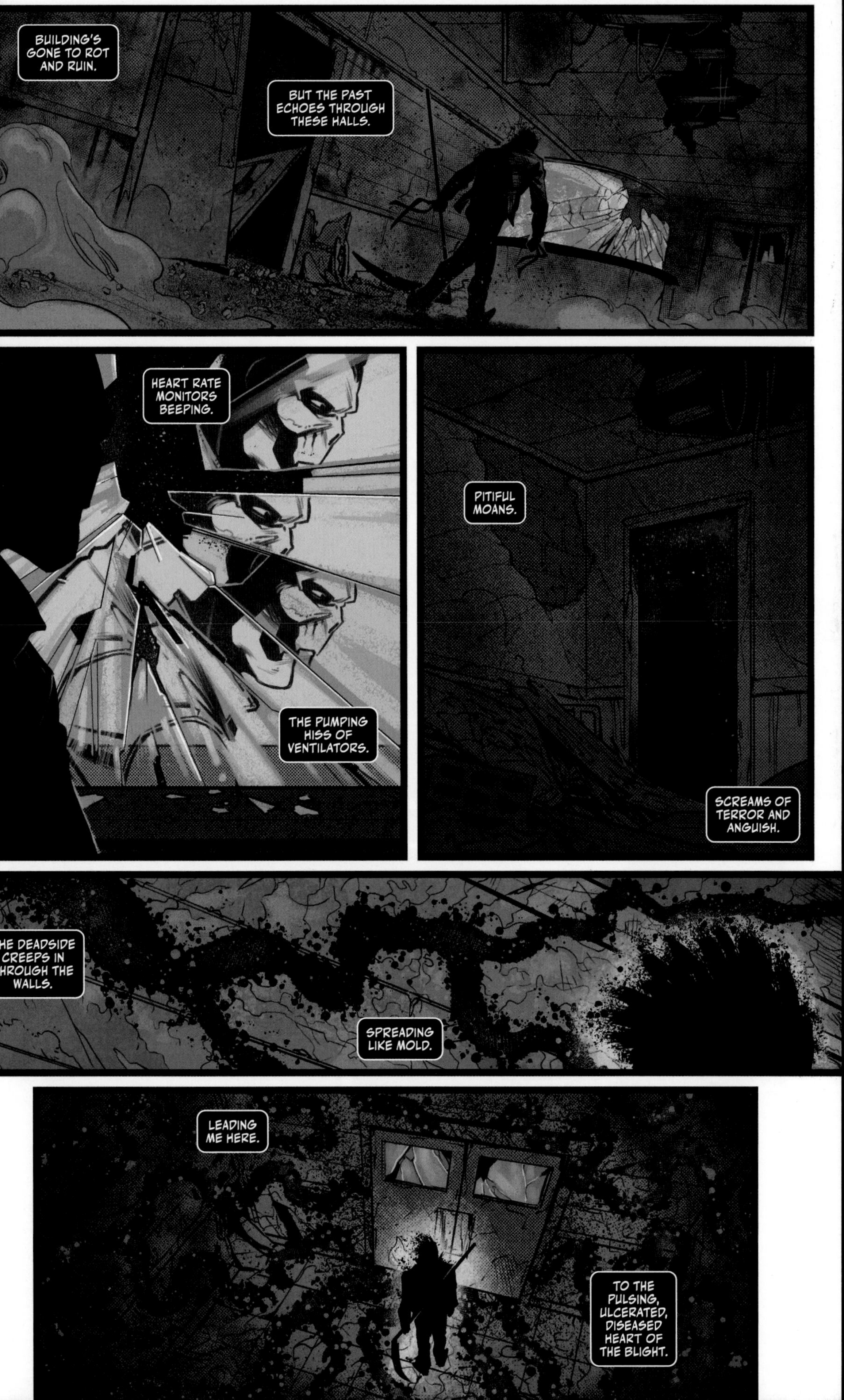

BUILDING'S GONE TO ROT AND RUIN.
BUT THE PAST ECHOES THROUGH THESE HALLS.
HEART RATE MONITORS BEEPING.
THE PUMPING HISS OF VENTILATORS.
PITIFUL MOANS.
SCREAMS OF TERROR AND ANGUISH.
HE DEADSIDE CREEPS IN HROUGH THE WALLS.
SPREADING LIKE MOLD.
LEADING ME HERE.
TO THE PULSING, ULCERATED, DISEASED HEART OF THE BLIGHT.

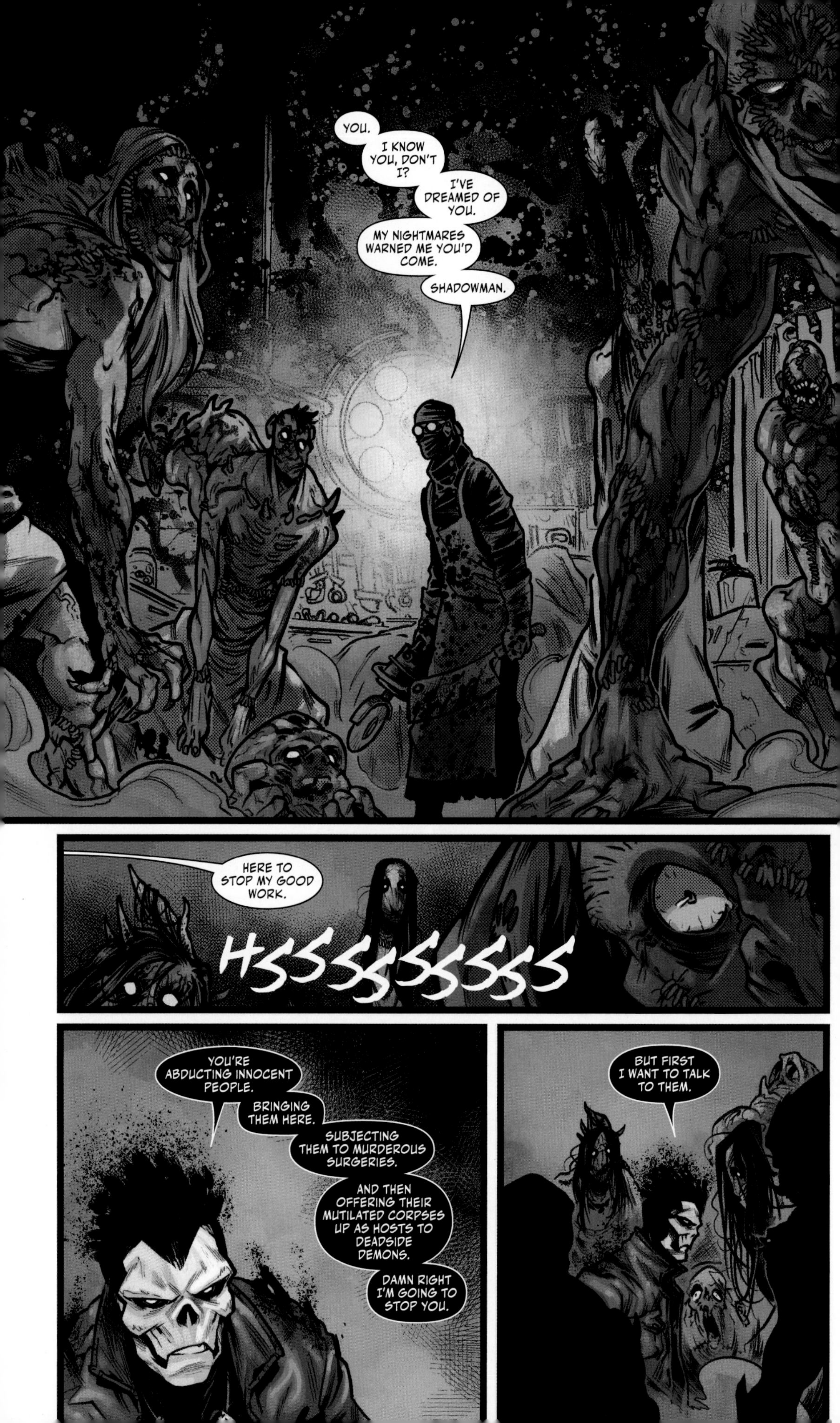
YOU.
I KNOW YOU, DON'T I?
I'VE DREAMED OF YOU.
MY NIGHTMARES WARNED ME YOU'D COME.
SHADOWMAN.
HERE TO STOP MY GOOD WORK.
HSSSSSSSSS
YOU'RE ABDUCTING INNOCENT PEOPLE.
BRINGING THEM HERE.
SUBJECTING THEM TO MURDEROUS SURGERIES.
AND THEN OFFERING THEIR MUTILATED CORPSES UP AS HOSTS TO DEADSIDE DEMONS.
DAMN RIGHT I'M GOING TO STOP YOU.
BUT FIRST I WANT TO TALK TO THEM.

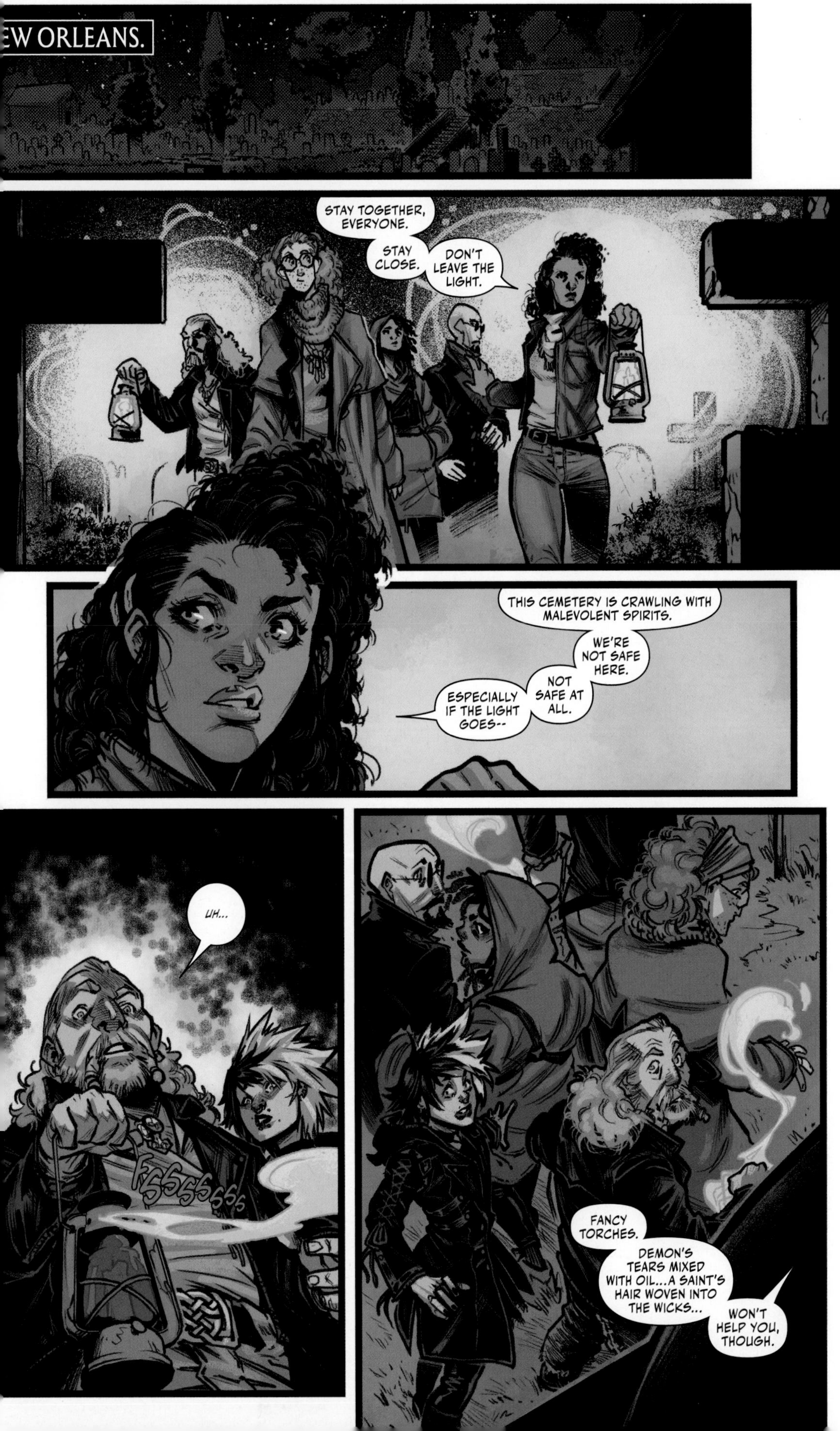
EW ORLEANS.
STAY TOGETHER, EVERYONE.
STAY CLOSE.
DON'T LEAVE THE LIGHT.
THIS CEMETERY IS CRAWLING WITH MALEVOLENT SPIRITS.
WE'RE NOT SAFE HERE.
NOT SAFE AT ALL.
ESPECIALLY IF THE LIGHT GOES--
UH...
FSSSSSSS
FANCY TORCHES.
DEMON'S TEARS MIXED WITH OIL...A SAINT'S HAIR WOVEN INTO THE WICKS...
WON'T HELP YOU, THOUGH.

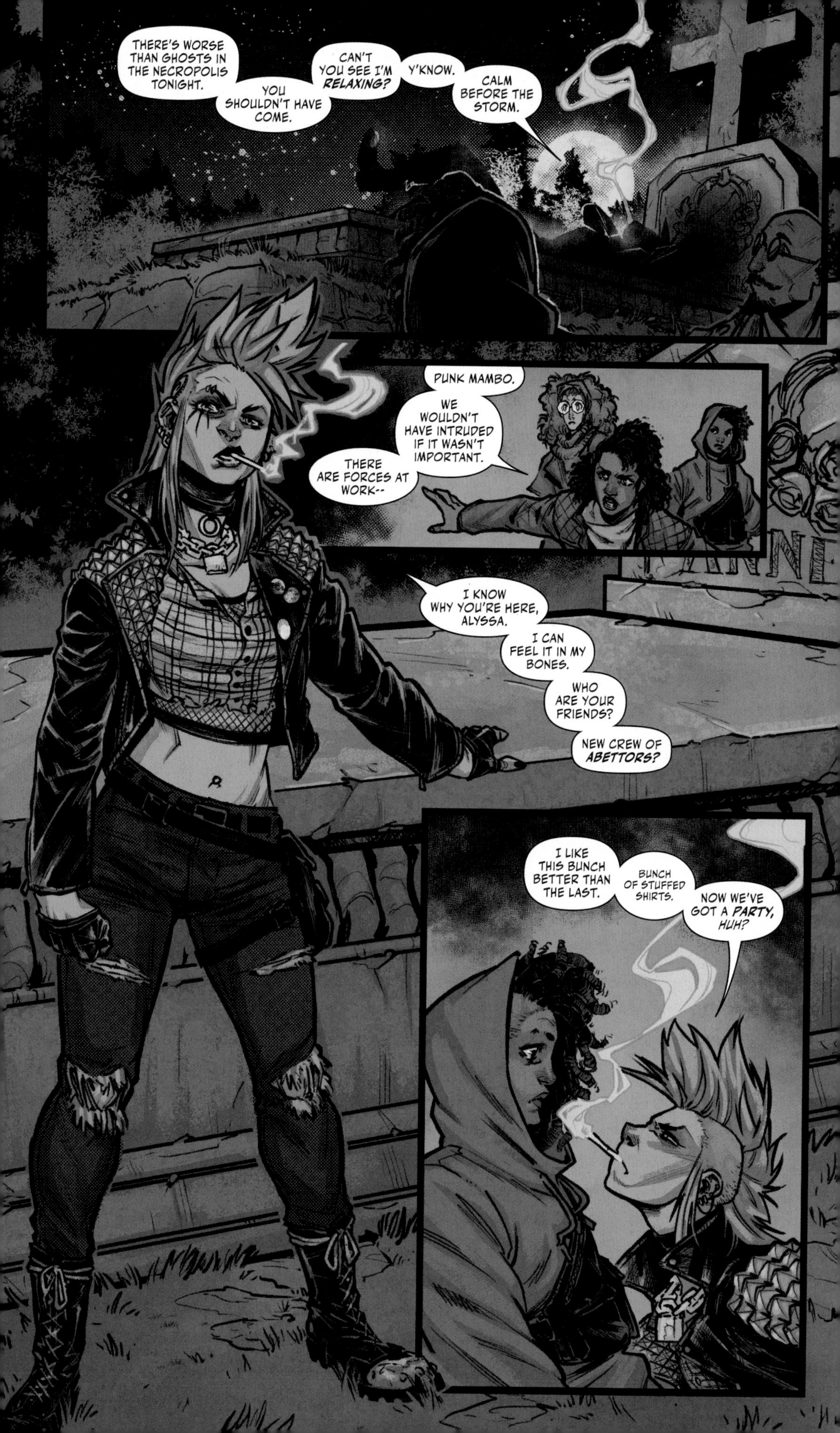
THERE'S WORSE THAN GHOSTS IN THE NECROPOLIS TONIGHT.
YOU SHOULDN'T HAVE COME.
CAN'T YOU SEE I'M *RELAXING?*
Y'KNOW.
CALM BEFORE THE STORM.
PUNK MAMBO.
WE WOULDN'T HAVE INTRUDED IF IT WASN'T IMPORTANT.
THERE ARE FORCES AT WORK--
I KNOW WHY YOU'RE HERE, ALYSSA.
I CAN FEEL IT IN MY BONES.
WHO ARE YOUR FRIENDS?
NEW CREW OF *ABETTORS?*
I LIKE THIS BUNCH BETTER THAN THE LAST.
BUNCH OF STUFFED SHIRTS.
NOW WE'VE GOT A *PARTY,* HUH?

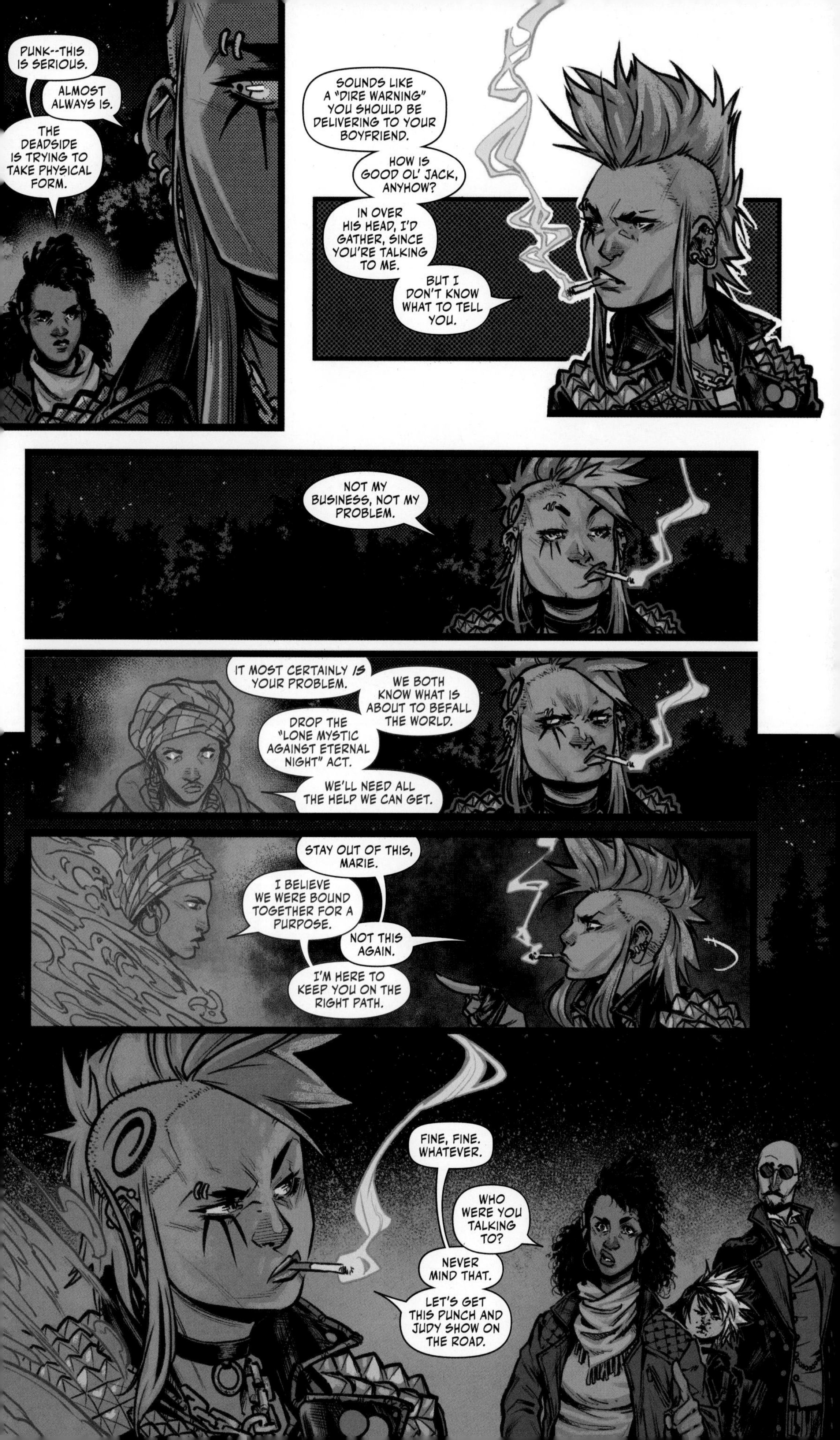
PUNK--THIS IS SERIOUS.
ALMOST ALWAYS IS.
THE DEADSIDE IS TRYING TO TAKE PHYSICAL FORM.
SOUNDS LIKE A "DIRE WARNING" YOU SHOULD BE DELIVERING TO YOUR BOYFRIEND.
HOW IS GOOD OL' JACK, ANYHOW?
IN OVER HIS HEAD, I'D GATHER, SINCE YOU'RE TALKING TO ME.
BUT I DON'T KNOW WHAT TO TELL YOU.
NOT MY BUSINESS, NOT MY PROBLEM.
IT MOST CERTAINLY *IS* YOUR PROBLEM.
WE BOTH KNOW WHAT IS ABOUT TO BEFALL THE WORLD.
DROP THE "LONE MYSTIC AGAINST ETERNAL NIGHT" ACT.
WE'LL NEED ALL THE HELP WE CAN GET.
STAY OUT OF THIS, MARIE.
I BELIEVE WE WERE BOUND TOGETHER FOR A PURPOSE.
NOT THIS AGAIN.
I'M HERE TO KEEP YOU ON THE RIGHT PATH.
FINE, FINE. WHATEVER.
WHO WERE YOU TALKING TO?
NEVER MIND THAT.
LET'S GET THIS PUNCH AND JUDY SHOW ON THE ROAD.

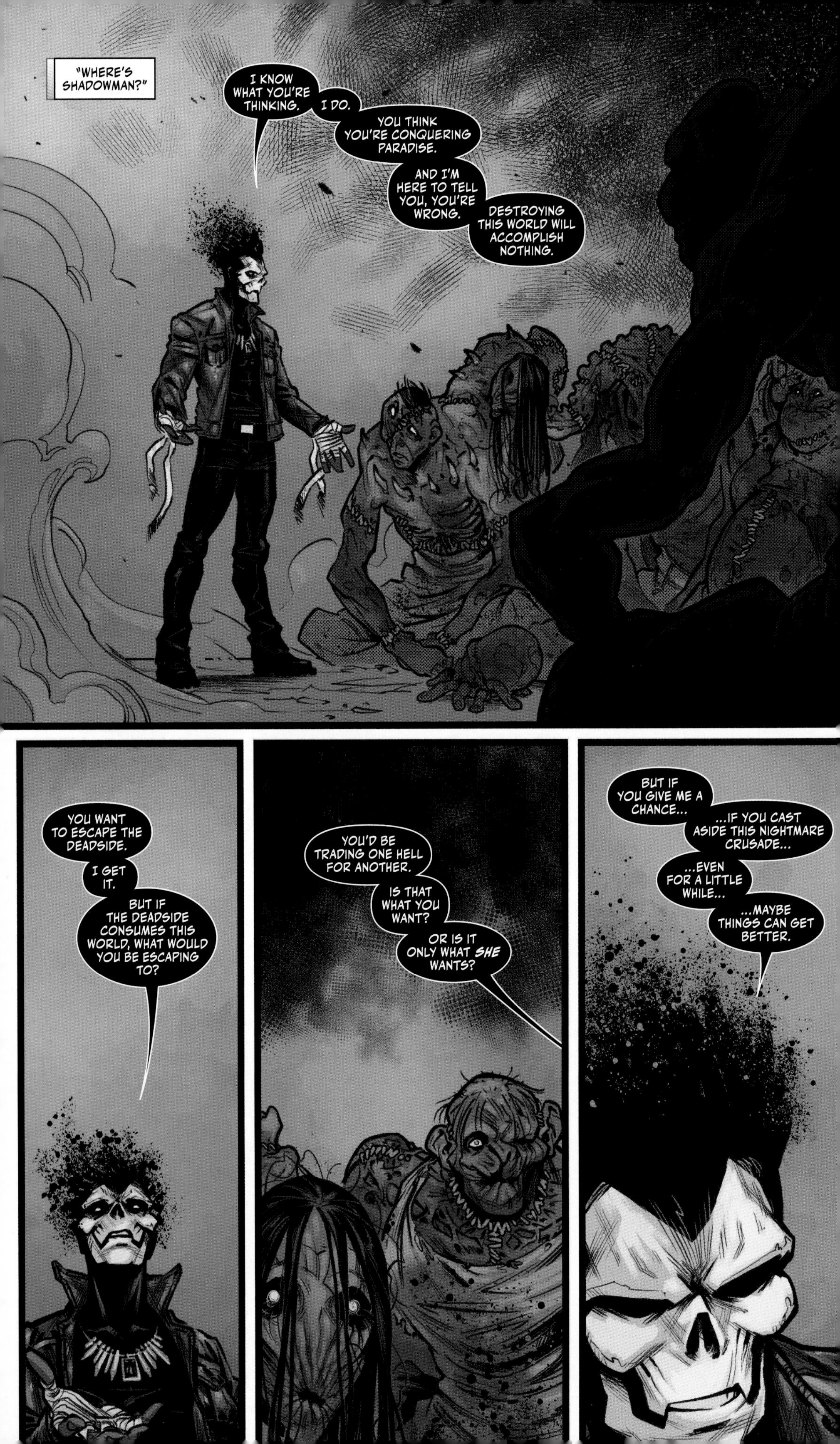
"WHERE'S SHADOWMAN?"
I KNOW WHAT YOU'RE THINKING.
I DO.
YOU THINK YOU'RE CONQUERING PARADISE.
AND I'M HERE TO TELL YOU, YOU'RE WRONG.
DESTROYING THIS WORLD WILL ACCOMPLISH NOTHING.
YOU WANT TO ESCAPE THE DEADSIDE.
I GET IT.
BUT IF THE DEADSIDE CONSUMES THIS WORLD, WHAT WOULD YOU BE ESCAPING TO?
YOU'D BE TRADING ONE HELL FOR ANOTHER.
IS THAT WHAT YOU WANT?
OR IS IT ONLY WHAT *SHE* WANTS?
BUT IF YOU GIVE ME A CHANCE...
...IF YOU CAST ASIDE THIS NIGHTMARE CRUSADE...
...EVEN FOR A LITTLE WHILE...
...MAYBE THINGS CAN GET BETTER.

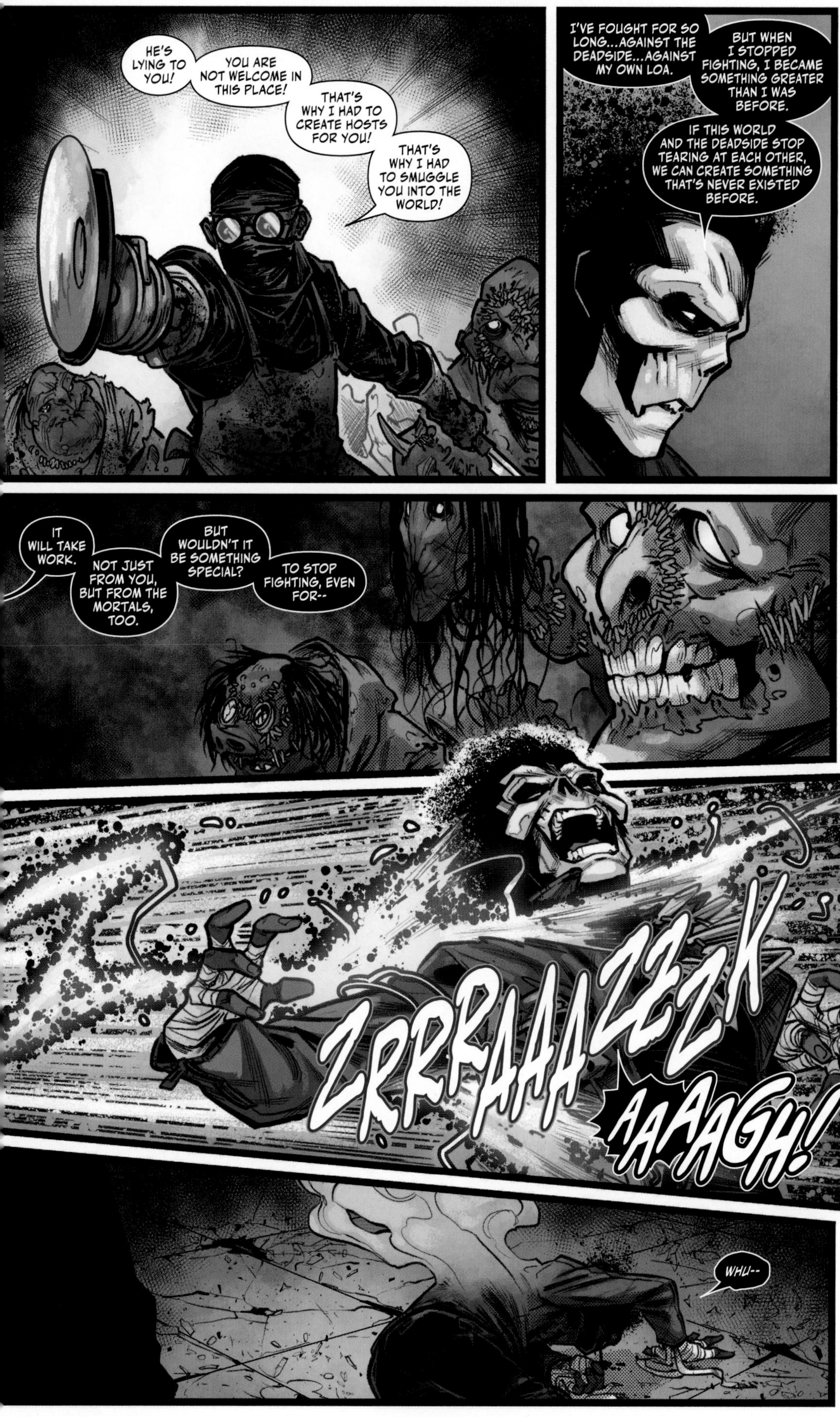
HE'S LYING TO YOU!
YOU ARE NOT WELCOME IN THIS PLACE!
THAT'S WHY I HAD TO CREATE HOSTS FOR YOU!
THAT'S WHY I HAD TO SMUGGLE YOU INTO THE WORLD!
I'VE FOUGHT FOR SO LONG...AGAINST THE DEADSIDE...AGAINST MY OWN LOA.
BUT WHEN I STOPPED FIGHTING, I BECAME SOMETHING GREATER THAN I WAS BEFORE.
IF THIS WORLD AND THE DEADSIDE STOP TEARING AT EACH OTHER, WE CAN CREATE SOMETHING THAT'S NEVER EXISTED BEFORE.
IT WILL TAKE WORK.
NOT JUST FROM YOU, BUT FROM THE MORTALS, TOO.
BUT WOULDN'T IT BE SOMETHING SPECIAL?
TO STOP FIGHTING, EVEN FOR--
ZRRRAAAZZZK
AAAAAGH!
WHU--

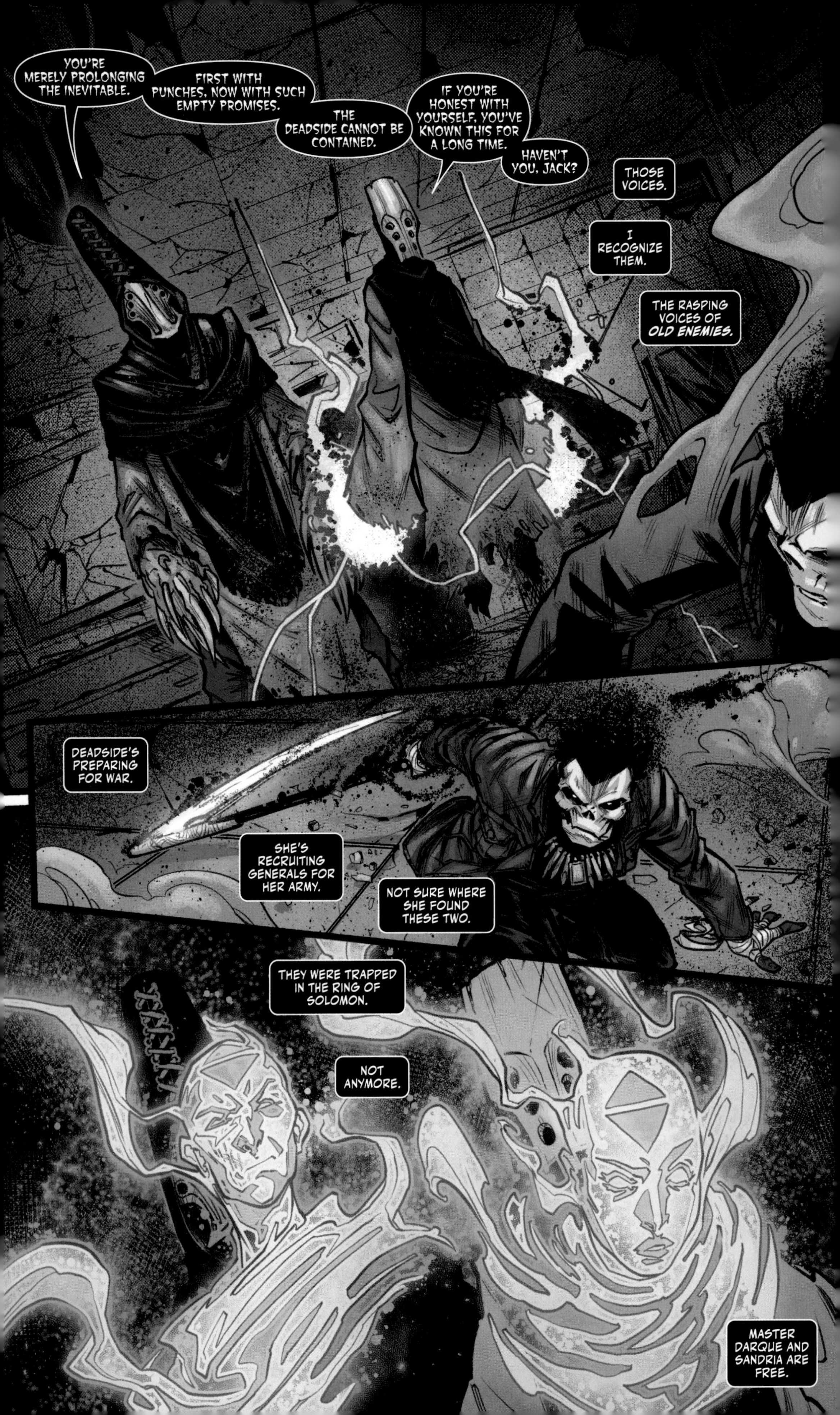
YOU'RE MERELY PROLONGING THE INEVITABLE.
FIRST WITH PUNCHES, NOW WITH SUCH EMPTY PROMISES.
THE DEADSIDE CANNOT BE CONTAINED.
IF YOU'RE HONEST WITH YOURSELF, YOU'VE KNOWN THIS FOR A LONG TIME.
HAVEN'T YOU, JACK?
THOSE VOICES.
I RECOGNIZE THEM.
THE RASPING VOICES OF *OLD ENEMIES.*
DEADSIDE'S PREPARING FOR WAR.
SHE'S RECRUITING GENERALS FOR HER ARMY.
NOT SURE WHERE SHE FOUND THESE TWO.
THEY WERE TRAPPED IN THE RING OF SOLOMON.
NOT ANYMORE.
MASTER DARQUE AND SANDRIA ARE FREE.

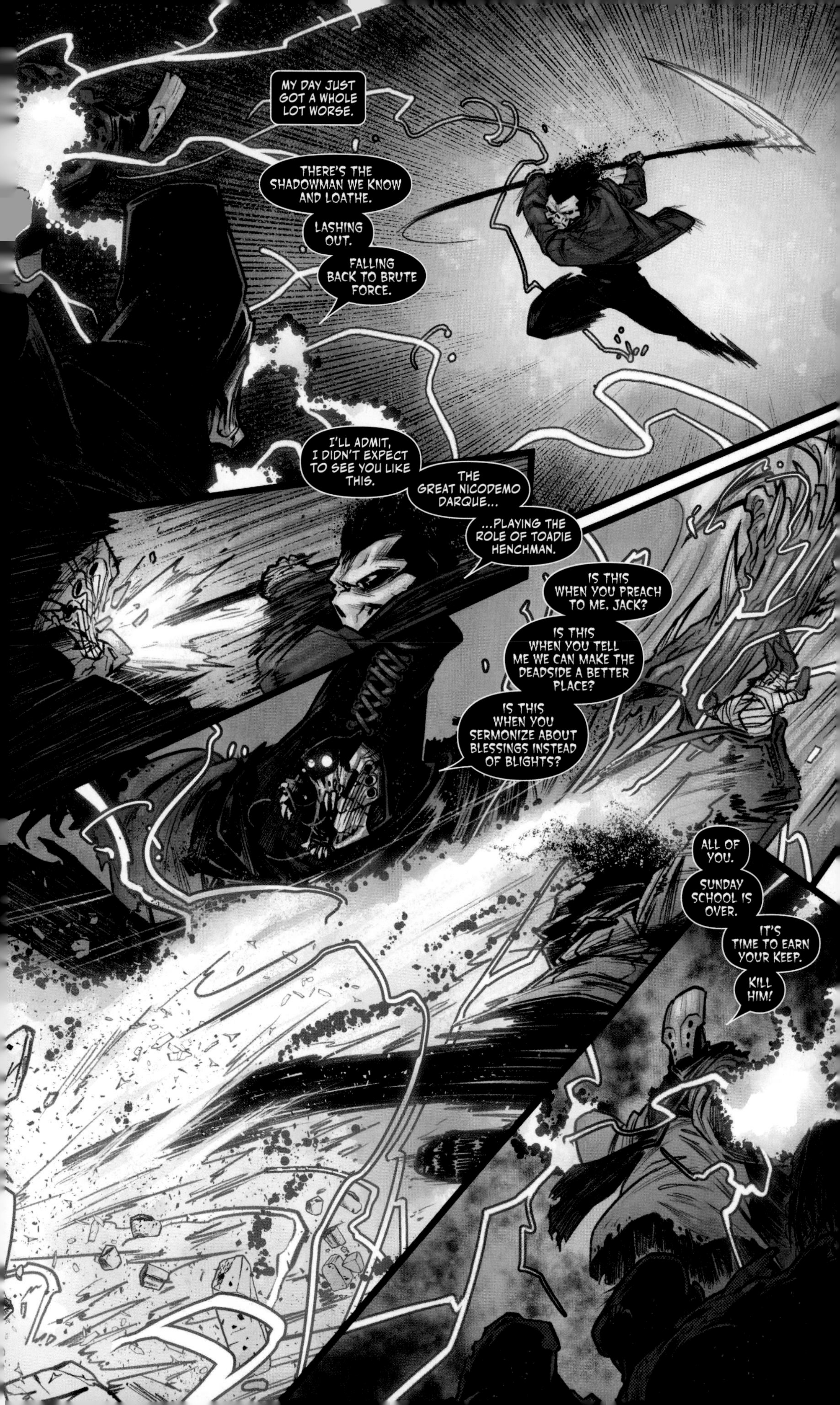

MY DAY JUST GOT A WHOLE LOT WORSE.
THERE'S THE SHADOWMAN WE KNOW AND LOATHE.
LASHING OUT.
FALLING BACK TO BRUTE FORCE.
I'LL ADMIT, I DIDN'T EXPECT TO SEE YOU LIKE THIS.
THE GREAT NICODEMO DARQUE...
...PLAYING THE ROLE OF TOADIE HENCHMAN.
IS THIS WHEN YOU PREACH TO ME, JACK?
IS THIS WHEN YOU TELL ME WE CAN MAKE THE DEADSIDE A BETTER PLACE?
IS THIS WHEN YOU SERMONIZE ABOUT BLESSINGS INSTEAD OF BLIGHTS?
ALL OF YOU.
SUNDAY SCHOOL IS OVER.
IT'S TIME TO EARN YOUR KEEP.
KILL HIM!

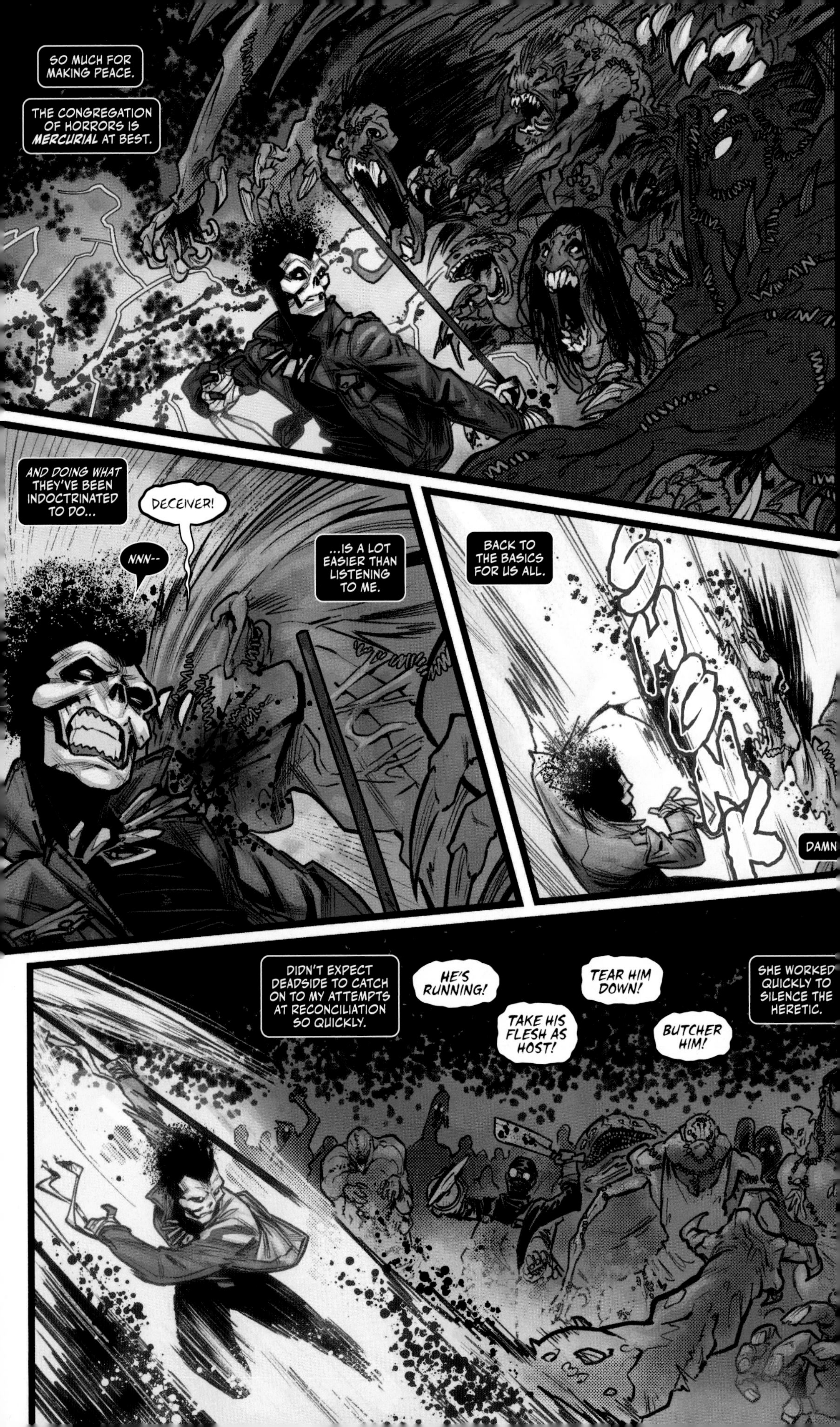
SO MUCH FOR MAKING PEACE.
THE CONGREGATION OF HORRORS IS *MERCURIAL* AT BEST.
AND DOING WHAT THEY'VE BEEN INDOCTRINATED TO DO...
DECEIVER!
NNN--
...IS A LOT EASIER THAN LISTENING TO ME.
BACK TO THE BASICS FOR US ALL.
DAMN
DIDN'T EXPECT DEADSIDE TO CATCH ON TO MY ATTEMPTS AT RECONCILIATION SO QUICKLY.
HE'S RUNNING!
TAKE HIS FLESH AS HOST!
TEAR HIM DOWN!
BUTCHER HIM!
SHE WORKED QUICKLY TO SILENCE THE HERETIC.

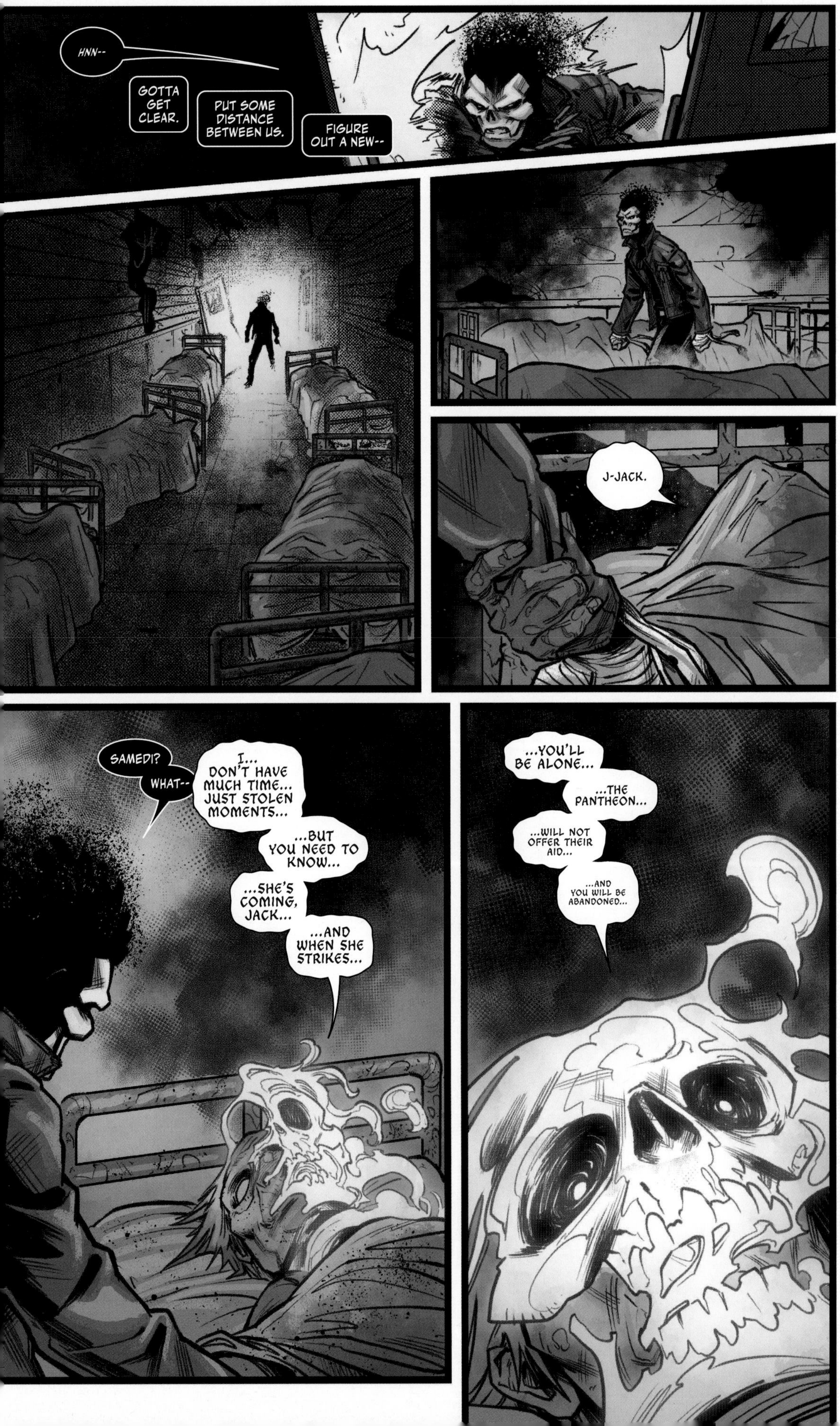
HNN--
GOTTA GET CLEAR.
PUT SOME DISTANCE BETWEEN US.
FIGURE OUT A NEW--
J-JACK.
SAMEDI?
WHAT--
I... DON'T HAVE MUCH TIME... JUST STOLEN MOMENTS...
...BUT YOU NEED TO KNOW...
...SHE'S COMING, JACK...
...AND WHEN SHE STRIKES...
...YOU'LL BE ALONE...
...THE PANTHEON...
...WILL NOT OFFER THEIR AID...
...AND YOU WILL BE ABANDONED...

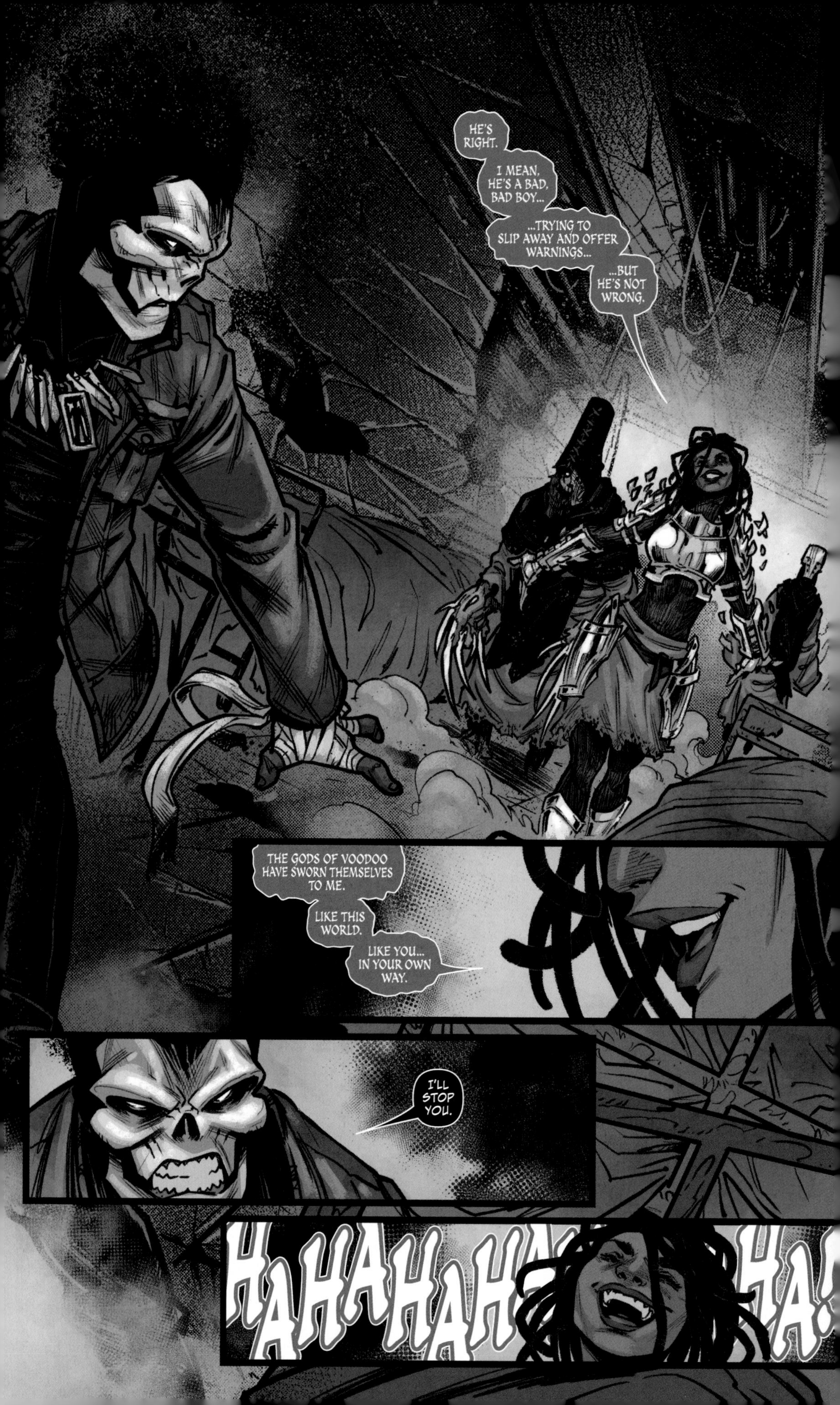
HE'S RIGHT.
I MEAN. HE'S A BAD, BAD BOY...
...TRYING TO SLIP AWAY AND OFFER WARNINGS...
...BUT HE'S NOT WRONG.
THE GODS OF VOODOO HAVE SWORN THEMSELVES TO ME.
LIKE THIS WORLD.
LIKE YOU... IN YOUR OWN WAY.
I'LL STOP YOU.
HAHAHAHAHA HAHA!

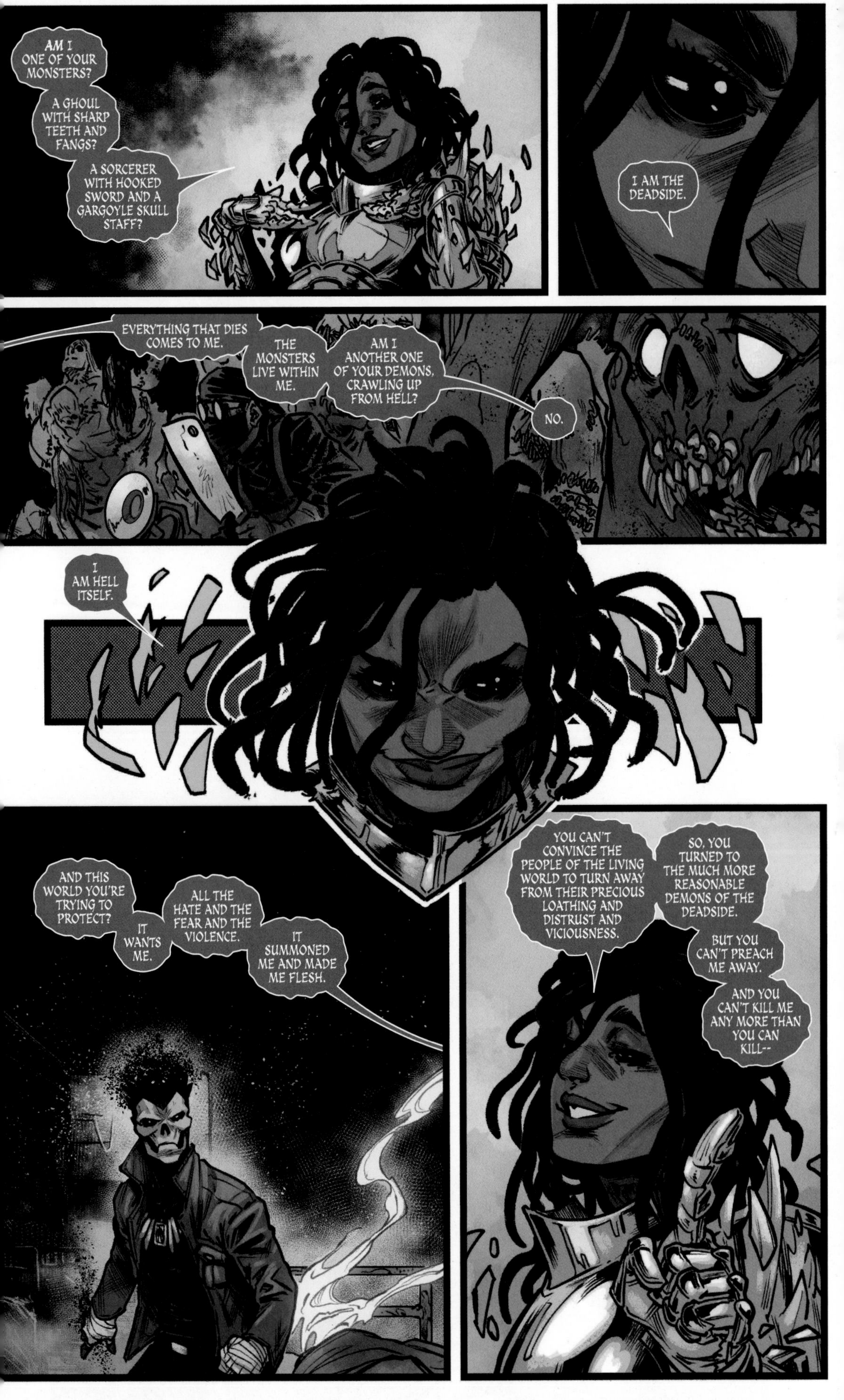
AM I ONE OF YOUR MONSTERS?
A GHOUL WITH SHARP TEETH AND FANGS?
A SORCERER WITH HOOKED SWORD AND A GARGOYLE SKULL STAFF?
I AM THE DEADSIDE.
EVERYTHING THAT DIES COMES TO ME.
THE MONSTERS LIVE WITHIN ME.
AM I ANOTHER ONE OF YOUR DEMONS, CRAWLING UP FROM HELL?
NO.
I AM HELL ITSELF.
AND THIS WORLD YOU'RE TRYING TO PROTECT?
IT WANTS ME.
ALL THE HATE AND THE FEAR AND THE VIOLENCE.
IT SUMMONED ME AND MADE ME FLESH.
YOU CAN'T CONVINCE THE PEOPLE OF THE LIVING WORLD TO TURN AWAY FROM THEIR PRECIOUS LOATHING AND DISTRUST AND VICIOUSNESS.
SO, YOU TURNED TO THE MUCH MORE REASONABLE DEMONS OF THE DEADSIDE.
BUT YOU CAN'T PREACH ME AWAY.
AND YOU CAN'T KILL ME ANY MORE THAN YOU CAN KILL--

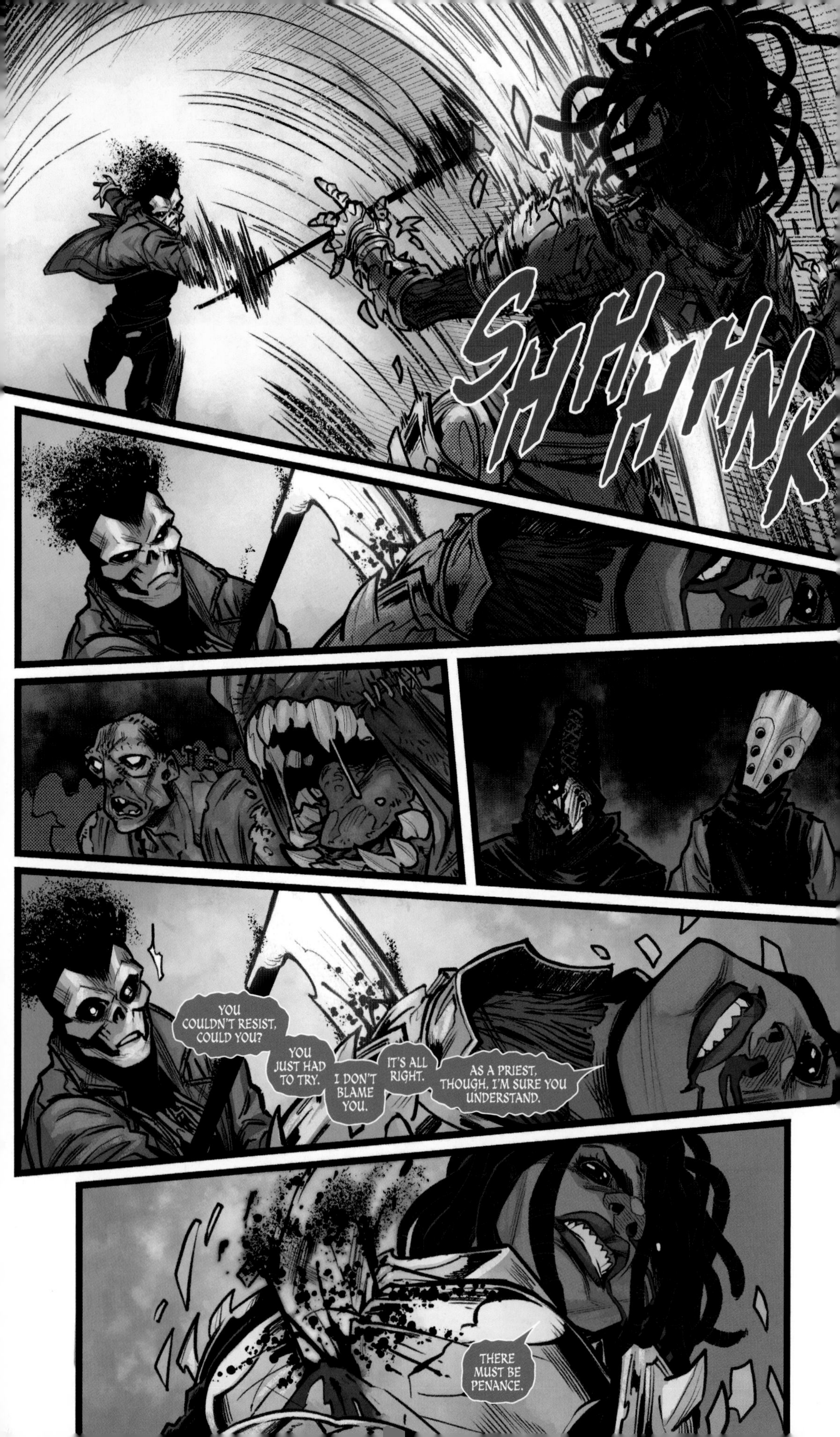
SHHHHNK
YOU COULDN'T RESIST, COULD YOU?
YOU JUST HAD TO TRY.
I DON'T BLAME YOU.
IT'S ALL RIGHT.
AS A PRIEST, THOUGH, I'M SURE YOU UNDERSTAND.
THERE MUST BE PENANCE.

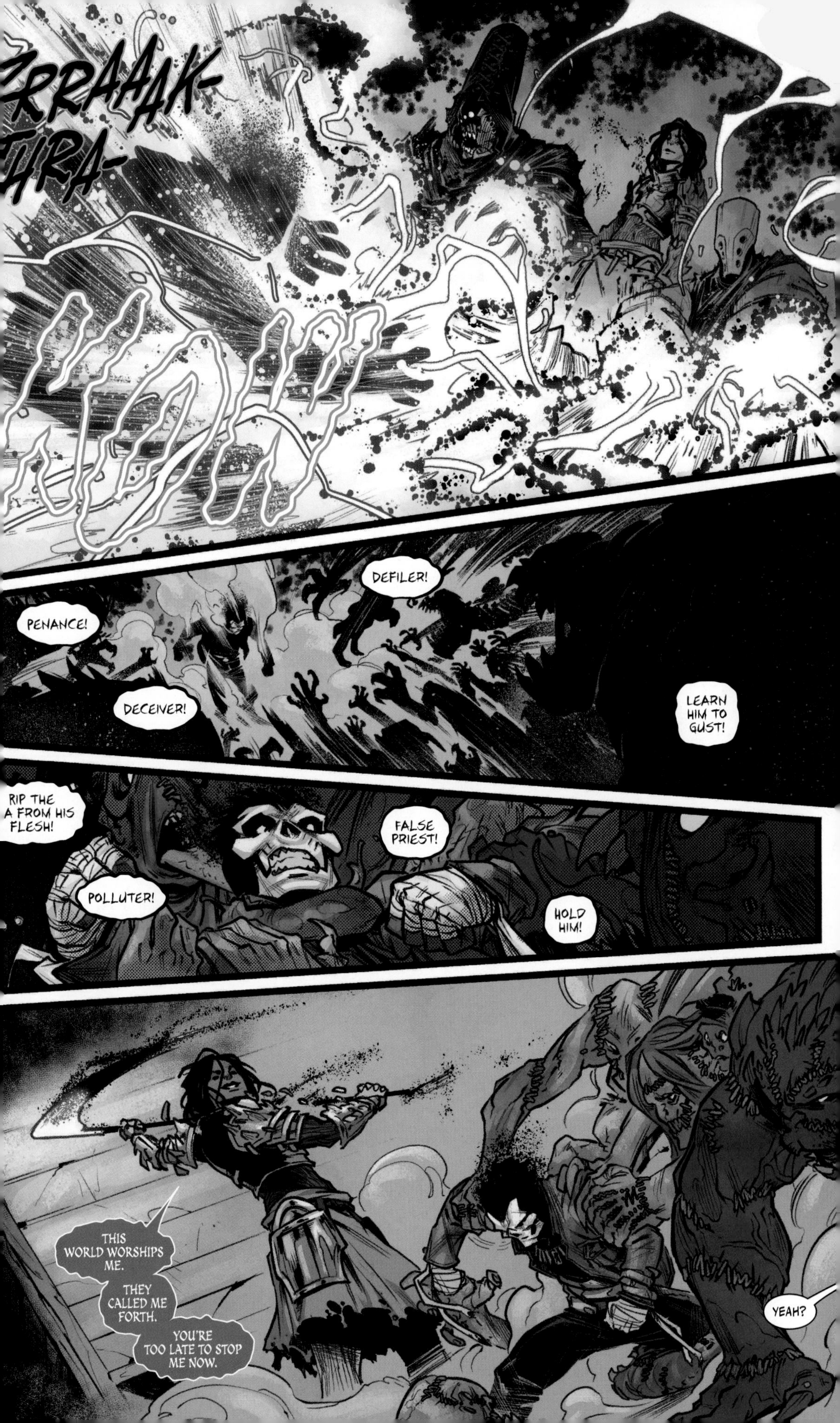
RRAAAK-
HRA-
PENANCE!
DEFILER!
DECEIVER!
LEARN HIM TO GUST!
RIP THE A FROM HIS FLESH!
FALSE PRIEST!
POLLUTER!
HOLD HIM!
THIS WORLD WORSHIPS ME.
THEY CALLED ME FORTH.
YOU'RE TOO LATE TO STOP ME NOW.
YEAH?

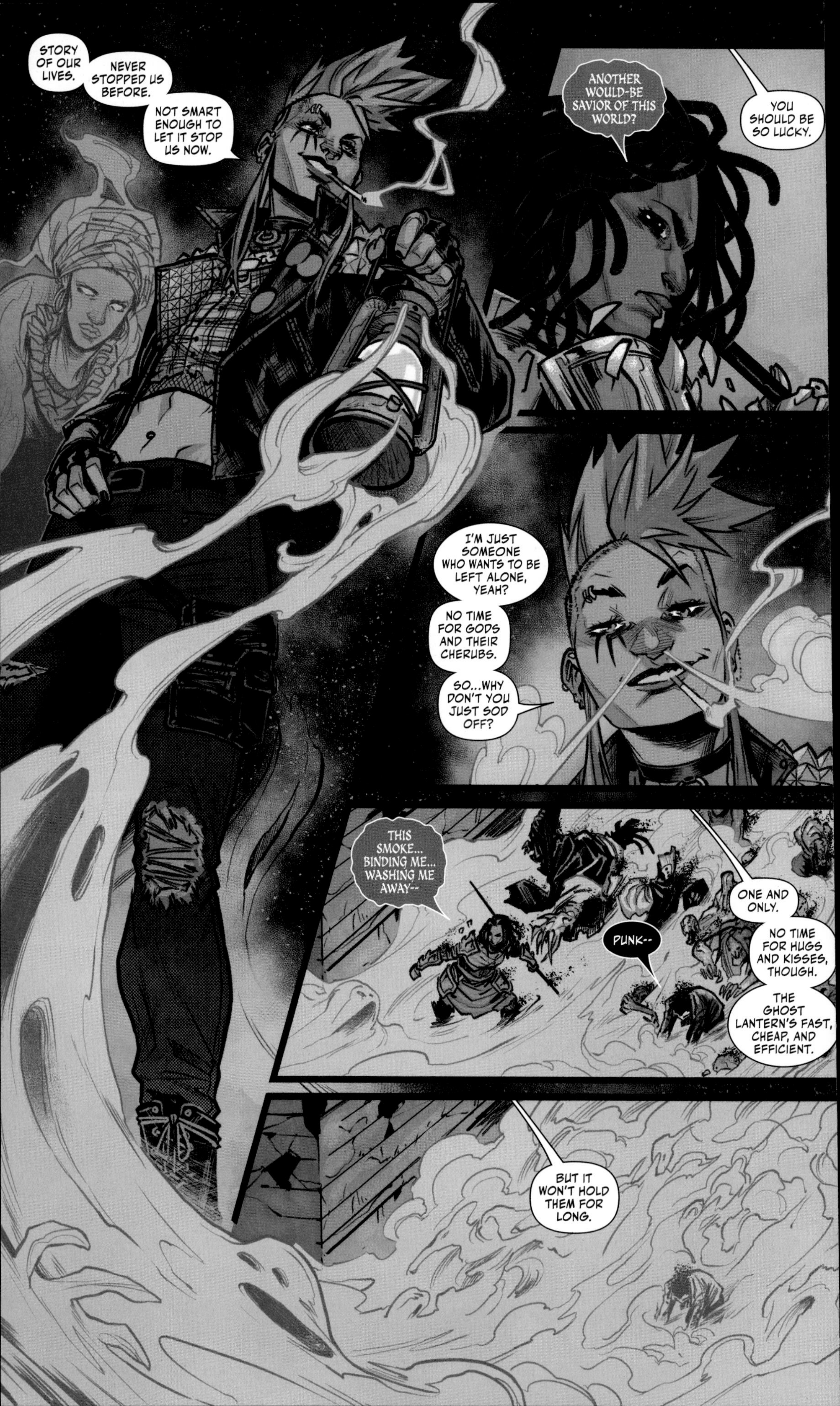
STORY OF OUR LIVES.
NEVER STOPPED US BEFORE.
NOT SMART ENOUGH TO LET IT STOP US NOW.
ANOTHER WOULD-BE SAVIOR OF THIS WORLD?
YOU SHOULD BE SO LUCKY.
I'M JUST SOMEONE WHO WANTS TO BE LEFT ALONE, YEAH?
NO TIME FOR GODS AND THEIR CHERUBS.
SO...WHY DON'T YOU JUST SOD OFF?
THIS SMOKE... BINDING ME... WASHING ME AWAY--
ONE AND ONLY.
PUNK--
NO TIME FOR HUGS AND KISSES, THOUGH.
THE GHOST LANTERN'S FAST, CHEAP, AND EFFICIENT.
BUT IT WON'T HOLD THEM FOR LONG.

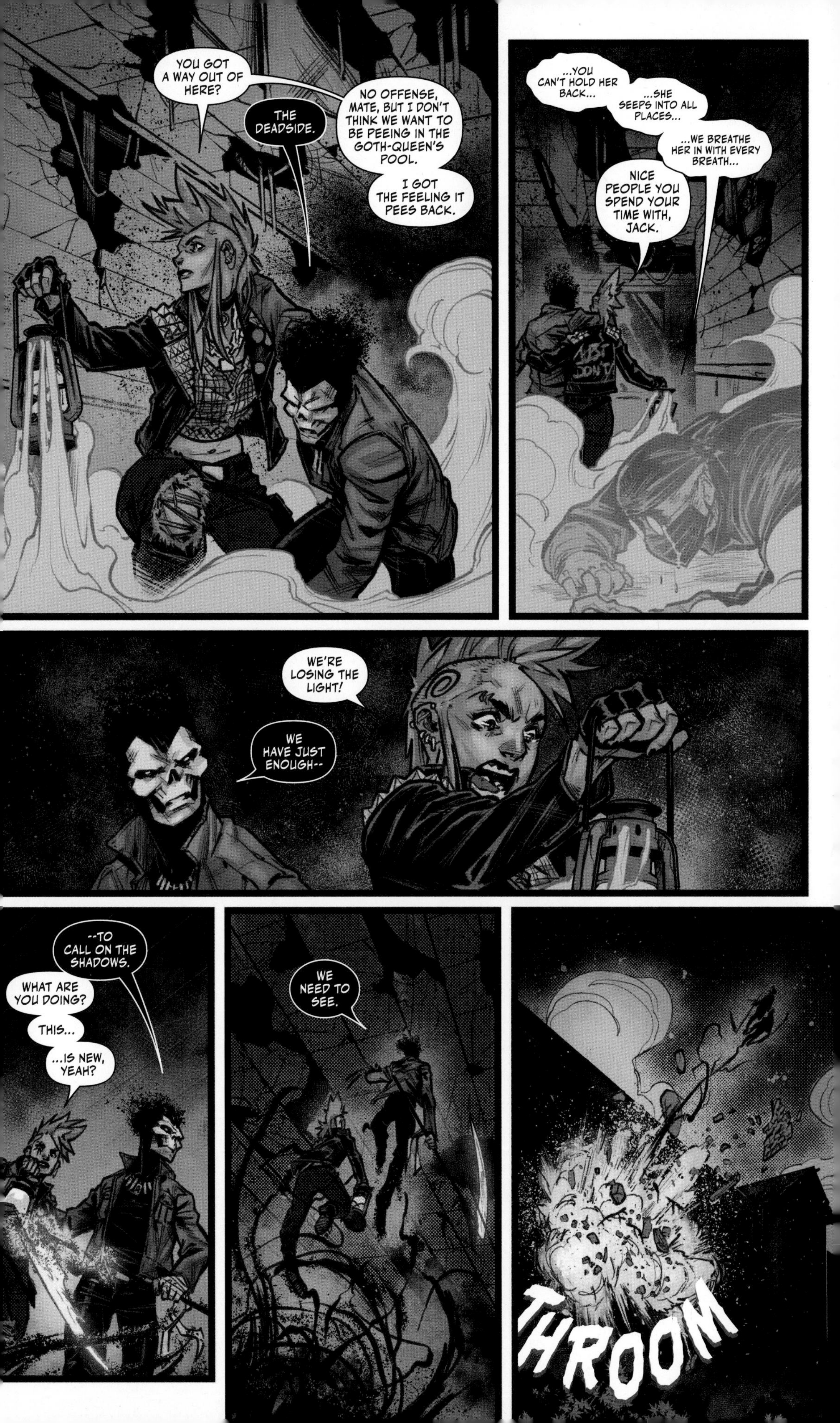

YOU GOT A WAY OUT OF HERE?
THE DEADSIDE.
NO OFFENSE, MATE, BUT I DON'T THINK WE WANT TO BE PEEING IN THE GOTH-QUEEN'S POOL.
I GOT THE FEELING IT PEES BACK.
...YOU CAN'T HOLD HER BACK...
...SHE SEEPS INTO ALL PLACES...
...WE BREATHE HER IN WITH EVERY BREATH...
NICE PEOPLE YOU SPEND YOUR TIME WITH, JACK.
WE'RE LOSING THE LIGHT!
WE HAVE JUST ENOUGH--
--TO CALL ON THE SHADOWS.
WHAT ARE YOU DOING?
THIS...
...IS NEW, YEAH?
WE NEED TO SEE.
THROOM

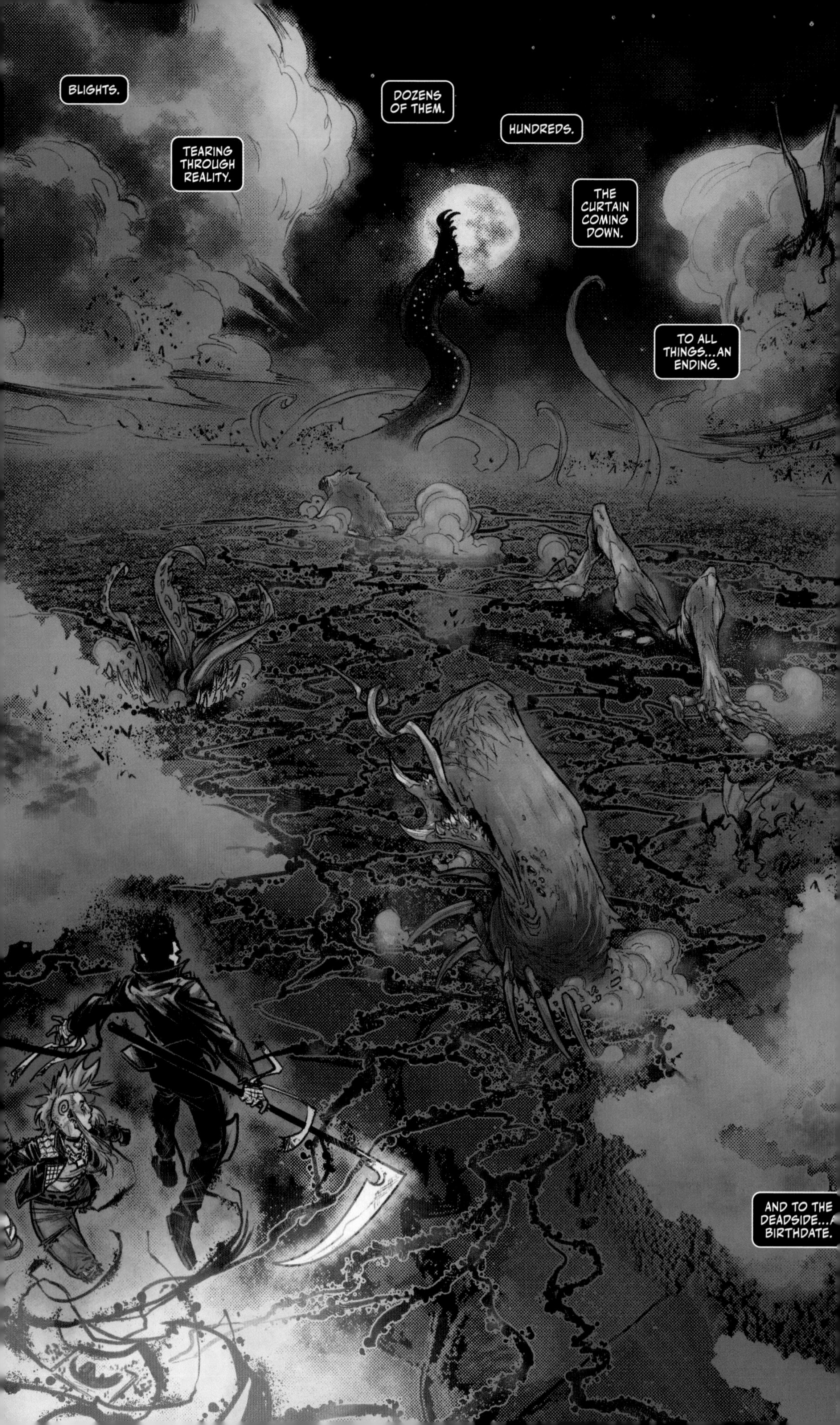
BLIGHTS.
TEARING THROUGH REALITY.
DOZENS OF THEM.
HUNDREDS.
THE CURTAIN COMING DOWN.
TO ALL THINGS...AN ENDING.
AND TO THE DEADSIDE...A BIRTHDATE.

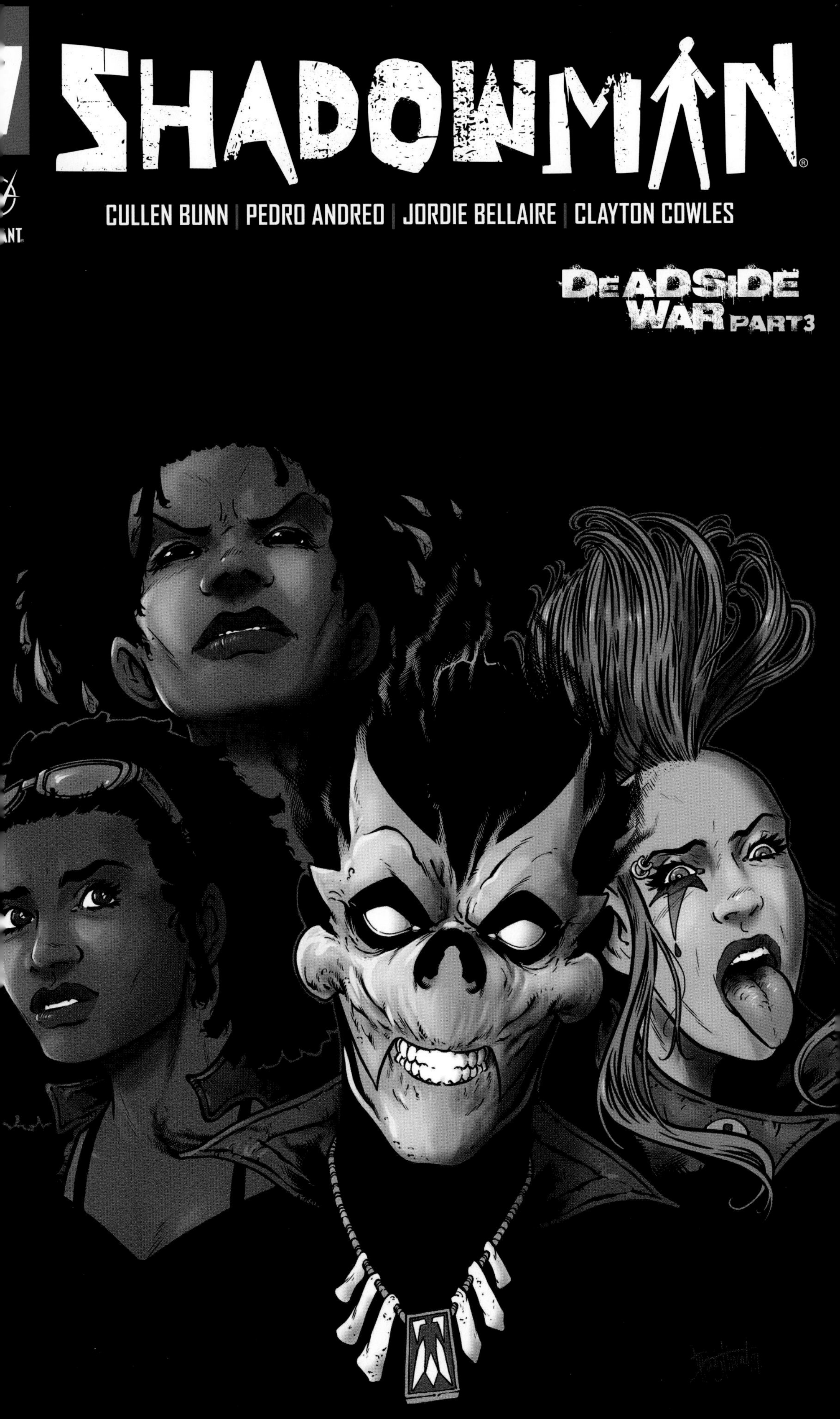

SHADOWMAN
CULLEN BUNN | PEDRO ANDREO | JORDIE BELLAIRE | CLAYTON COWLES
DEADSIDE WAR PART 3

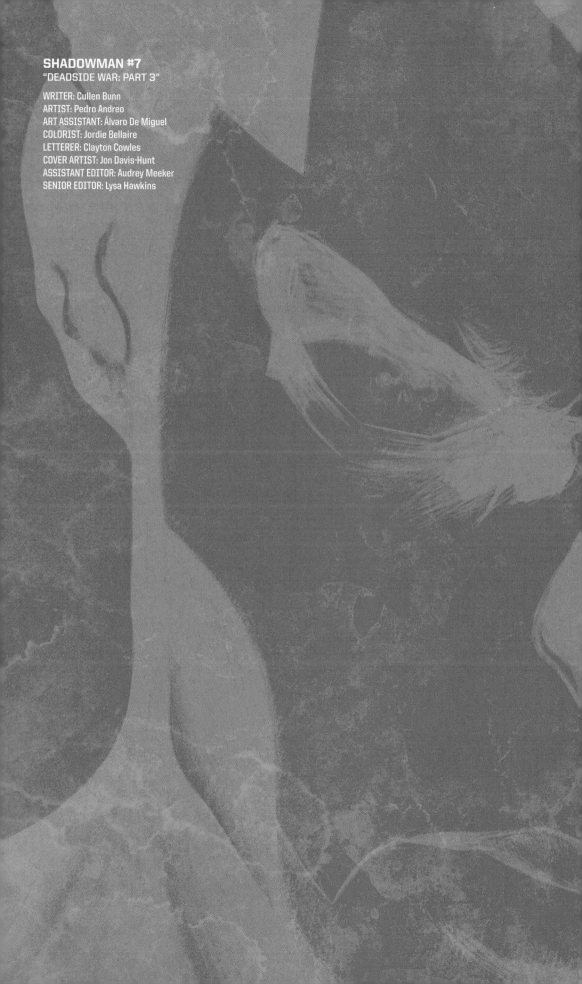

SHADOWMAN #7
"DEADSIDE WAR: PART 3"

WRITER: Cullen Bunn
ARTIST: Pedro Andreo
ART ASSISTANT: Álvaro De Miguel
COLORIST: Jordie Bellaire
LETTERER: Clayton Cowles
COVER ARTIST: Jon Davis-Hunt
ASSISTANT EDITOR: Audrey Meeker
SENIOR EDITOR: Lysa Hawkins

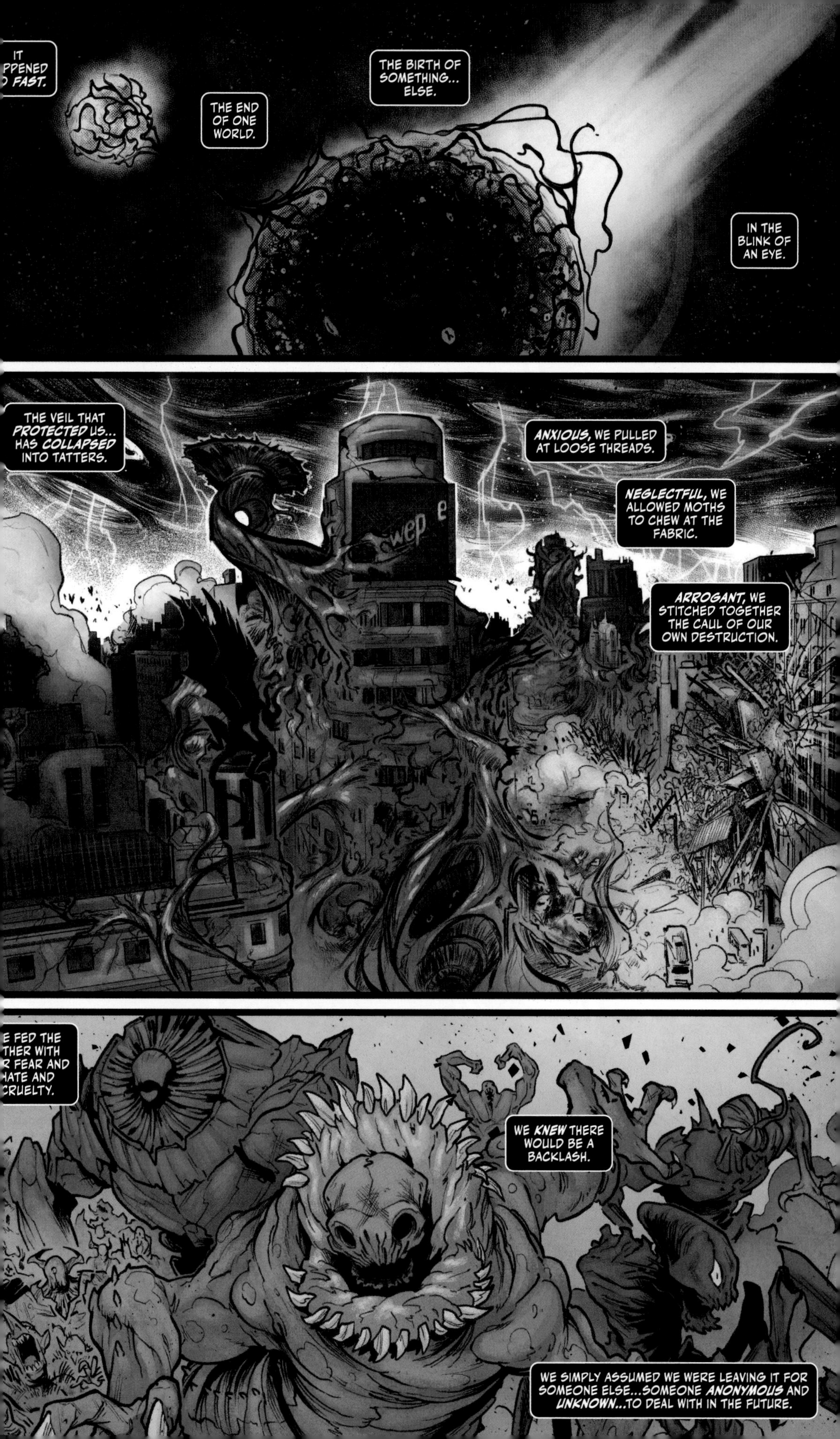
IT
PPENED
FAST.
THE END OF ONE WORLD.
THE BIRTH OF SOMETHING... ELSE.
IN THE BLINK OF AN EYE.
THE VEIL THAT PROTECTED US... HAS COLLAPSED INTO TATTERS.
ANXIOUS, WE PULLED AT LOOSE THREADS.
NEGLECTFUL, WE ALLOWED MOTHS TO CHEW AT THE FABRIC.
ARROGANT, WE STITCHED TOGETHER THE CAUL OF OUR OWN DESTRUCTION.
E FED THE
THER WITH
R FEAR AND
HATE AND
CRUELTY.
WE KNEW THERE WOULD BE A BACKLASH.
WE SIMPLY ASSUMED WE WERE LEAVING IT FOR SOMEONE ELSE...SOMEONE ANONYMOUS AND UNKNOWN...TO DEAL WITH IN THE FUTURE.

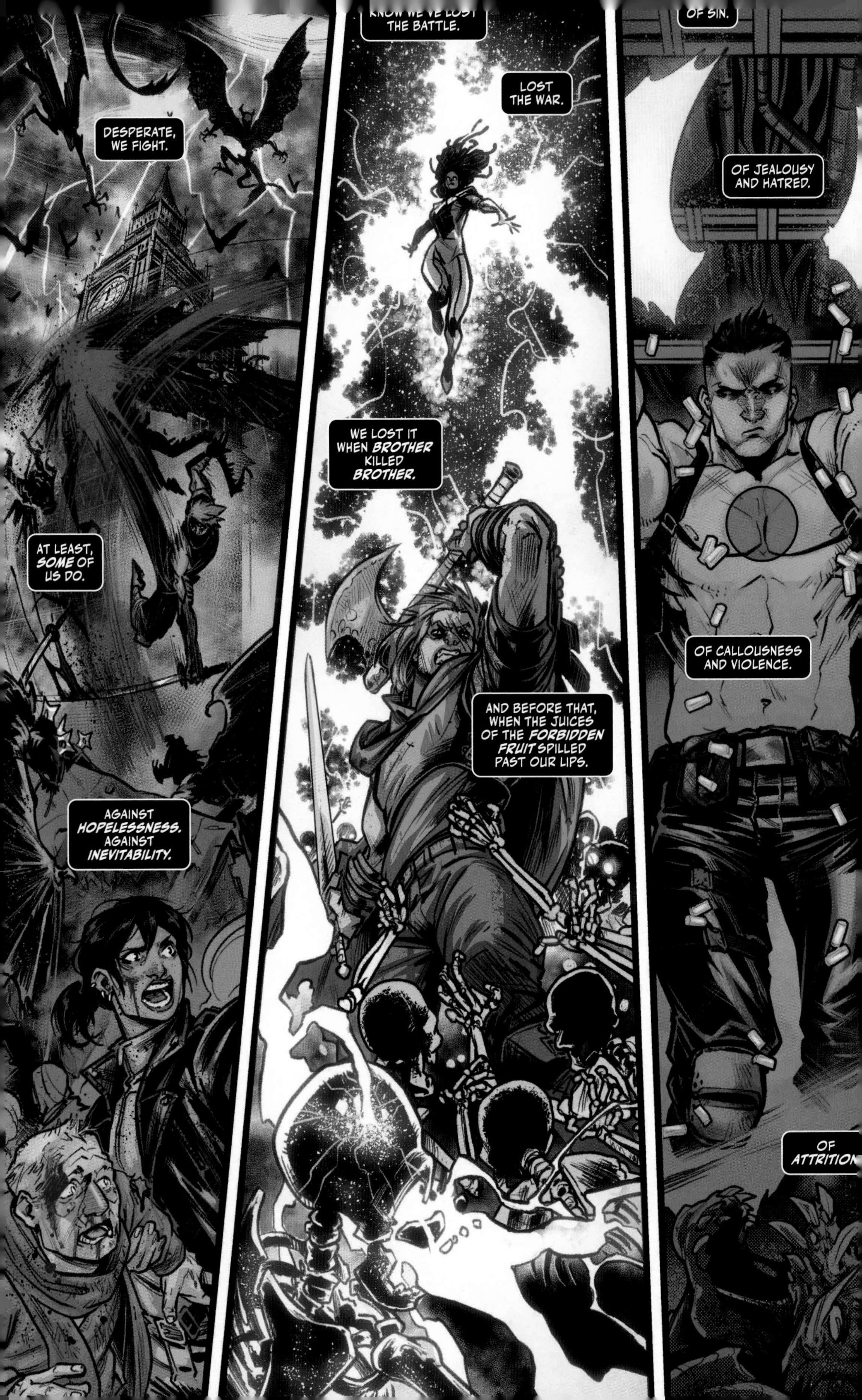
DESPERATE, WE FIGHT.
AT LEAST, SOME OF US DO.
AGAINST HOPELESSNESS. AGAINST INEVITABILITY.
THE BATTLE.
LOST THE WAR.
WE LOST IT WHEN BROTHER KILLED BROTHER.
AND BEFORE THAT, WHEN THE JUICES OF THE FORBIDDEN FRUIT SPILLED PAST OUR LIPS.
OF SIN.
OF JEALOUSY AND HATRED.
OF CALLOUSNESS AND VIOLENCE.
OF ATTRITION

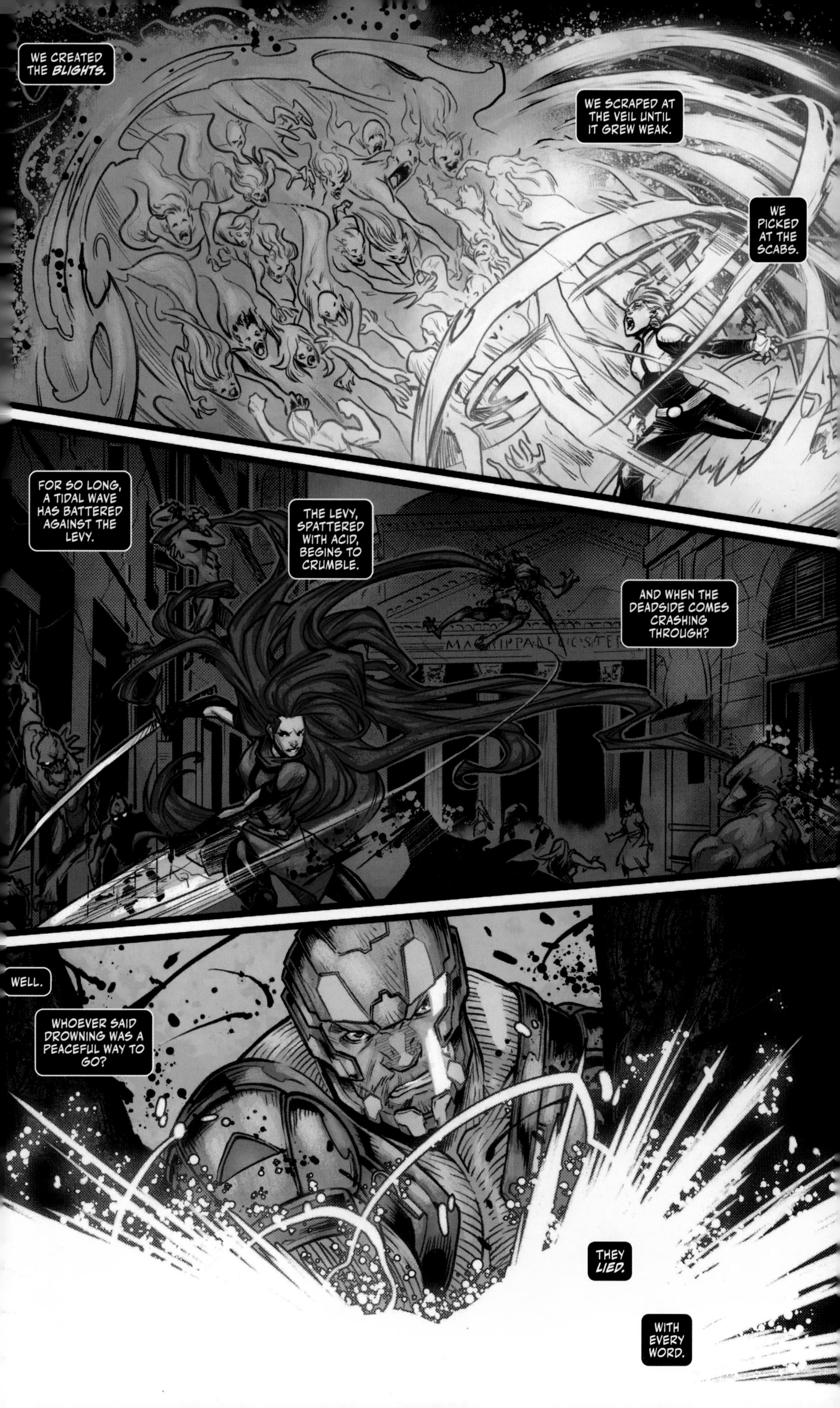

WE CREATED THE *BLIGHTS.*
WE SCRAPED AT THE VEIL UNTIL IT GREW WEAK.
WE PICKED AT THE SCABS.
FOR SO LONG, A TIDAL WAVE HAS BATTERED AGAINST THE LEVY.
THE LEVY, SPATTERED WITH ACID, BEGINS TO CRUMBLE.
AND WHEN THE DEADSIDE COMES CRASHING THROUGH?
WELL.
WHOEVER SAID DROWNING WAS A PEACEFUL WAY TO GO?
THEY *LIED.*
WITH EVERY WORD.

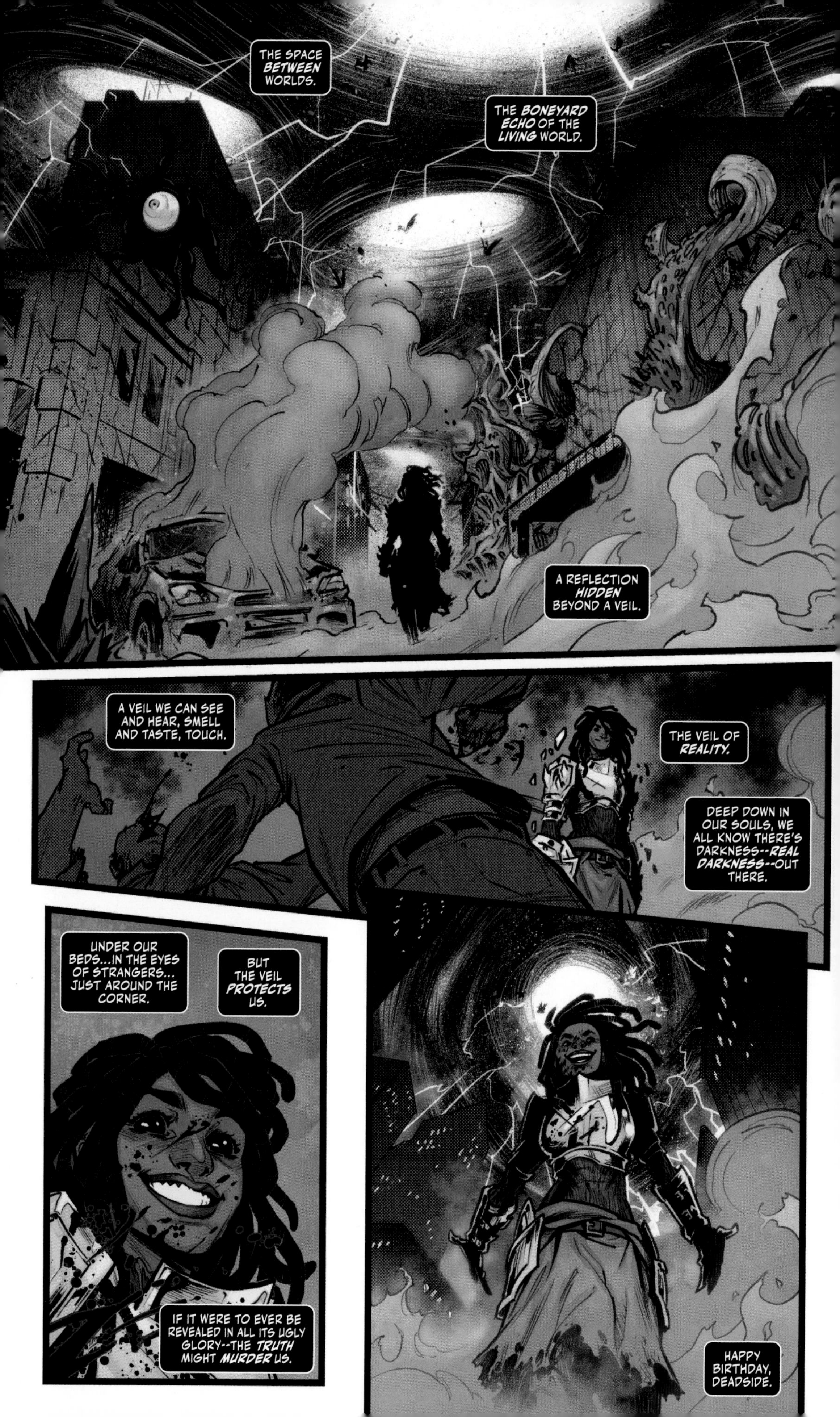
THE SPACE BETWEEN WORLDS.
THE BONEYARD ECHO OF THE LIVING WORLD.
A REFLECTION HIDDEN BEYOND A VEIL.
A VEIL WE CAN SEE AND HEAR, SMELL AND TASTE, TOUCH.
THE VEIL OF REALITY.
DEEP DOWN IN OUR SOULS, WE ALL KNOW THERE'S DARKNESS--REAL DARKNESS--OUT THERE.
UNDER OUR BEDS...IN THE EYES OF STRANGERS... JUST AROUND THE CORNER.
BUT THE VEIL PROTECTS US.
IF IT WERE TO EVER BE REVEALED IN ALL ITS UGLY GLORY--THE TRUTH MIGHT MURDER US.
HAPPY BIRTHDAY, DEADSIDE.

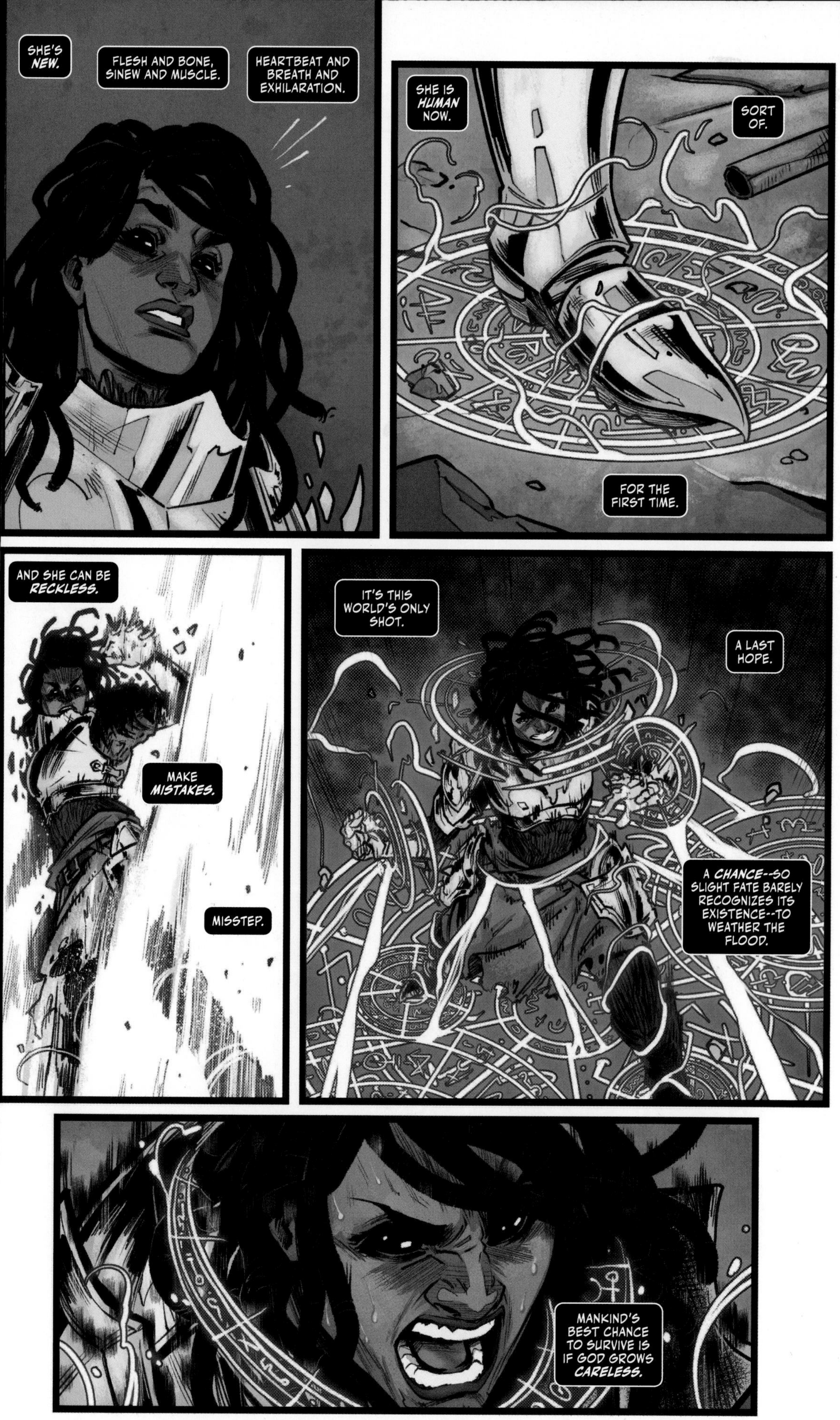
SHE'S NEW.
FLESH AND BONE, SINEW AND MUSCLE.
HEARTBEAT AND BREATH AND EXHILARATION.
SHE IS HUMAN NOW.
SORT OF.
FOR THE FIRST TIME.
AND SHE CAN BE RECKLESS.
MAKE MISTAKES.
MISSTEP.
IT'S THIS WORLD'S ONLY SHOT.
A LAST HOPE.
A CHANCE--SO SLIGHT FATE BARELY RECOGNIZES ITS EXISTENCE--TO WEATHER THE FLOOD.
MANKIND'S BEST CHANCE TO SURVIVE IS IF GOD GROWS CARELESS.

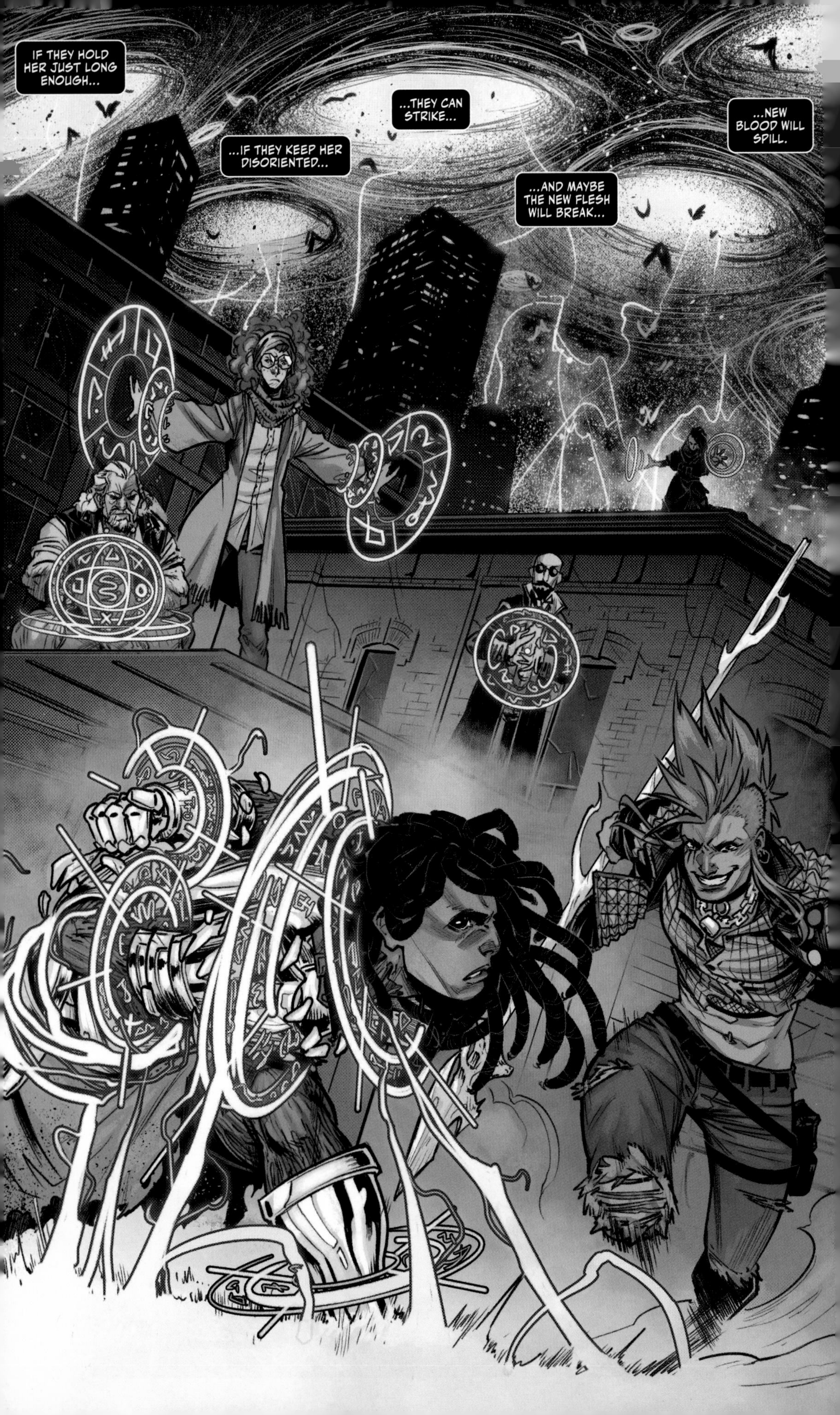

IF THEY HOLD HER JUST LONG ENOUGH...
...IF THEY KEEP HER DISORIENTED...
...THEY CAN STRIKE...
...AND MAYBE THE NEW FLESH WILL BREAK...
...NEW BLOOD WILL SPILL.

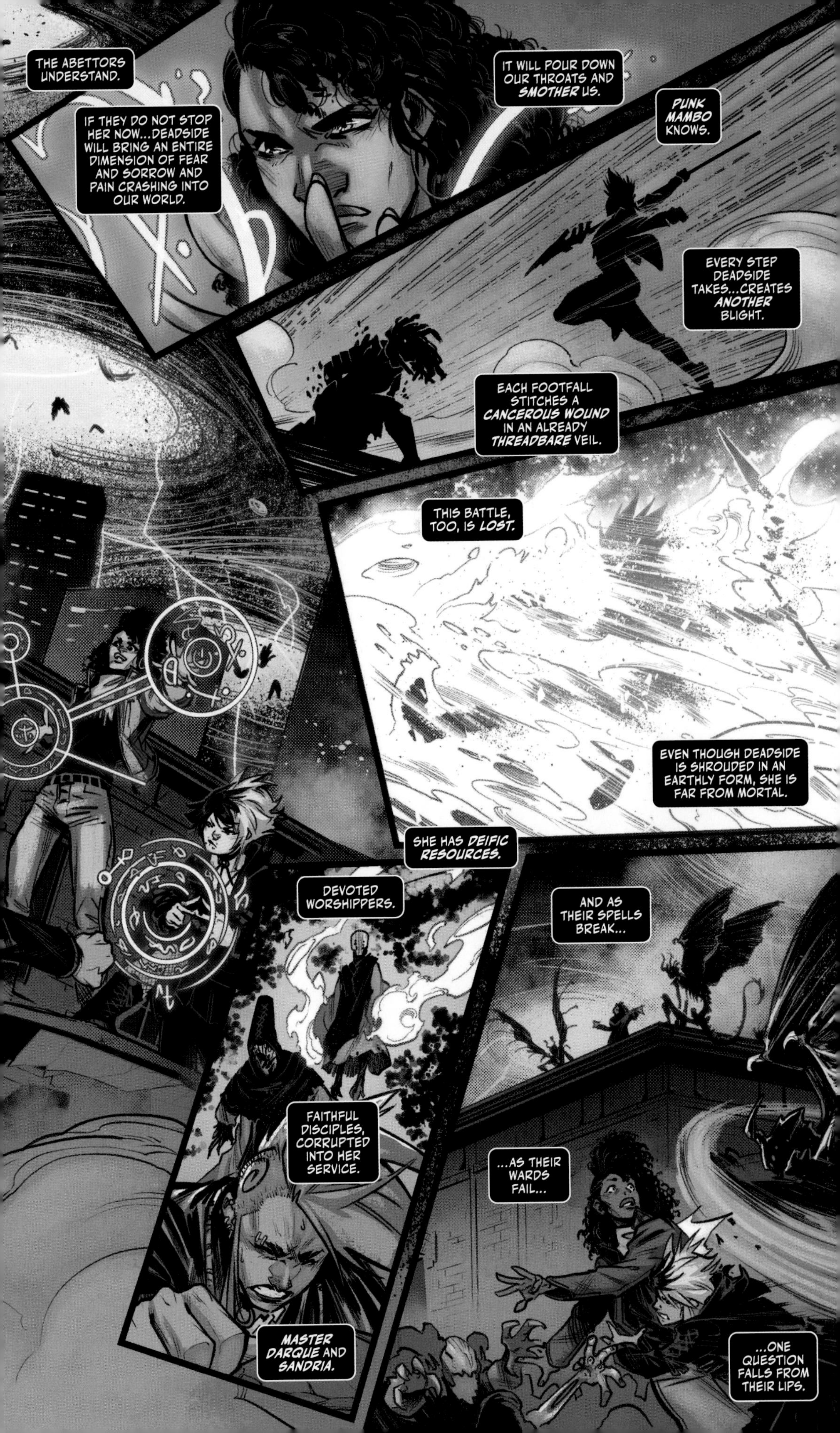
THE ABETTORS UNDERSTAND.
IF THEY DO NOT STOP HER NOW...DEADSIDE WILL BRING AN ENTIRE DIMENSION OF FEAR AND SORROW AND PAIN CRASHING INTO OUR WORLD.
IT WILL POUR DOWN OUR THROATS AND SMOTHER US.
PUNK MAMBO KNOWS.
EVERY STEP DEADSIDE TAKES...CREATES ANOTHER BLIGHT.
EACH FOOTFALL STITCHES A CANCEROUS WOUND IN AN ALREADY THREADBARE VEIL.
THIS BATTLE, TOO, IS LOST.
EVEN THOUGH DEADSIDE IS SHROUDED IN AN EARTHLY FORM, SHE IS FAR FROM MORTAL.
SHE HAS DEIFIC RESOURCES.
DEVOTED WORSHIPPERS.
FAITHFUL DISCIPLES, CORRUPTED INTO HER SERVICE.
MASTER DARQUE AND SANDRIA.
AND AS THEIR SPELLS BREAK...
...AS THEIR WARDS FAIL...
...ONE QUESTION FALLS FROM THEIR LIPS.

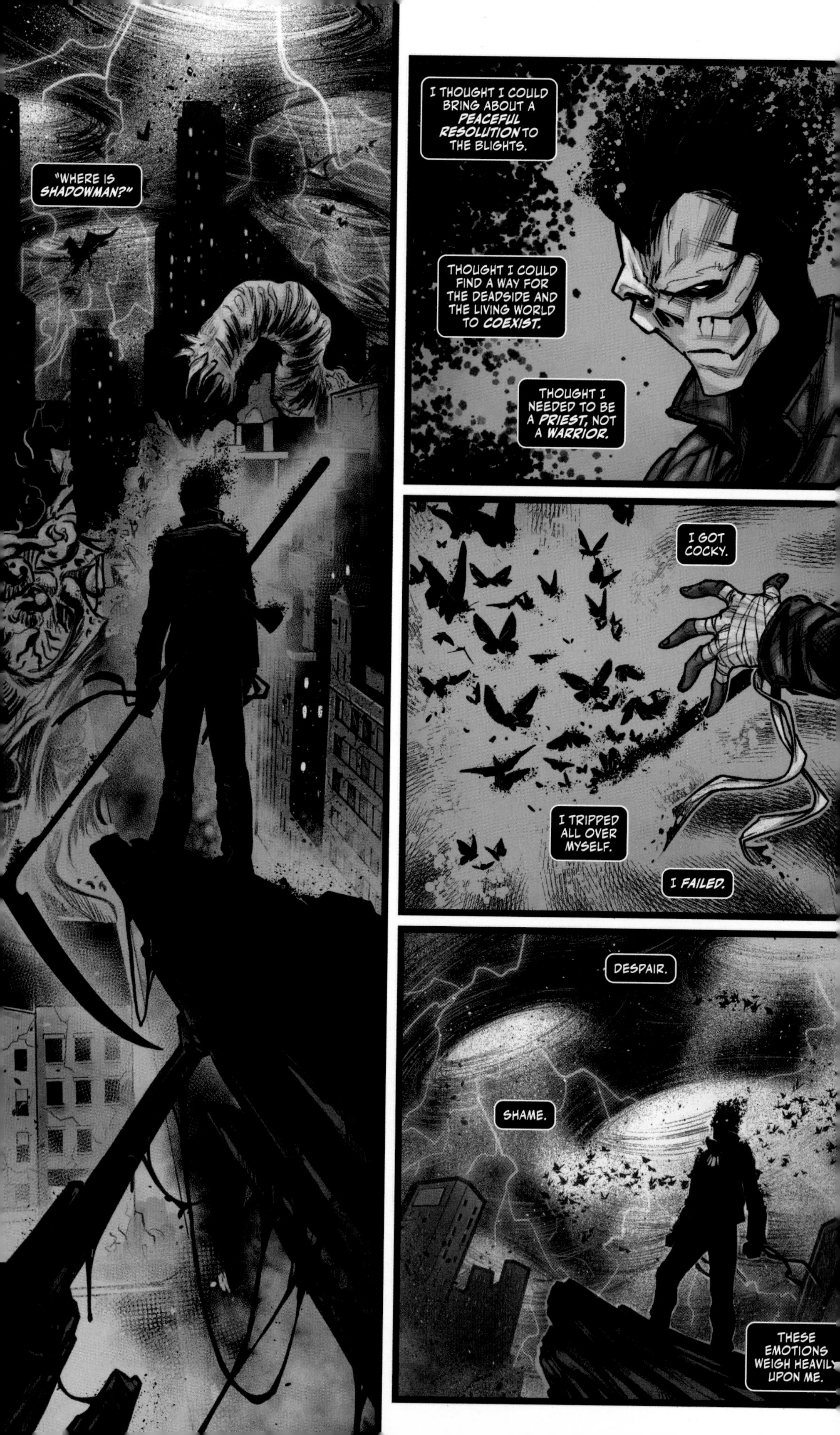
"WHERE IS SHADOWMAN?"
I THOUGHT I COULD BRING ABOUT A PEACEFUL RESOLUTION TO THE BLIGHTS.
THOUGHT I COULD FIND A WAY FOR THE DEADSIDE AND THE LIVING WORLD TO COEXIST.
THOUGHT I NEEDED TO BE A PRIEST, NOT A WARRIOR.
I GOT COCKY.
I TRIPPED ALL OVER MYSELF.
I FAILED.
DESPAIR.
SHAME.
THESE EMOTIONS WEIGH HEAVILY UPON ME.

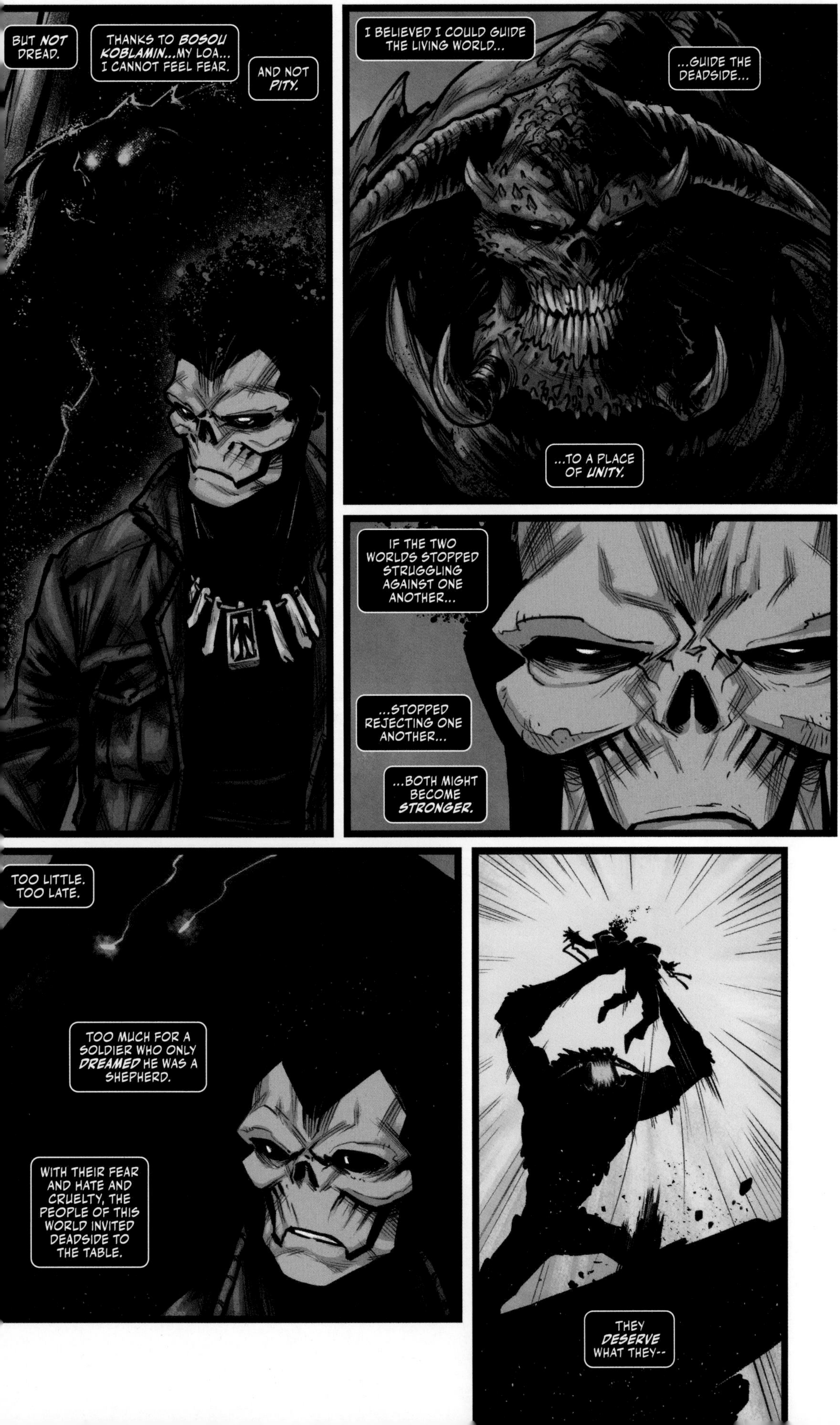
BUT NOT DREAD.
THANKS TO BOSOU KOBLAMIN...MY LOA... I CANNOT FEEL FEAR.
AND NOT PITY.
I BELIEVED I COULD GUIDE THE LIVING WORLD...
...GUIDE THE DEADSIDE...
...TO A PLACE OF UNITY.
IF THE TWO WORLDS STOPPED STRUGGLING AGAINST ONE ANOTHER...
...STOPPED REJECTING ONE ANOTHER...
...BOTH MIGHT BECOME STRONGER.
TOO LITTLE. TOO LATE.
TOO MUCH FOR A SOLDIER WHO ONLY DREAMED HE WAS A SHEPHERD.
WITH THEIR FEAR AND HATE AND CRUELTY, THE PEOPLE OF THIS WORLD INVITED DEADSIDE TO THE TABLE.
THEY DESERVE WHAT THEY--

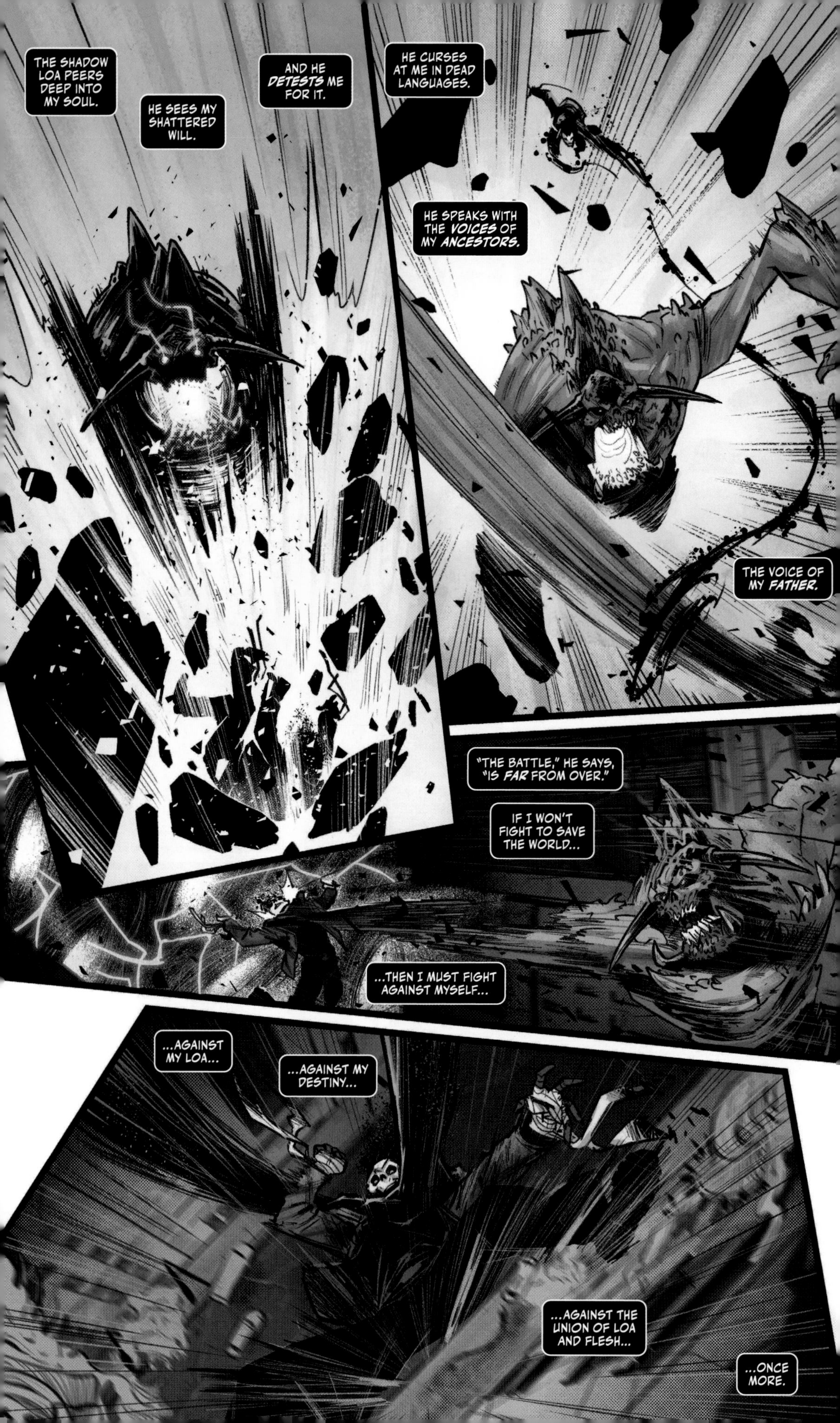
THE SHADOW LOA PEERS DEEP INTO MY SOUL.
HE SEES MY SHATTERED WILL.
AND HE *DETESTS* ME FOR IT.
HE CURSES AT ME IN DEAD LANGUAGES.
HE SPEAKS WITH THE *VOICES* OF MY *ANCESTORS.*
THE VOICE OF MY *FATHER.*
"THE BATTLE," HE SAYS, "IS *FAR* FROM OVER."
IF I WON'T FIGHT TO SAVE THE WORLD...
...THEN I MUST FIGHT AGAINST MYSELF...
...AGAINST MY LOA...
...AGAINST MY DESTINY...
...AGAINST THE UNION OF LOA AND FLESH...
...ONCE MORE.

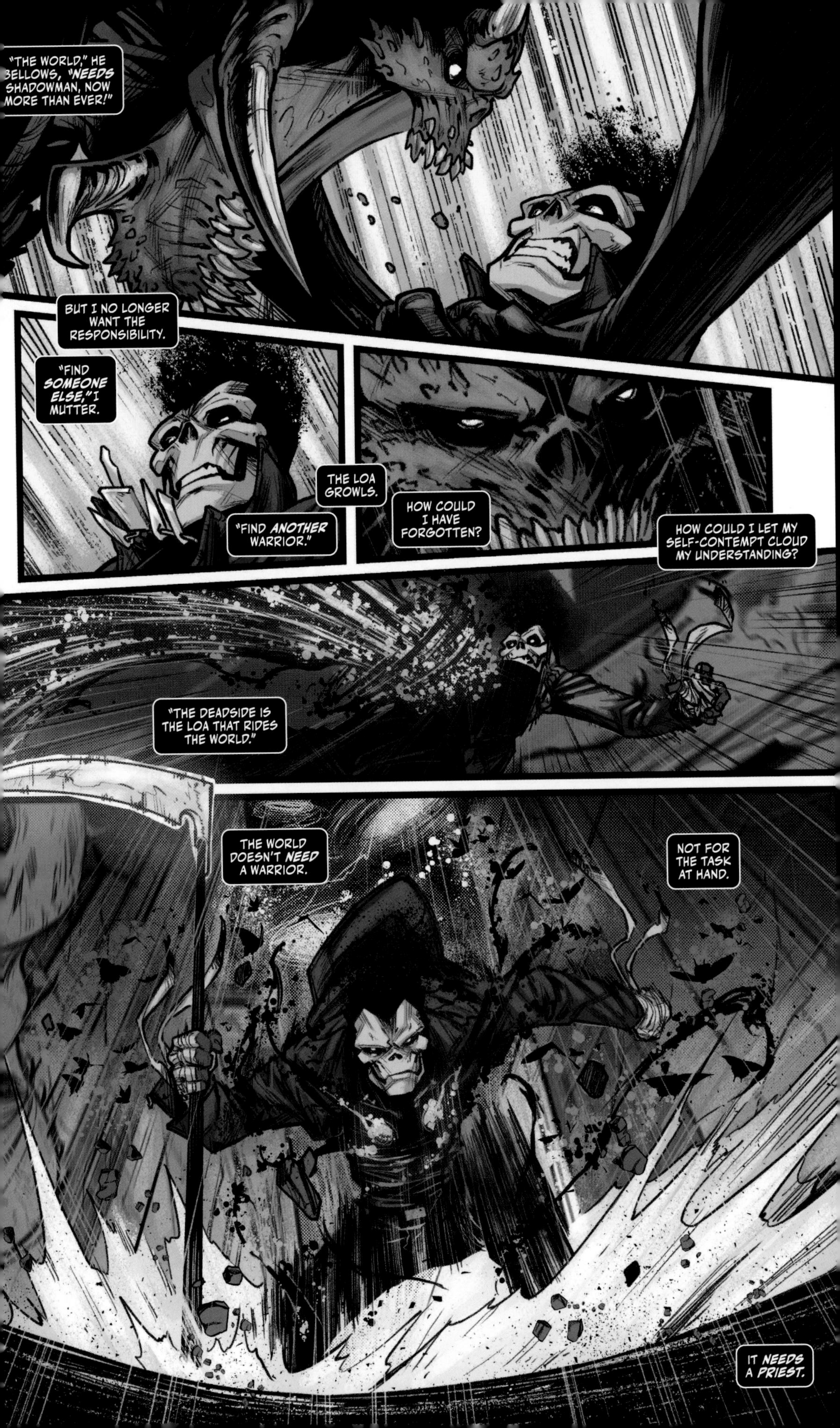
"THE WORLD," HE BELLOWS, "NEEDS SHADOWMAN, NOW MORE THAN EVER!"
BUT I NO LONGER WANT THE RESPONSIBILITY.
"FIND SOMEONE ELSE," I MUTTER.
"FIND ANOTHER WARRIOR."
THE LOA GROWLS.
HOW COULD I HAVE FORGOTTEN?
HOW COULD I LET MY SELF-CONTEMPT CLOUD MY UNDERSTANDING?
"THE DEADSIDE IS THE LOA THAT RIDES THE WORLD."
THE WORLD DOESN'T NEED A WARRIOR.
NOT FOR THE TASK AT HAND.
IT NEEDS A PRIEST.

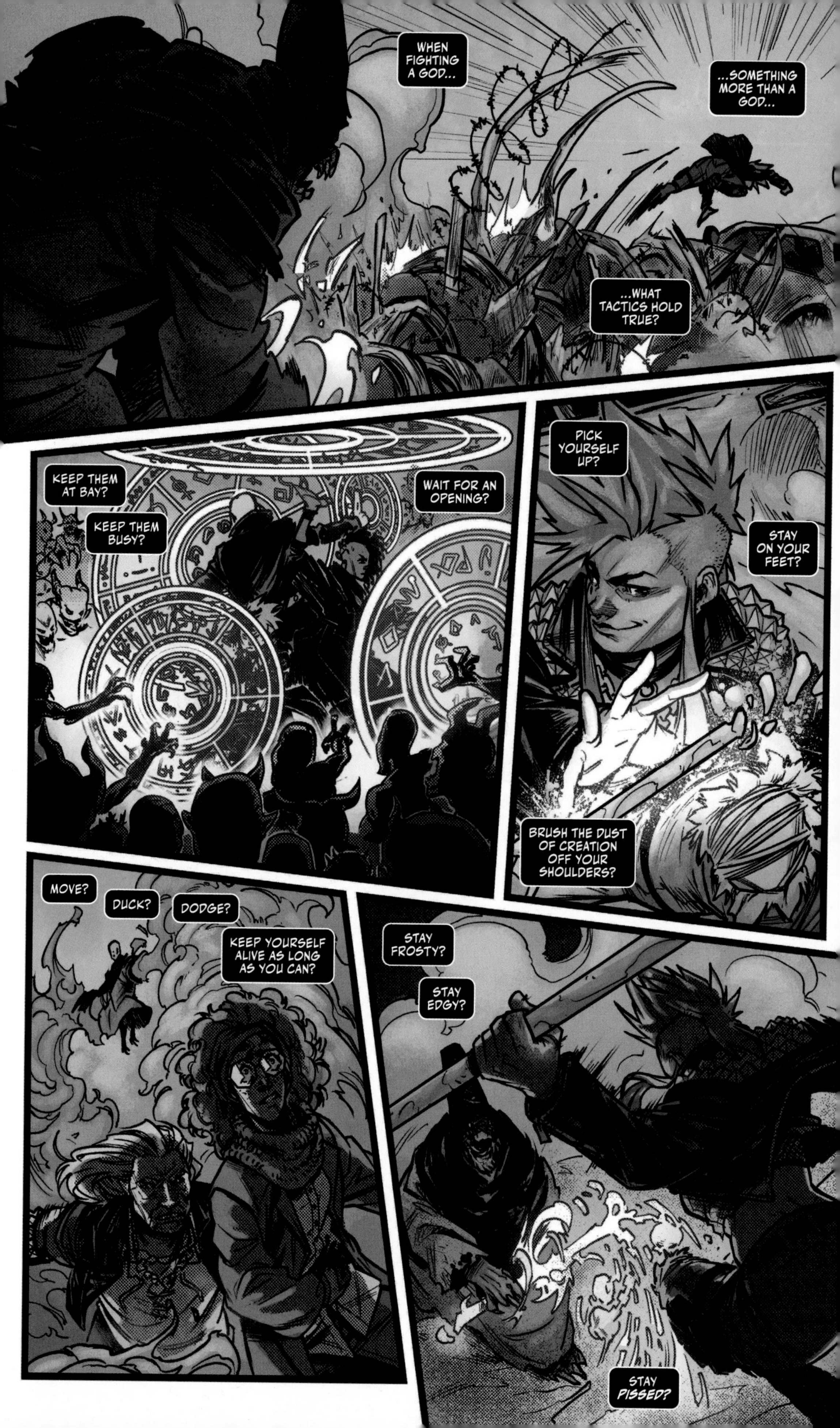
WHEN FIGHTING A GOD...
...SOMETHING MORE THAN A GOD...
...WHAT TACTICS HOLD TRUE?
KEEP THEM AT BAY?
KEEP THEM BUSY?
WAIT FOR AN OPENING?
PICK YOURSELF UP?
STAY ON YOUR FEET?
BRUSH THE DUST OF CREATION OFF YOUR SHOULDERS?
MOVE?
DUCK?
DODGE?
KEEP YOURSELF ALIVE AS LONG AS YOU CAN?
STAY FROSTY?
STAY EDGY?
STAY *PISSED?*

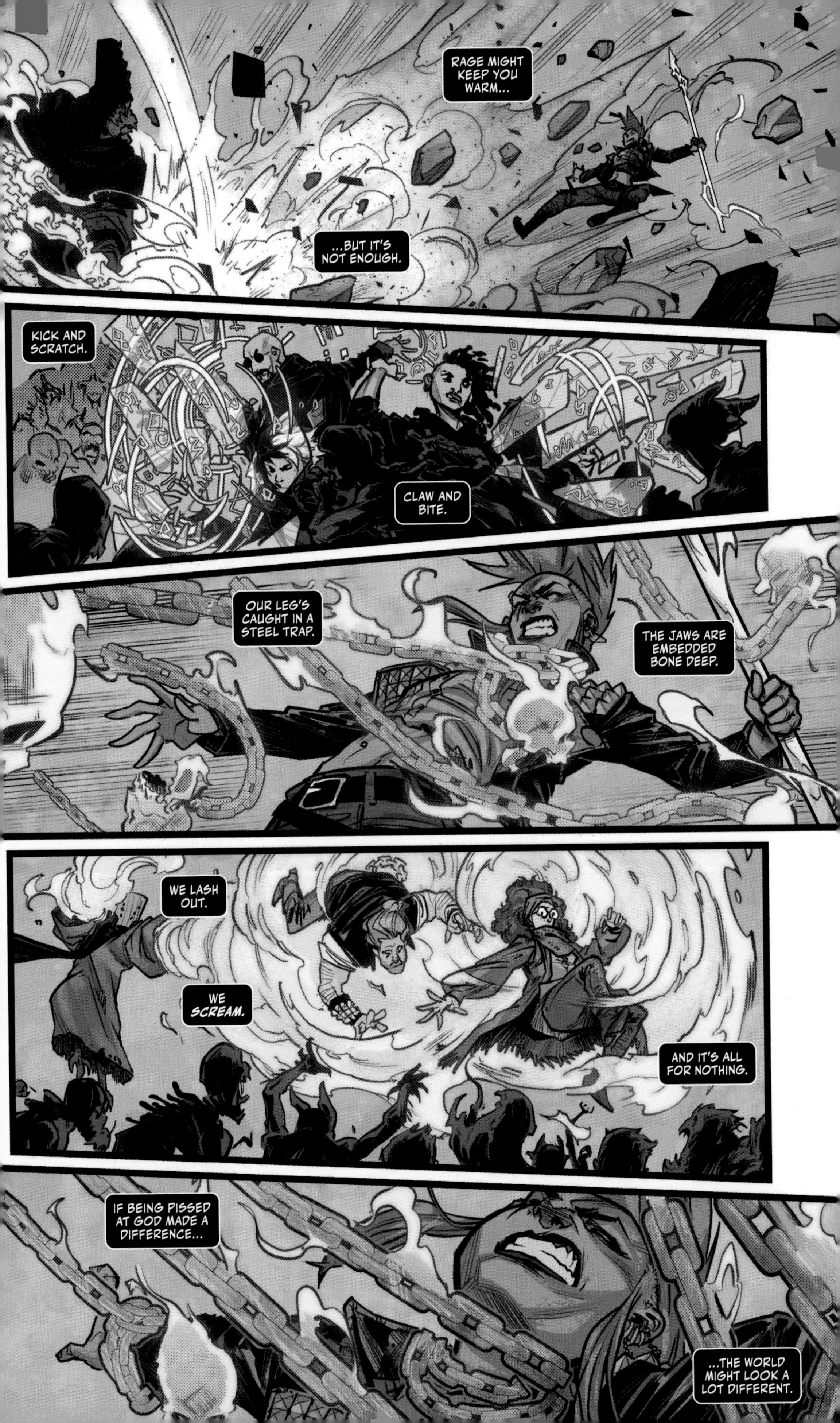
RAGE MIGHT KEEP YOU WARM...
...BUT IT'S NOT ENOUGH.
KICK AND SCRATCH.
CLAW AND BITE.
OUR LEG'S CAUGHT IN A STEEL TRAP.
THE JAWS ARE EMBEDDED BONE DEEP.
WE LASH OUT.
WE *SCREAM.*
AND IT'S ALL FOR NOTHING.
IF BEING PISSED AT GOD MADE A DIFFERENCE...
...THE WORLD MIGHT LOOK A LOT DIFFERENT.

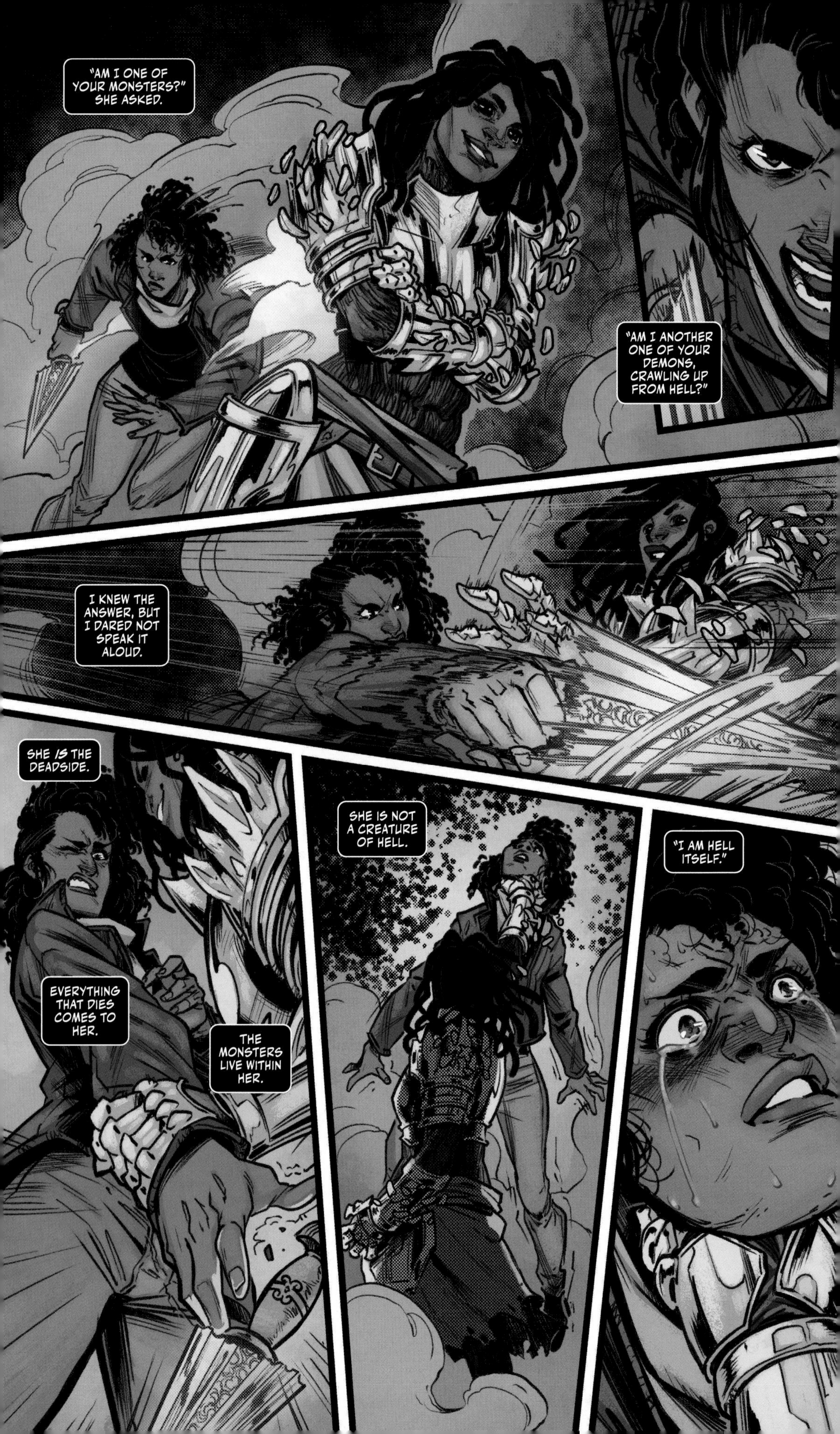
"AM I ONE OF YOUR MONSTERS?" SHE ASKED.
"AM I ANOTHER ONE OF YOUR DEMONS, CRAWLING UP FROM HELL?"
I KNEW THE ANSWER, BUT I DARED NOT SPEAK IT ALOUD.
SHE *IS* THE DEADSIDE.
EVERYTHING THAT DIES COMES TO HER.
THE MONSTERS LIVE WITHIN HER.
SHE IS NOT A CREATURE OF HELL.
"I AM HELL ITSELF."

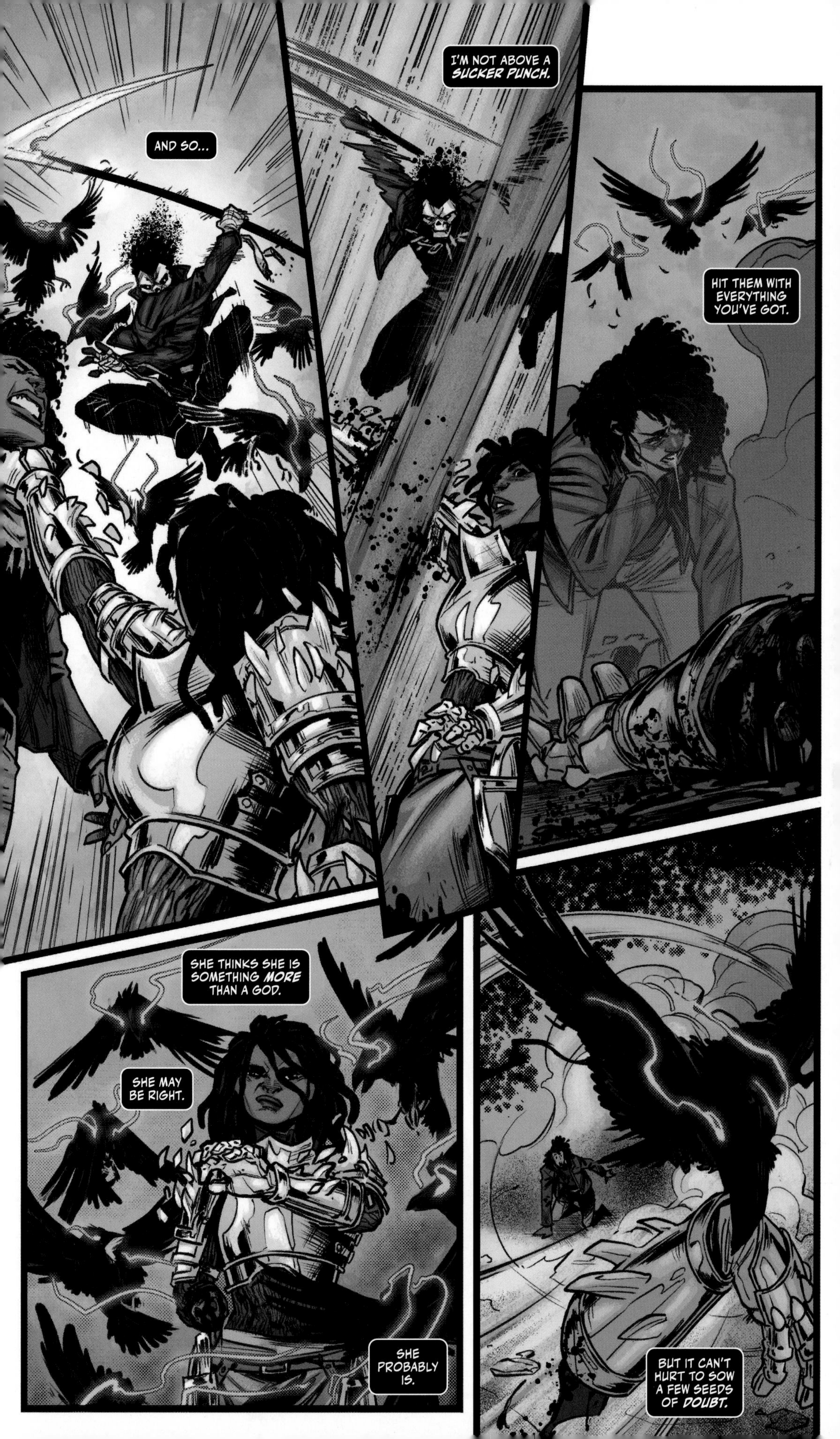

AND SO...
I'M NOT ABOVE A SUCKER PUNCH.
HIT THEM WITH EVERYTHING YOU'VE GOT.
SHE THINKS SHE IS SOMETHING MORE THAN A GOD.
SHE MAY BE RIGHT.
SHE PROBABLY IS.
BUT IT CAN'T HURT TO SOW A FEW SEEDS OF DOUBT.

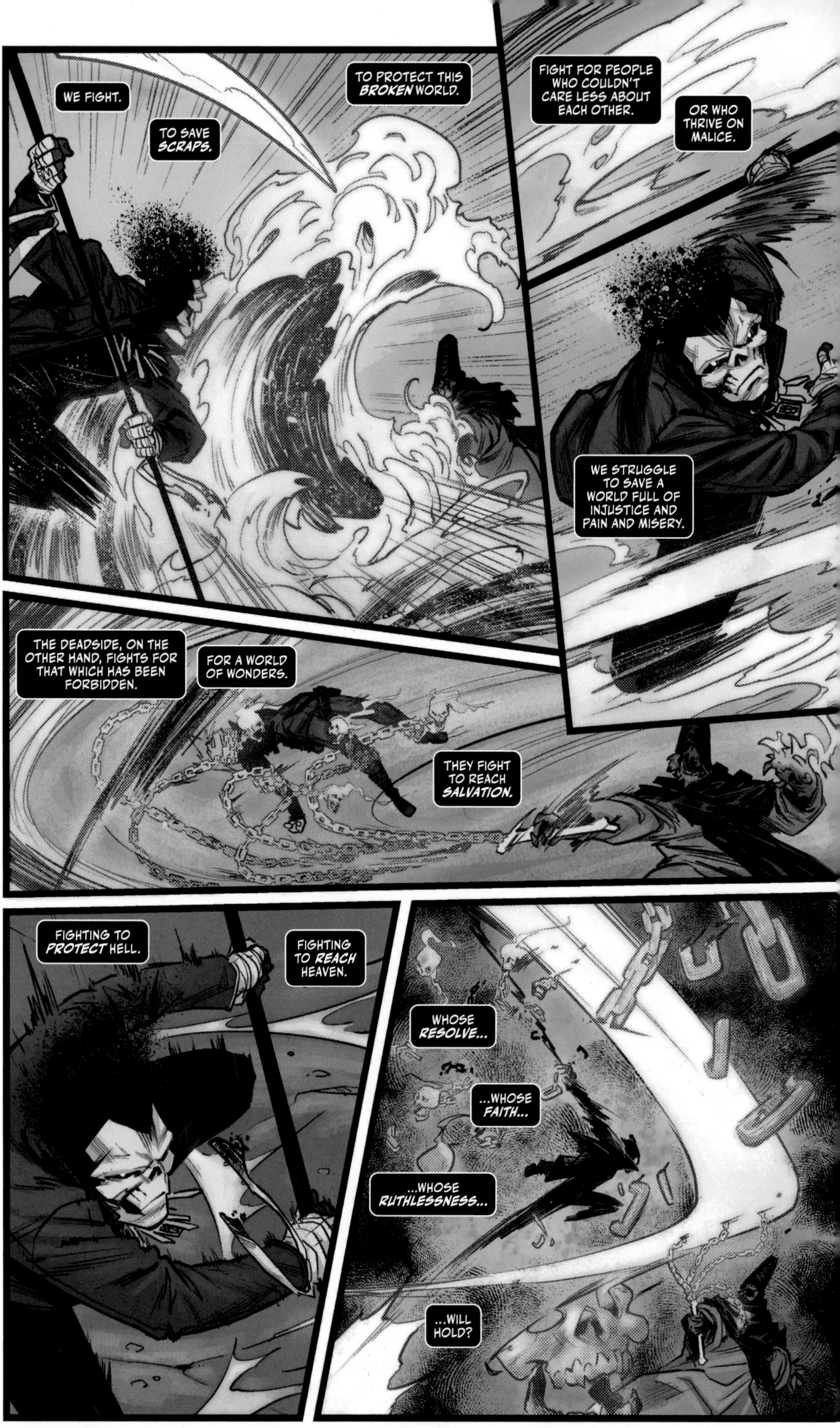
WE FIGHT.
TO SAVE *SCRAPS.*
TO PROTECT THIS *BROKEN* WORLD.
FIGHT FOR PEOPLE WHO COULDN'T CARE LESS ABOUT EACH OTHER.
OR WHO THRIVE ON MALICE.
WE STRUGGLE TO SAVE A WORLD FULL OF INJUSTICE AND PAIN AND MISERY.
THE DEADSIDE, ON THE OTHER HAND, FIGHTS FOR THAT WHICH HAS BEEN FORBIDDEN.
FOR A WORLD OF WONDERS.
THEY FIGHT TO REACH *SALVATION.*
FIGHTING TO *PROTECT* HELL.
FIGHTING TO *REACH* HEAVEN.
WHOSE *RESOLVE...*
...WHOSE *FAITH...*
...WHOSE *RUTHLESSNESS...*
...WILL HOLD?

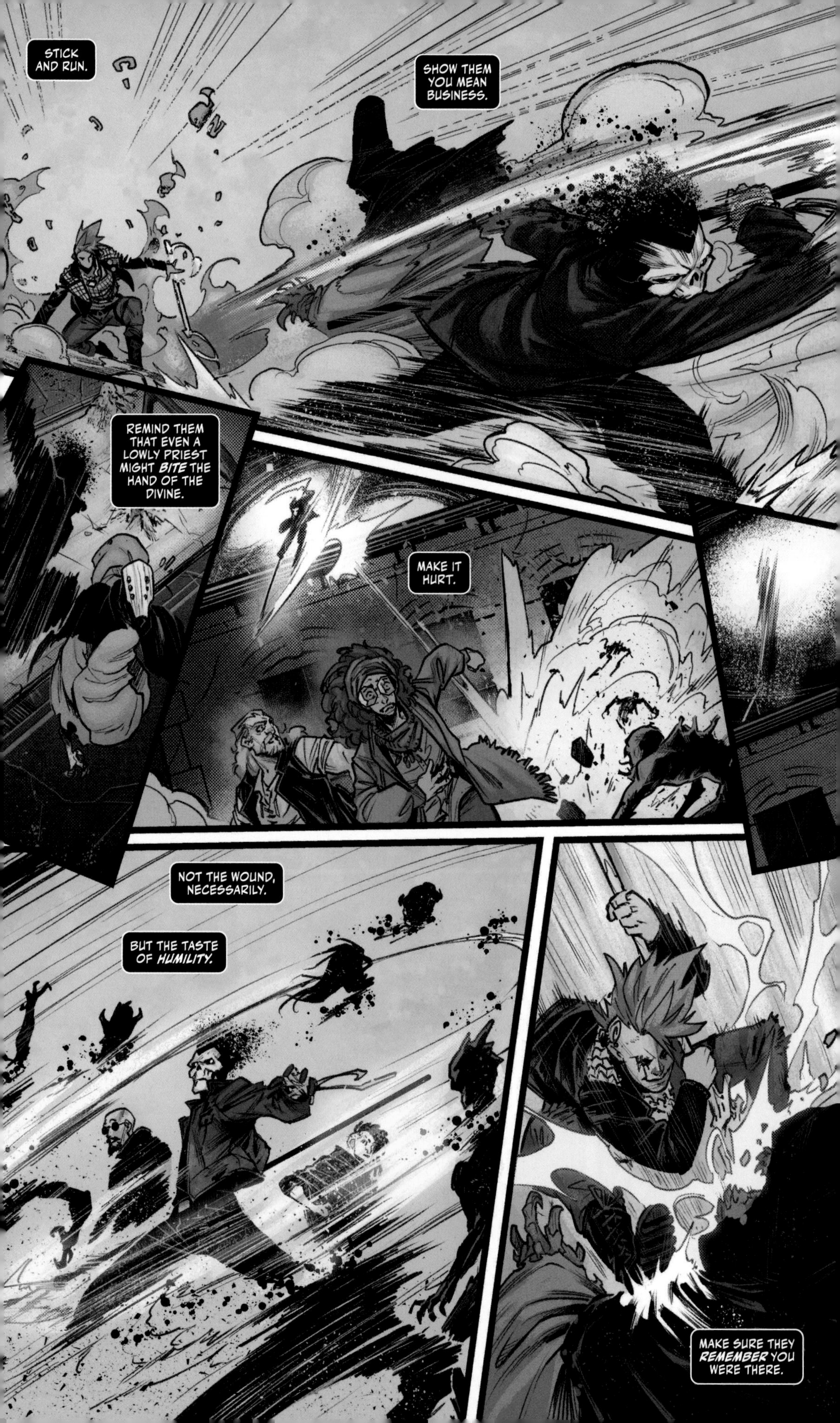
STICK AND RUN.
SHOW THEM YOU MEAN BUSINESS.
REMIND THEM THAT EVEN A LOWLY PRIEST MIGHT *BITE* THE HAND OF THE DIVINE.
MAKE IT HURT.
NOT THE WOUND, NECESSARILY.
BUT THE TASTE OF *HUMILITY.*
MAKE SURE THEY *REMEMBER* YOU WERE THERE.

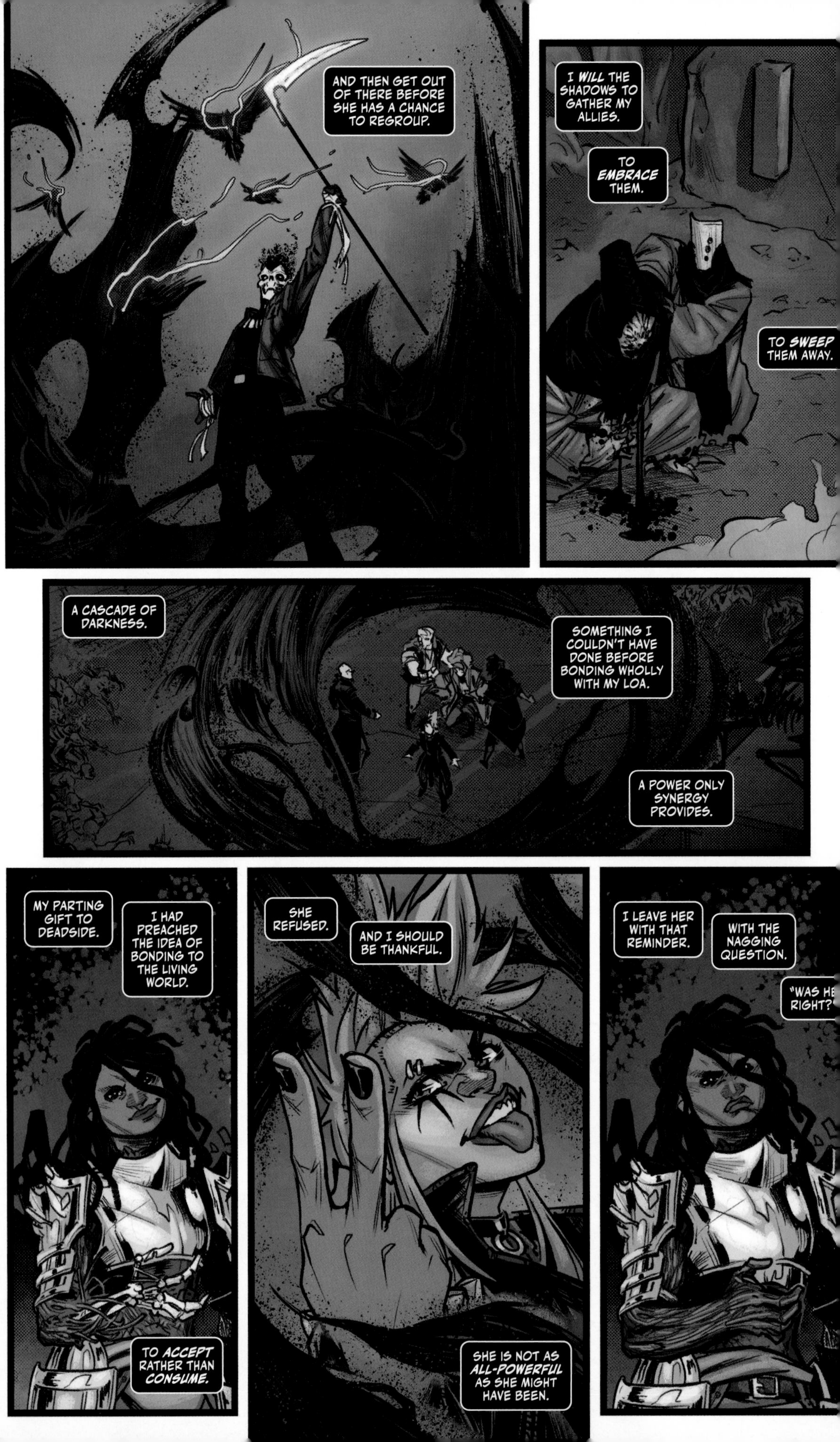
AND THEN GET OUT OF THERE BEFORE SHE HAS A CHANCE TO REGROUP.
I *WILL* THE SHADOWS TO GATHER MY ALLIES.
TO *EMBRACE* THEM.
TO *SWEEP* THEM AWAY.
A CASCADE OF DARKNESS.
SOMETHING I COULDN'T HAVE DONE BEFORE BONDING WHOLLY WITH MY LOA.
A POWER ONLY SYNERGY PROVIDES.
MY PARTING GIFT TO DEADSIDE.
I HAD PREACHED THE IDEA OF BONDING TO THE LIVING WORLD.
TO *ACCEPT* RATHER THAN *CONSUME.*
SHE REFUSED.
AND I SHOULD BE THANKFUL.
SHE IS NOT AS *ALL-POWERFUL* AS SHE MIGHT HAVE BEEN.
I LEAVE HER WITH THAT REMINDER.
WITH THE NAGGING QUESTION.

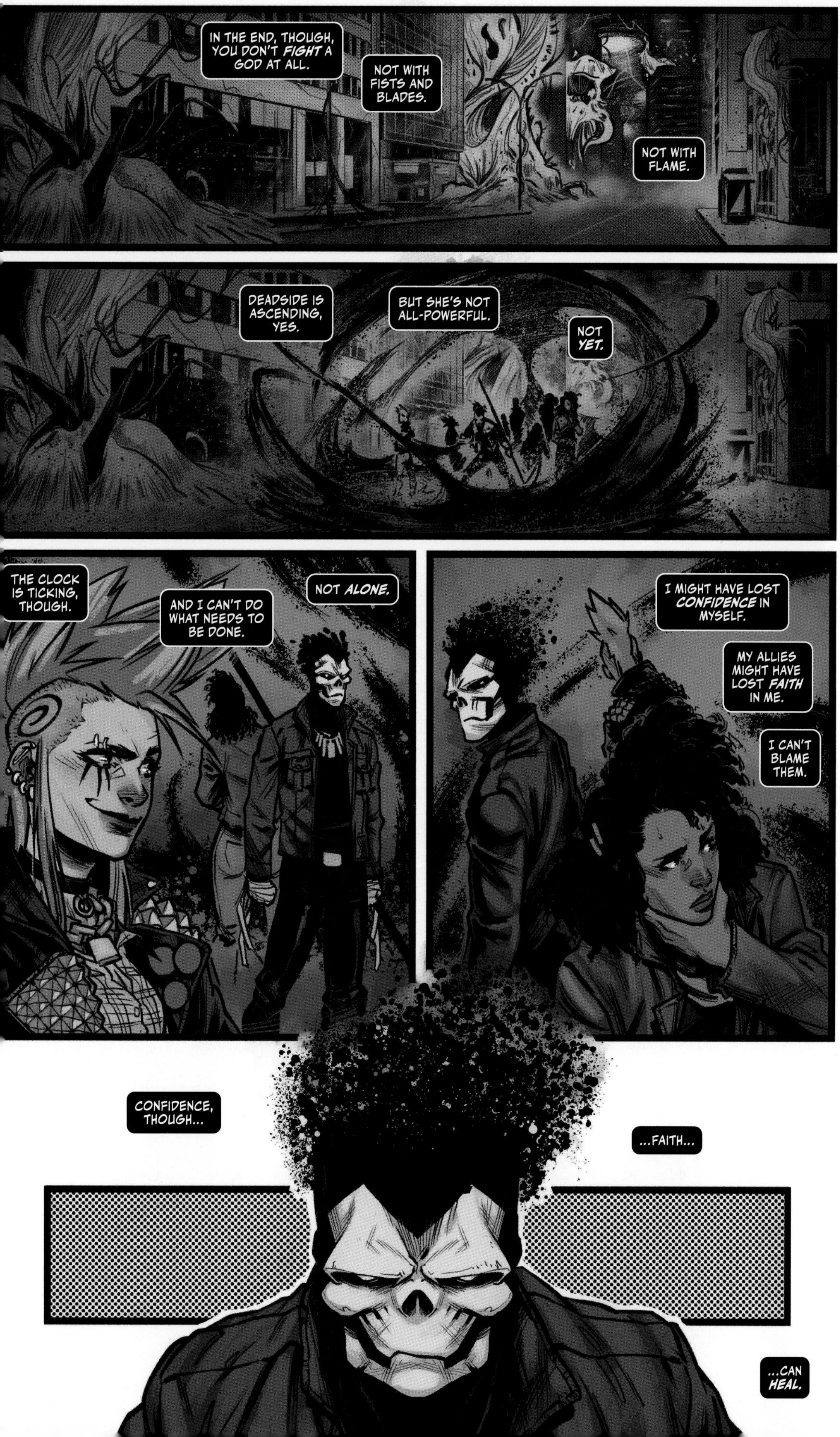
IN THE END, THOUGH, YOU DON'T FIGHT A GOD AT ALL.
NOT WITH FISTS AND BLADES.
NOT WITH FLAME.
DEADSIDE IS ASCENDING, YES.
BUT SHE'S NOT ALL-POWERFUL.
NOT YET.
THE CLOCK IS TICKING, THOUGH.
AND I CAN'T DO WHAT NEEDS TO BE DONE.
NOT ALONE.
I MIGHT HAVE LOST CONFIDENCE IN MYSELF.
MY ALLIES MIGHT HAVE LOST FAITH IN ME.
I CAN'T BLAME THEM.
CONFIDENCE, THOUGH...
...FAITH...
...CAN HEAL.

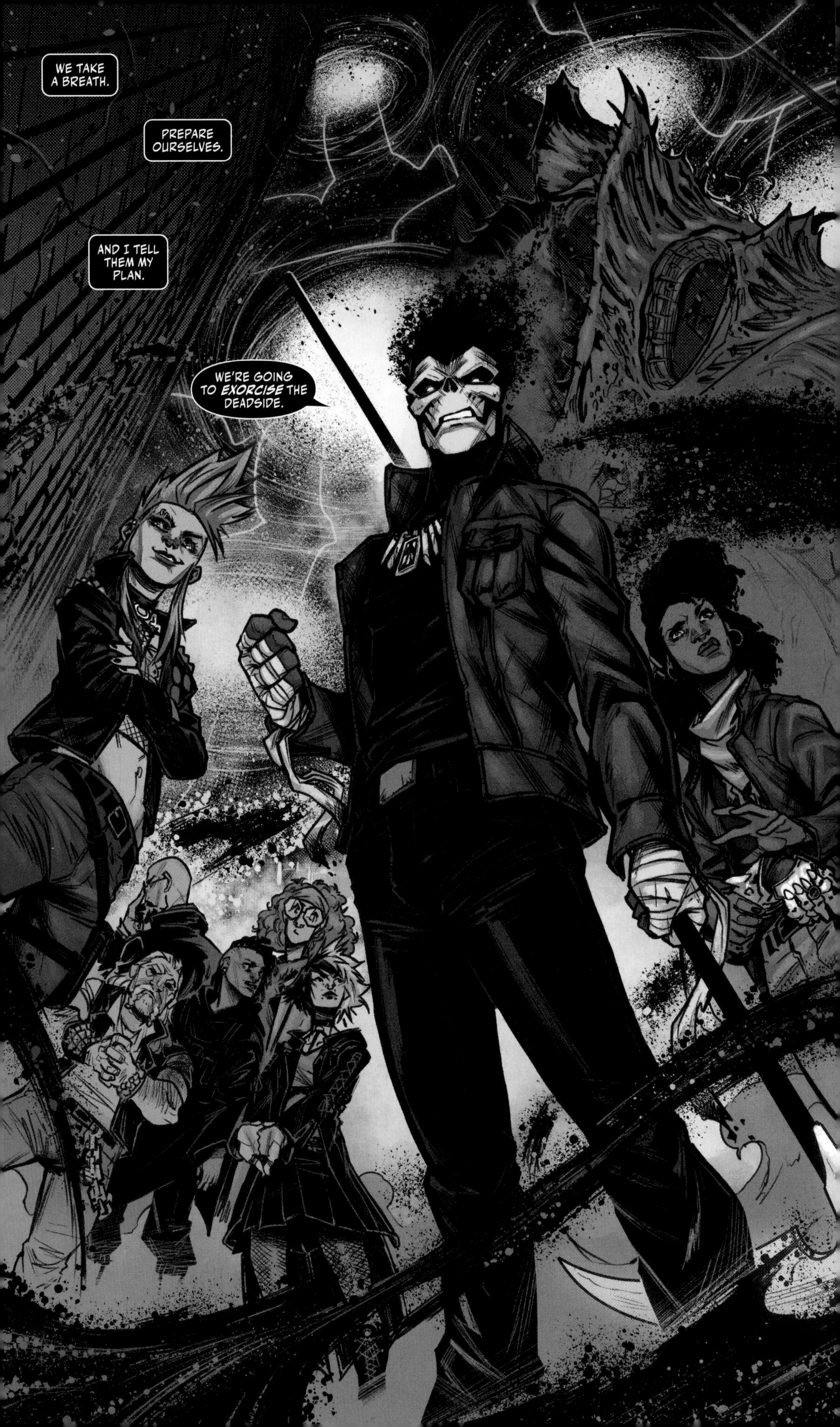

WE TAKE A BREATH.
PREPARE OURSELVES.
AND I TELL THEM MY PLAN.
WE'RE GOING TO *EXORCISE* THE DEADSIDE.

SHADOWMAN®
CULLEN BUNN | PEDRO ANDREO | JORDIE BELLAIRE | CLAYTON COWLES
DEADSIDE WAR PART 4

SHADOWMAN #8

"DEADSIDE WAR: PART 4"

WRITER: Cullen Bunn
ARTIST: Pedro Andreo
ART ASSISTANT: Álvaro De Miguel
COLORIST: Jordie Bellaire
LETTERER: Clayton Cowles
COVER ARTIST: Jon Davis-Hunt
ASSISTANT EDITOR: Audrey Meeker
SENIOR EDITOR: Lysa Hawkins

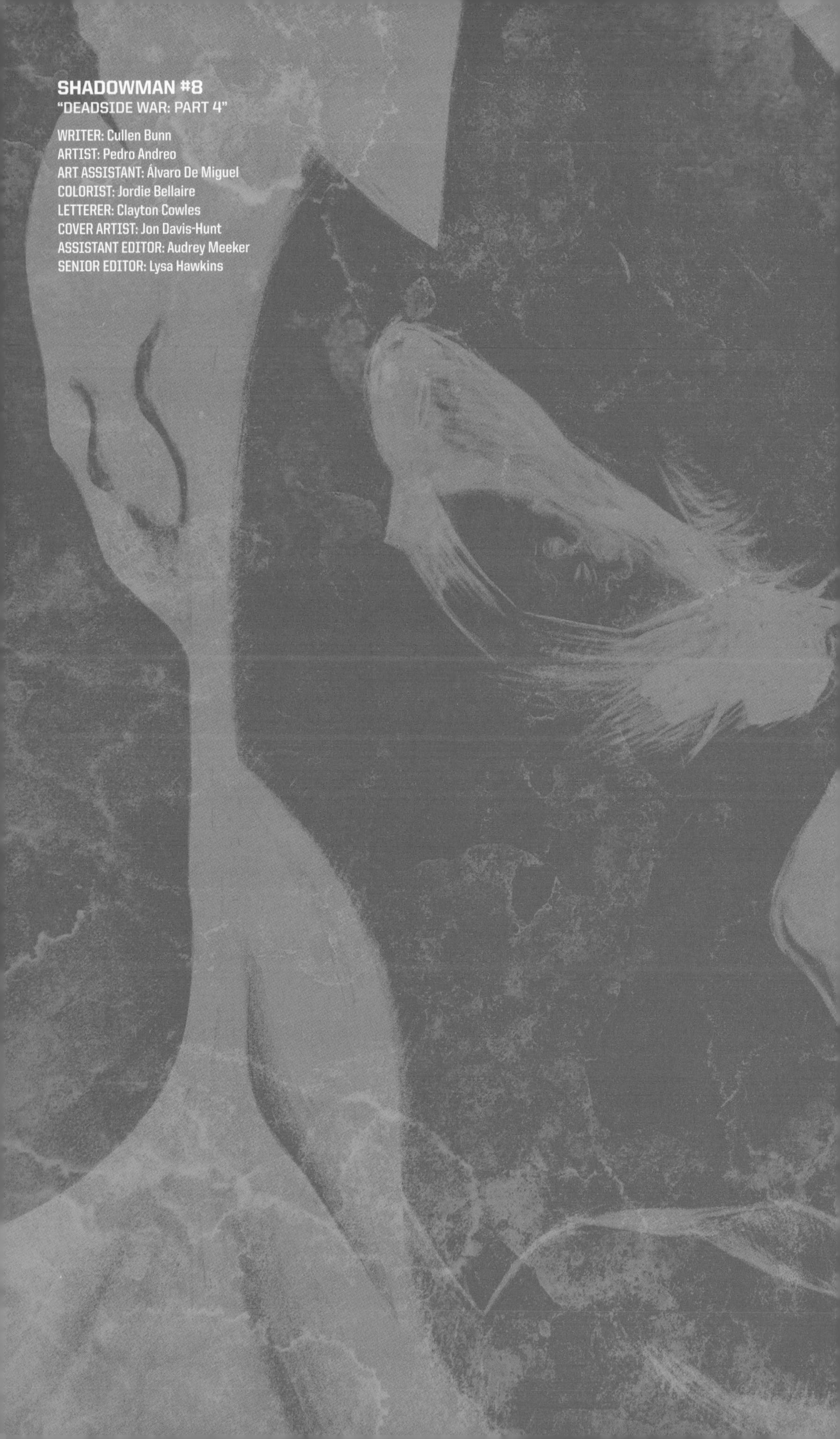

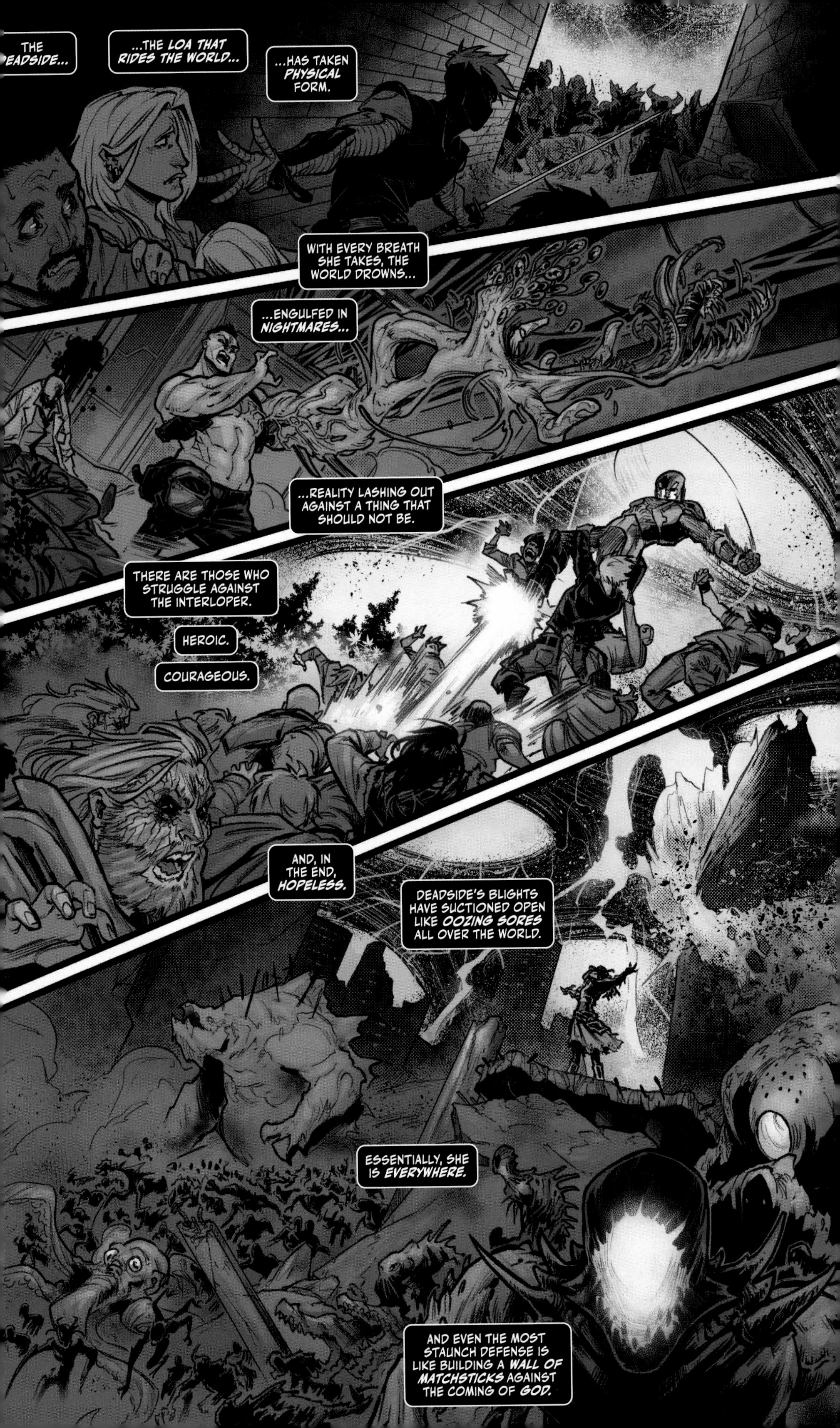
THE DEADSIDE...
...THE LOA THAT RIDES THE WORLD...
...HAS TAKEN PHYSICAL FORM.
WITH EVERY BREATH SHE TAKES, THE WORLD DROWNS...
...ENGULFED IN NIGHTMARES...
...REALITY LASHING OUT AGAINST A THING THAT SHOULD NOT BE.
THERE ARE THOSE WHO STRUGGLE AGAINST THE INTERLOPER.
HEROIC.
COURAGEOUS.
AND, IN THE END, HOPELESS.
DEADSIDE'S BLIGHTS HAVE SUCTIONED OPEN LIKE OOZING SORES ALL OVER THE WORLD.
ESSENTIALLY, SHE IS EVERYWHERE.
AND EVEN THE MOST STAUNCH DEFENSE IS LIKE BUILDING A WALL OF MATCHSTICKS AGAINST THE COMING OF GOD.

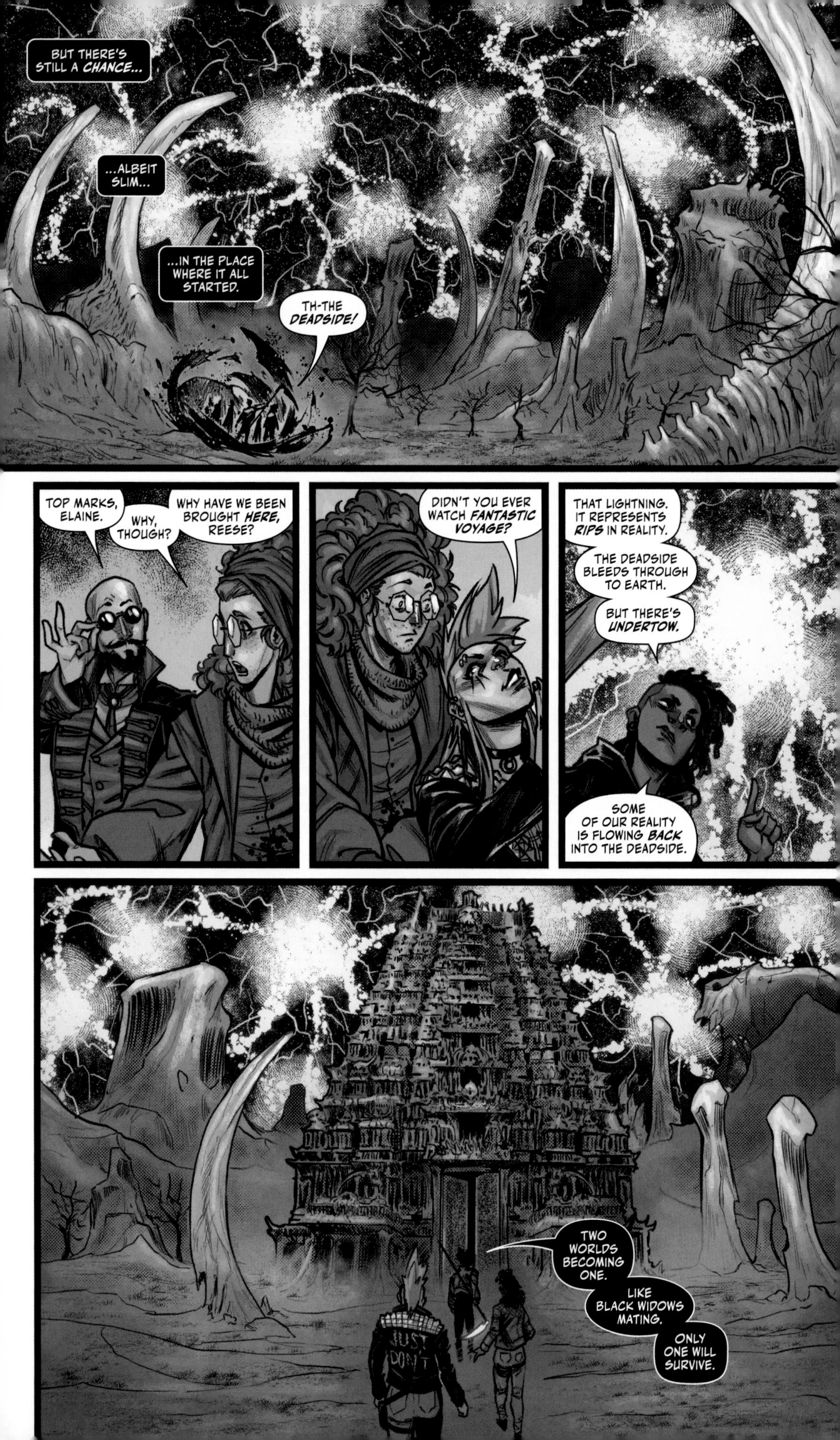
BUT THERE'S STILL A *CHANCE*...
...ALBEIT SLIM...
...IN THE PLACE WHERE IT ALL STARTED.
TH-THE *DEADSIDE!*
TOP MARKS, ELAINE.
WHY, THOUGH?
WHY HAVE WE BEEN BROUGHT *HERE,* REESE?
DIDN'T YOU EVER WATCH *FANTASTIC VOYAGE?*
THAT LIGHTNING. IT REPRESENTS *RIPS* IN REALITY.
THE DEADSIDE BLEEDS THROUGH TO EARTH.
BUT THERE'S *UNDERTOW.*
SOME OF OUR REALITY IS FLOWING *BACK* INTO THE DEADSIDE.
TWO WORLDS BECOMING ONE.
LIKE BLACK WIDOWS MATING.
ONLY ONE WILL SURVIVE.
JUST DON'T

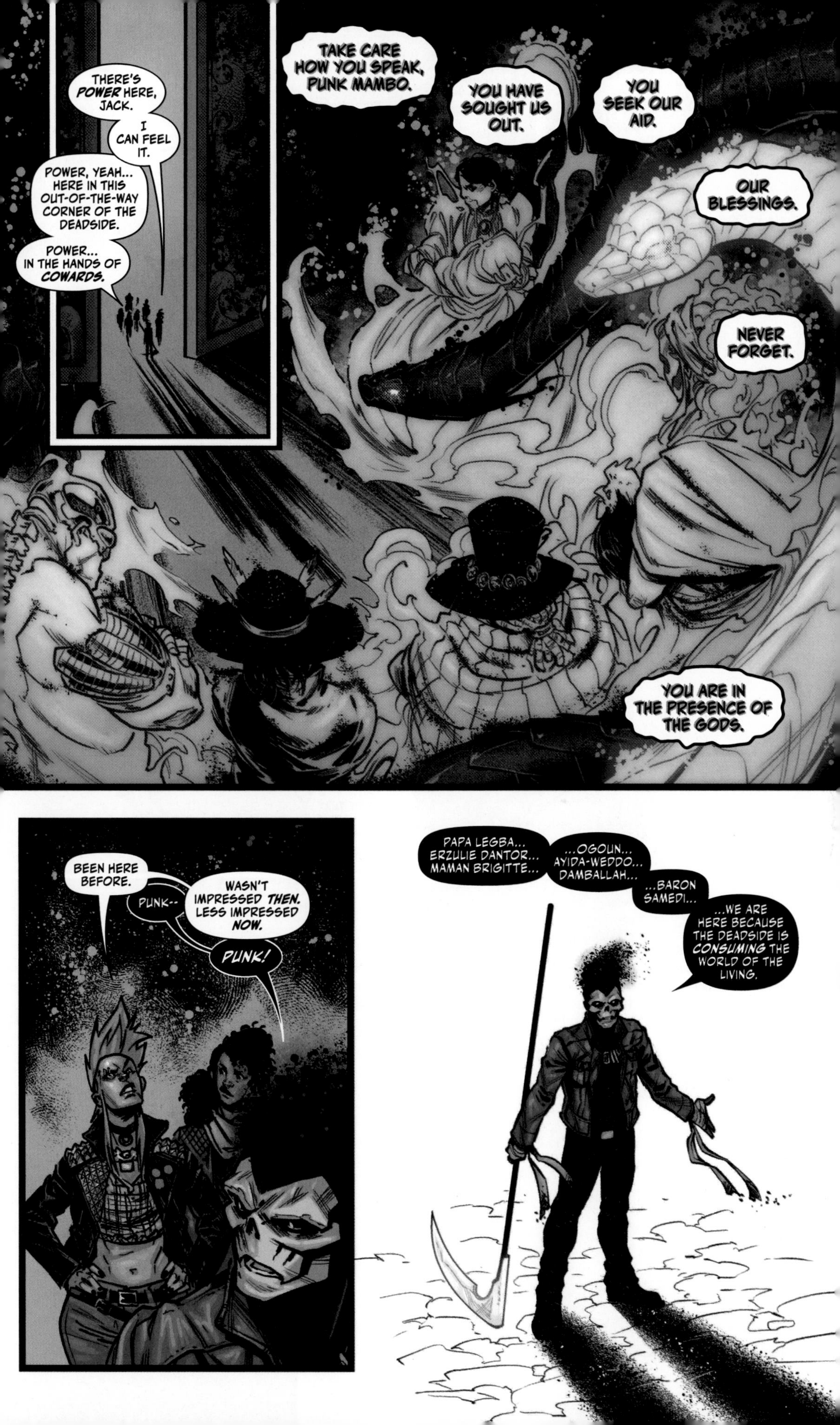
THERE'S POWER HERE, JACK.
I CAN FEEL IT.
POWER, YEAH... HERE IN THIS OUT-OF-THE-WAY CORNER OF THE DEADSIDE.
POWER... IN THE HANDS OF COWARDS.
TAKE CARE HOW YOU SPEAK, PUNK MAMBO.
YOU HAVE SOUGHT US OUT.
YOU SEEK OUR AID.
OUR BLESSINGS.
NEVER FORGET.
YOU ARE IN THE PRESENCE OF THE GODS.
BEEN HERE BEFORE.
PUNK--
WASN'T IMPRESSED THEN. LESS IMPRESSED NOW.
PUNK!
PAPA LEGBA... ERZULIE DANTOR... MAMAN BRIGITTE...
...OGOUN... AYIDA-WEDDO... DAMBALLAH...
...BARON SAMEDI...
...WE ARE HERE BECAUSE THE DEADSIDE IS CONSUMING THE WORLD OF THE LIVING.

WE KNOW THIS, JACK BONIFACE.

I GUIDED YOU MYSELF IN AN EFFORT TO STEM THE *BLIGHT-TIDE.*

THE EFFORT, I'D SAY, WAS *WASTED.*

BUT YOU NEVER TOLD ME THE *WHOLE* STORY.

YOU *KNEW* WHAT DEADSIDE WAS TRYING TO DO.

YOU *KNEW* SHE SOUGHT PHYSICAL FORM.

IF YOU HAD TOLD ME--

AND *WHAT* DO YOU INTEND TO DO NOW?

YOU CAME HERE FOR A *REASON,* DID YOU NOT?

WHAT DO YOU WANT FROM US?

HOW WILL YOU *STOP* DEADSIDE?

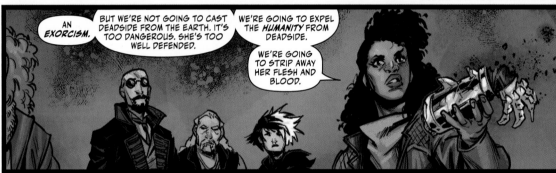

AN *EXORCISM.*

BUT WE'RE NOT GOING TO CAST DEADSIDE FROM THE EARTH. IT'S TOO DANGEROUS. SHE'S TOO WELL DEFENDED.

WE'RE GOING TO EXPEL THE *HUMANITY* FROM DEADSIDE.

WE'RE GOING TO STRIP AWAY HER FLESH AND BLOOD.

WITHOUT THE *ANCHOR,* THE LOA WILL BE DRAGGED BACK TO ITS PROPER PLACE.

THE SPIRIT WILL HAVE NOWHERE ELSE TO GO.

BUT YOU KNEW THAT ALREADY, DIDN'T YOU?

YOU WOULD NEED THE POWER OF THE GODS TO FUEL SUCH A RITE.

AND THE PANTHEON HAS PLEDGED AN ALLEGIANCE TO DEADSIDE.

WE WILL NOT STAND IN HER WAY.

WE WILL NOT OFFER YOU AID.

GOOD THING WE *DIDN'T* COME HERE TO ASK *PERMISSION.*

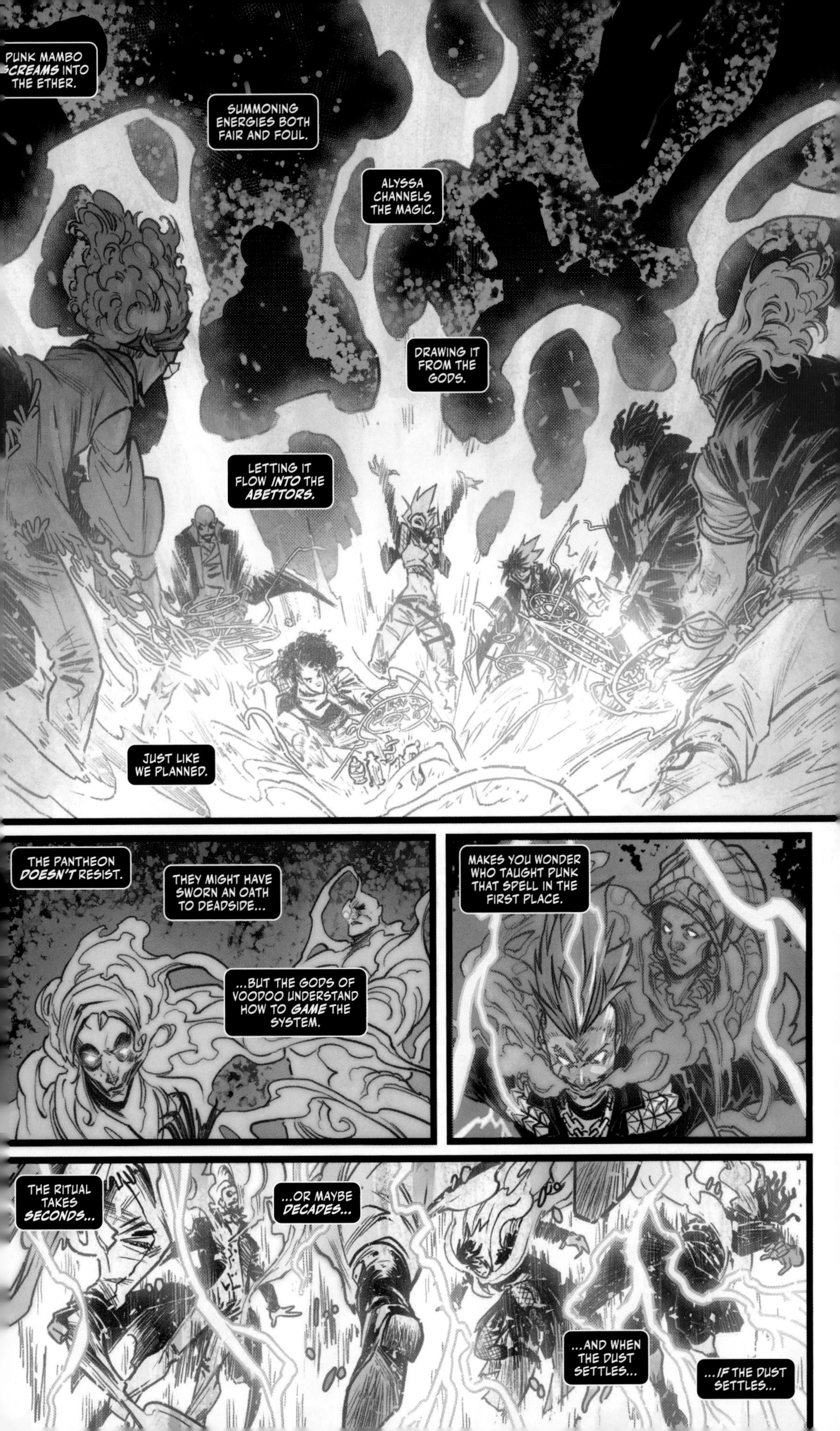
PUNK MAMBO SCREAMS INTO THE ETHER.
SUMMONING ENERGIES BOTH FAIR AND FOUL.
ALYSSA CHANNELS THE MAGIC.
DRAWING IT FROM THE GODS.
LETTING IT FLOW INTO THE ABETTORS.
JUST LIKE WE PLANNED.
THE PANTHEON DOESN'T RESIST.
THEY MIGHT HAVE SWORN AN OATH TO DEADSIDE...
...BUT THE GODS OF VOODOO UNDERSTAND HOW TO GAME THE SYSTEM.
MAKES YOU WONDER WHO TAUGHT PUNK THAT SPELL IN THE FIRST PLACE.
THE RITUAL TAKES SECONDS...
...OR MAYBE DECADES...
...AND WHEN THE DUST SETTLES...
...IF THE DUST SETTLES...

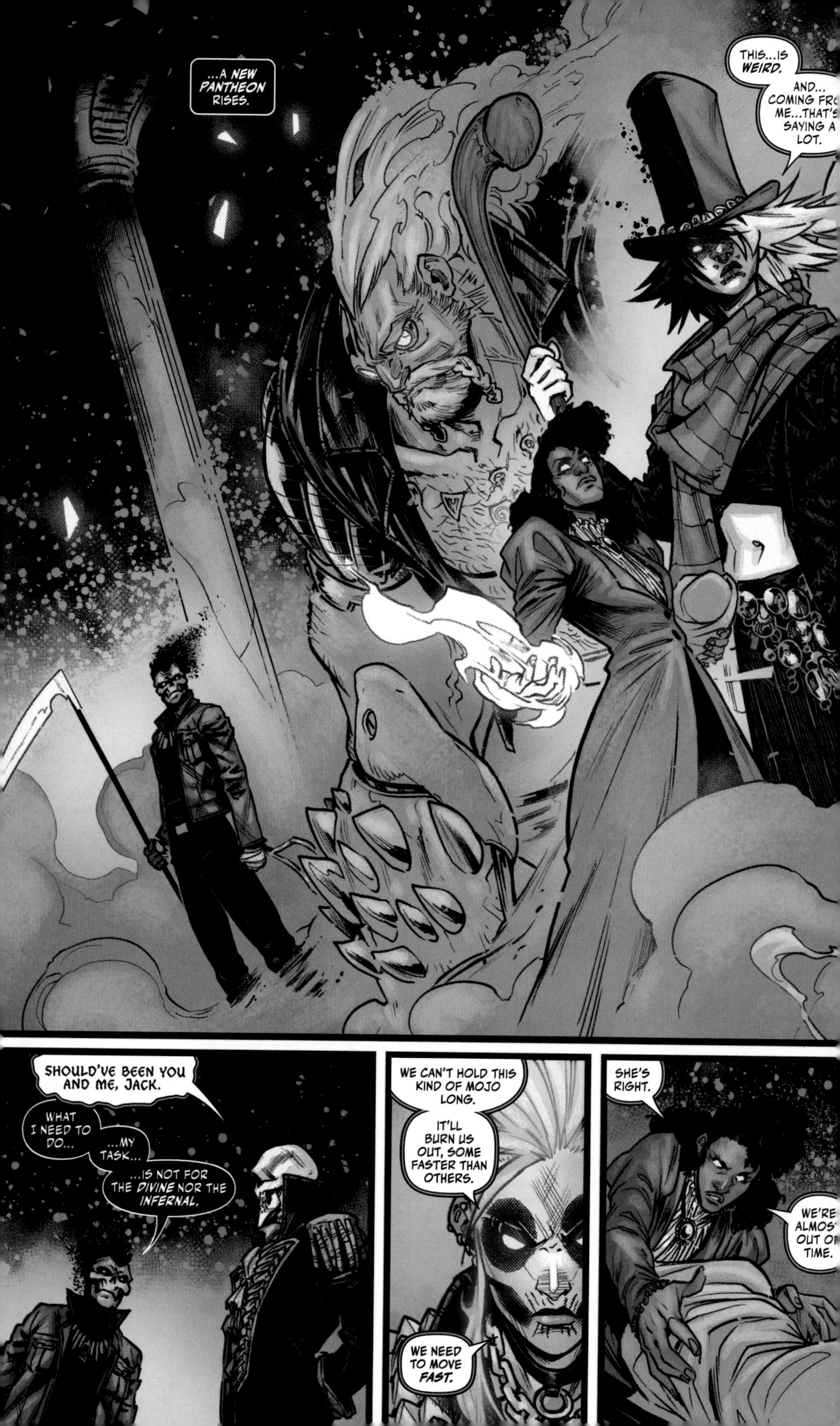
...A NEW PANTHEON RISES.
THIS...IS WEIRD.
AND... COMING FR ME...THAT'S SAYING A LOT.
SHOULD'VE BEEN YOU AND ME, JACK.
WHAT I NEED TO DO...
...MY TASK...
...IS NOT FOR THE DIVINE NOR THE INFERNAL.
WE CAN'T HOLD THIS KIND OF MOJO LONG.
IT'LL BURN US OUT, SOME FASTER THAN OTHERS.
WE NEED TO MOVE FAST.
SHE'S RIGHT.
WE'RE ALMOS OUT O TIME.

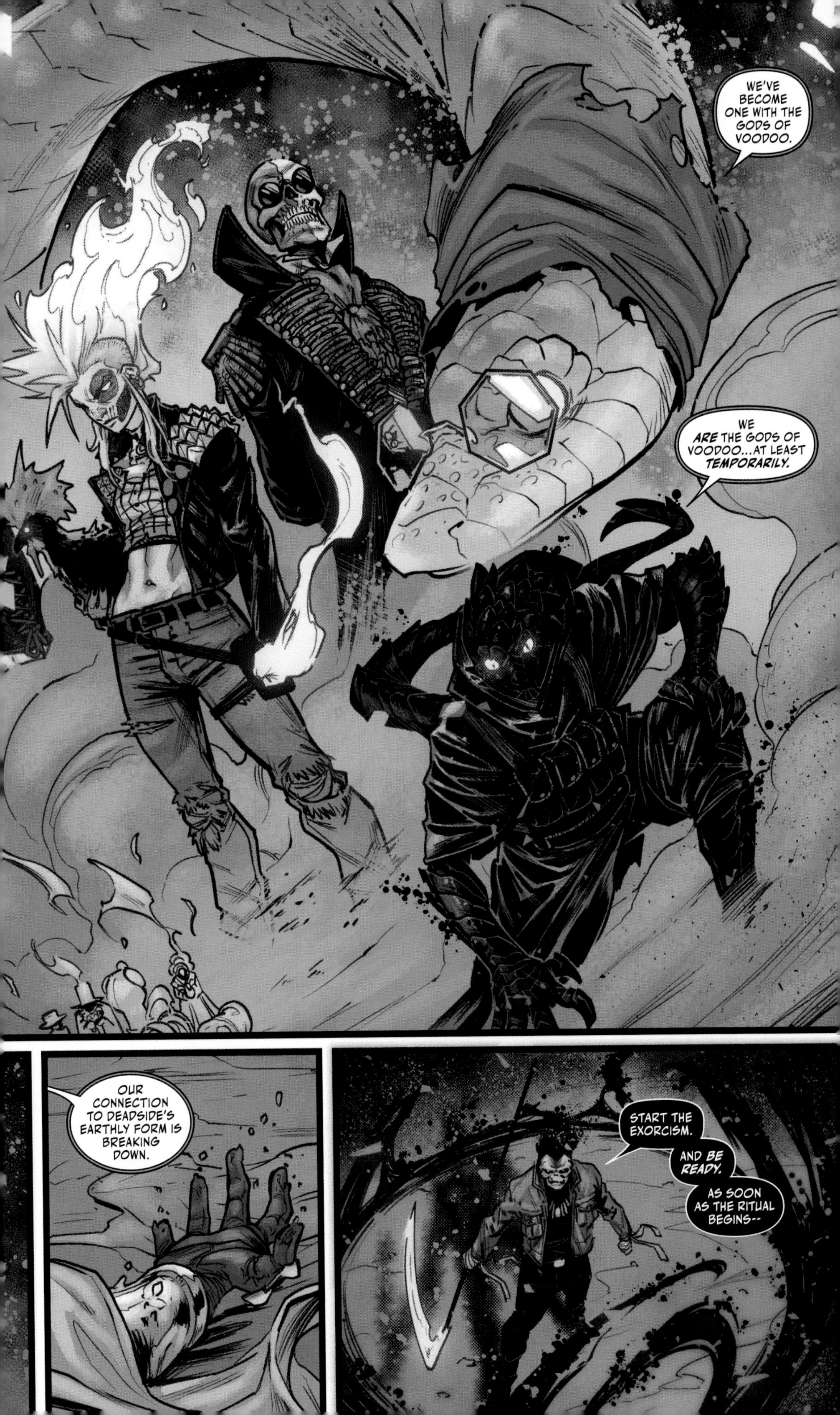
WE'VE BECOME ONE WITH THE GODS OF VOODOO.
WE ARE THE GODS OF VOODOO...AT LEAST TEMPORARILY.
OUR CONNECTION TO DEADSIDE'S EARTHLY FORM IS BREAKING DOWN.
START THE EXORCISM.
AND BE READY.
AS SOON AS THE RITUAL BEGINS--

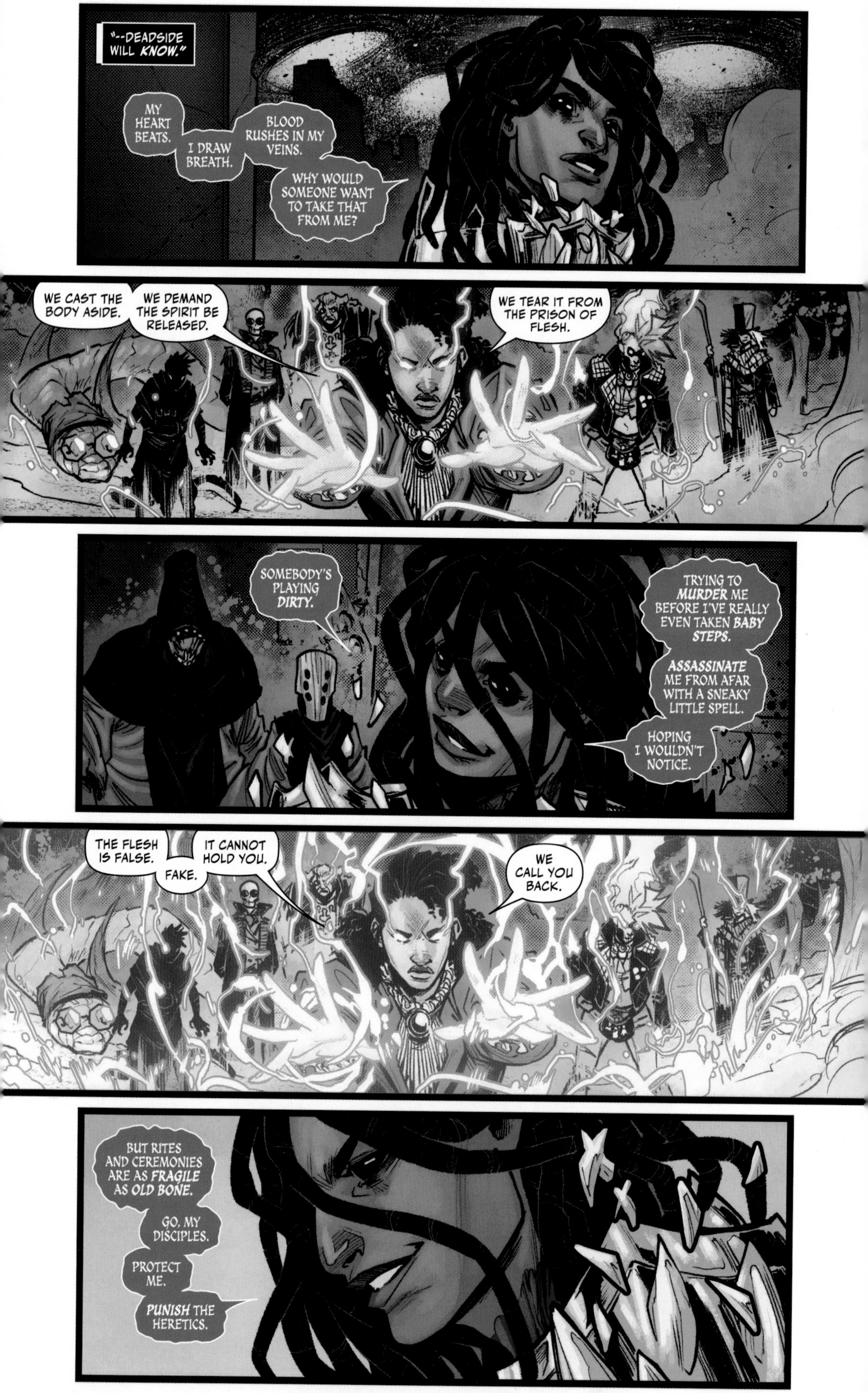
"--DEADSIDE WILL *KNOW.*"
MY HEART BEATS.
I DRAW BREATH.
BLOOD RUSHES IN MY VEINS.
WHY WOULD SOMEONE WANT TO TAKE THAT FROM ME?
WE CAST THE BODY ASIDE.
WE DEMAND THE SPIRIT BE RELEASED.
WE TEAR IT FROM THE PRISON OF FLESH.
SOMEBODY'S PLAYING *DIRTY.*
TRYING TO *MURDER* ME BEFORE I'VE REALLY EVEN TAKEN *BABY STEPS.*
ASSASSINATE ME FROM AFAR WITH A SNEAKY LITTLE SPELL.
HOPING I WOULDN'T NOTICE.
THE FLESH IS FALSE.
FAKE.
IT CANNOT HOLD YOU.
WE CALL YOU BACK.
BUT RITES AND CEREMONIES ARE AS *FRAGILE* AS *OLD BONE.*
GO, MY DISCIPLES.
PROTECT ME.
PUNISH THE HERETICS.

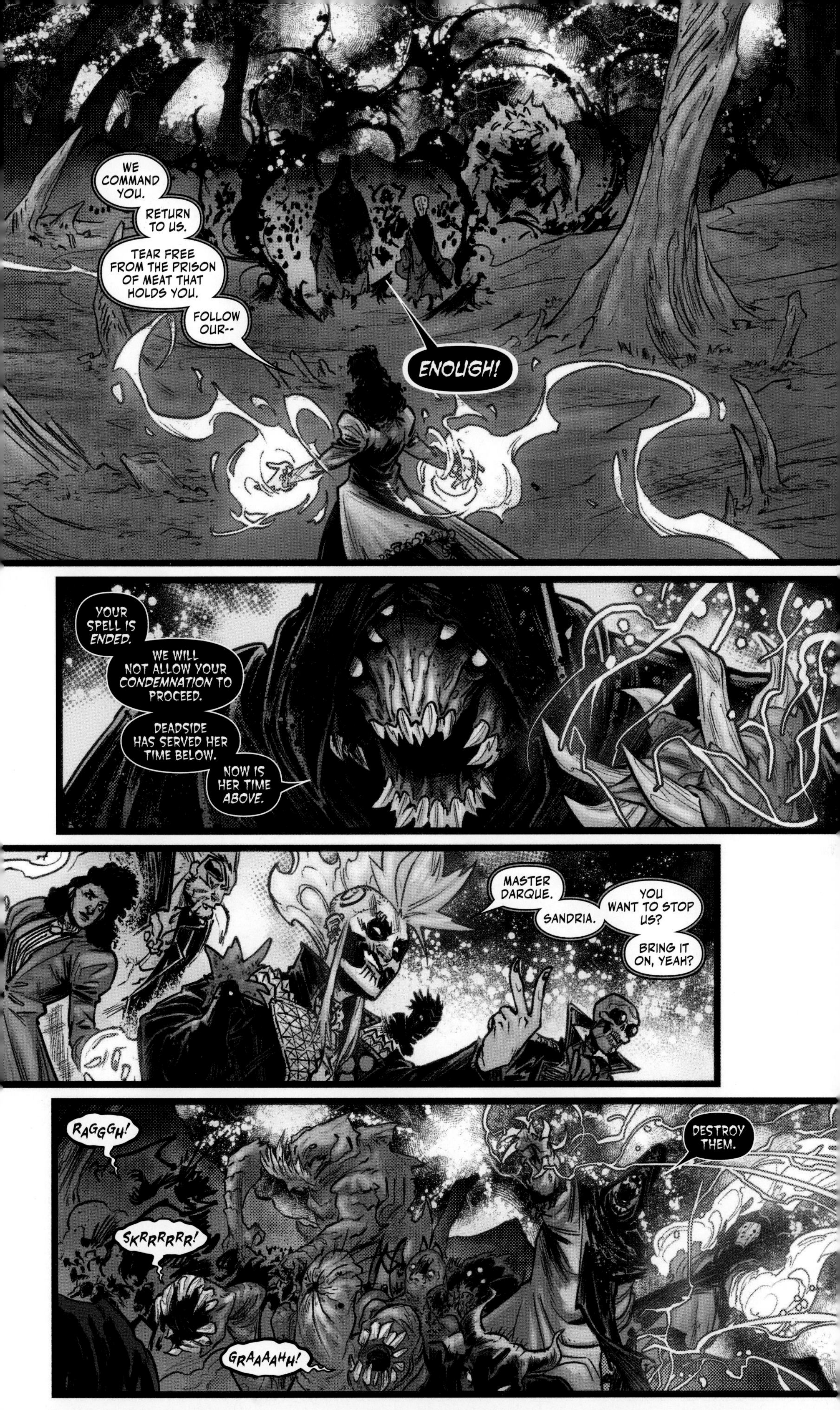
WE COMMAND YOU.
RETURN TO US.
TEAR FREE FROM THE PRISON OF MEAT THAT HOLDS YOU.
FOLLOW OUR--
ENOUGH!
YOUR SPELL IS *ENDED.*
WE WILL NOT ALLOW YOUR *CONDEMNATION* TO PROCEED.
DEADSIDE HAS SERVED HER TIME BELOW.
NOW IS HER TIME *ABOVE.*
MASTER DARQUE.
SANDRIA.
YOU WANT TO STOP US?
BRING IT ON, YEAH?
RAGGGH!
SKRRRRRR!
GRAAAAHH!
DESTROY THEM.

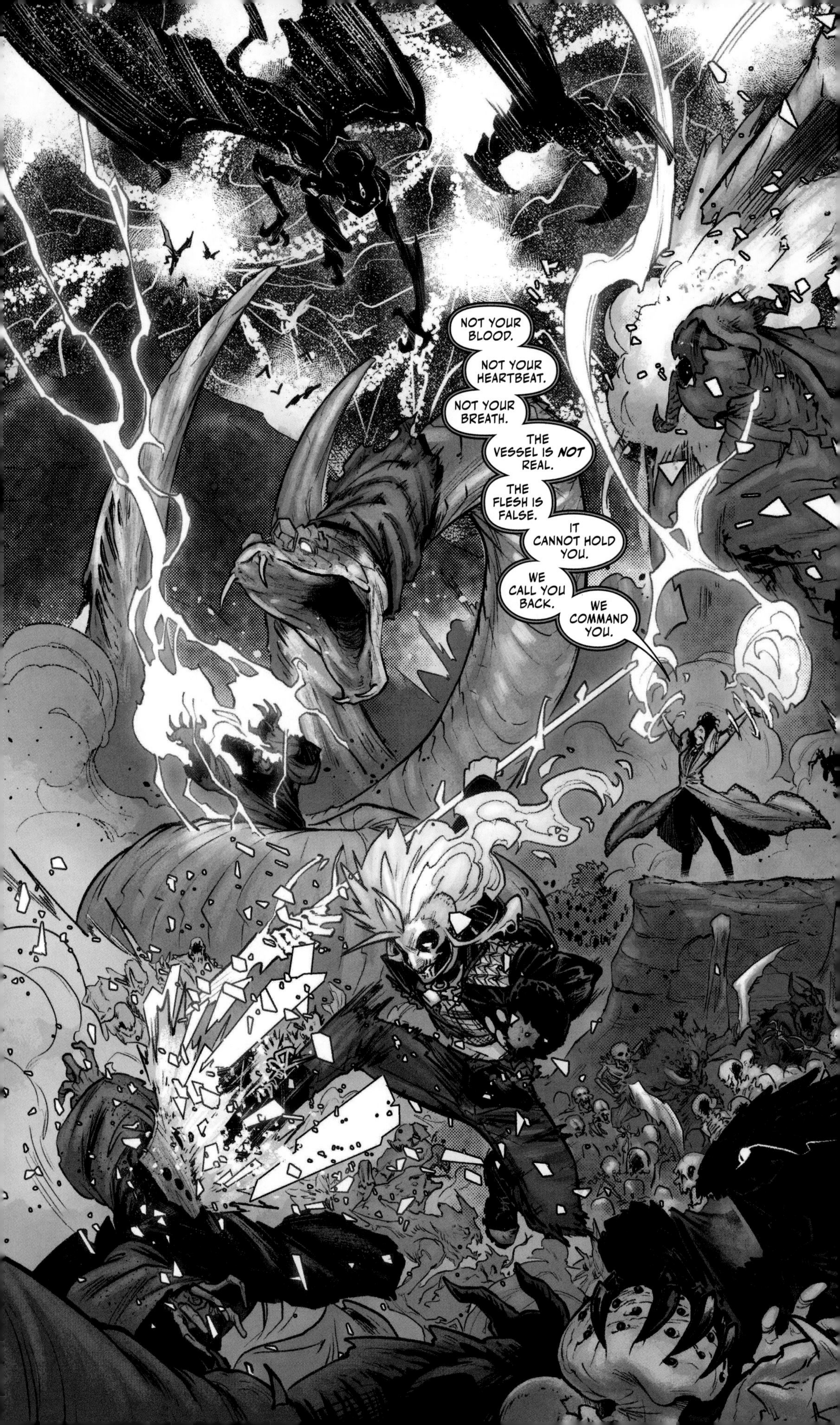
NOT YOUR BLOOD.
NOT YOUR HEARTBEAT.
NOT YOUR BREATH.
THE VESSEL IS NOT REAL.
THE FLESH IS FALSE.
IT CANNOT HOLD YOU.
WE CALL YOU BACK.
WE COMMAND YOU.

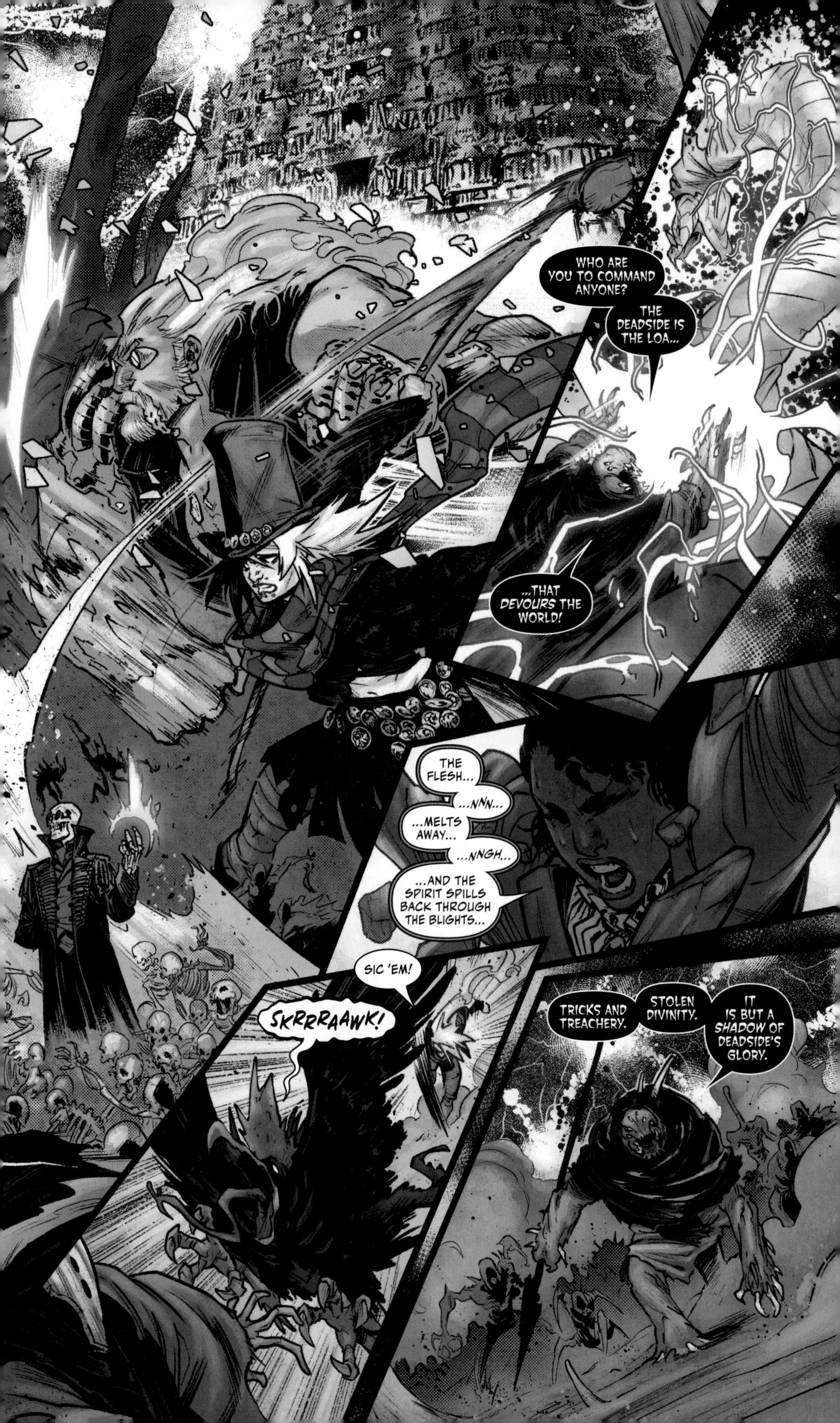
WHO ARE YOU TO COMMAND ANYONE?
THE DEADSIDE IS THE LOA...
...THAT DEVOURS THE WORLD!
THE FLESH...
...NNN...
...MELTS AWAY...
...NNGH...
...AND THE SPIRIT SPILLS BACK THROUGH THE BLIGHTS...
SIC 'EM!
SKRRRAAWK!
TRICKS AND TREACHERY.
STOLEN DIVINITY.
IT IS BUT A SHADOW OF DEADSIDE'S GLORY.

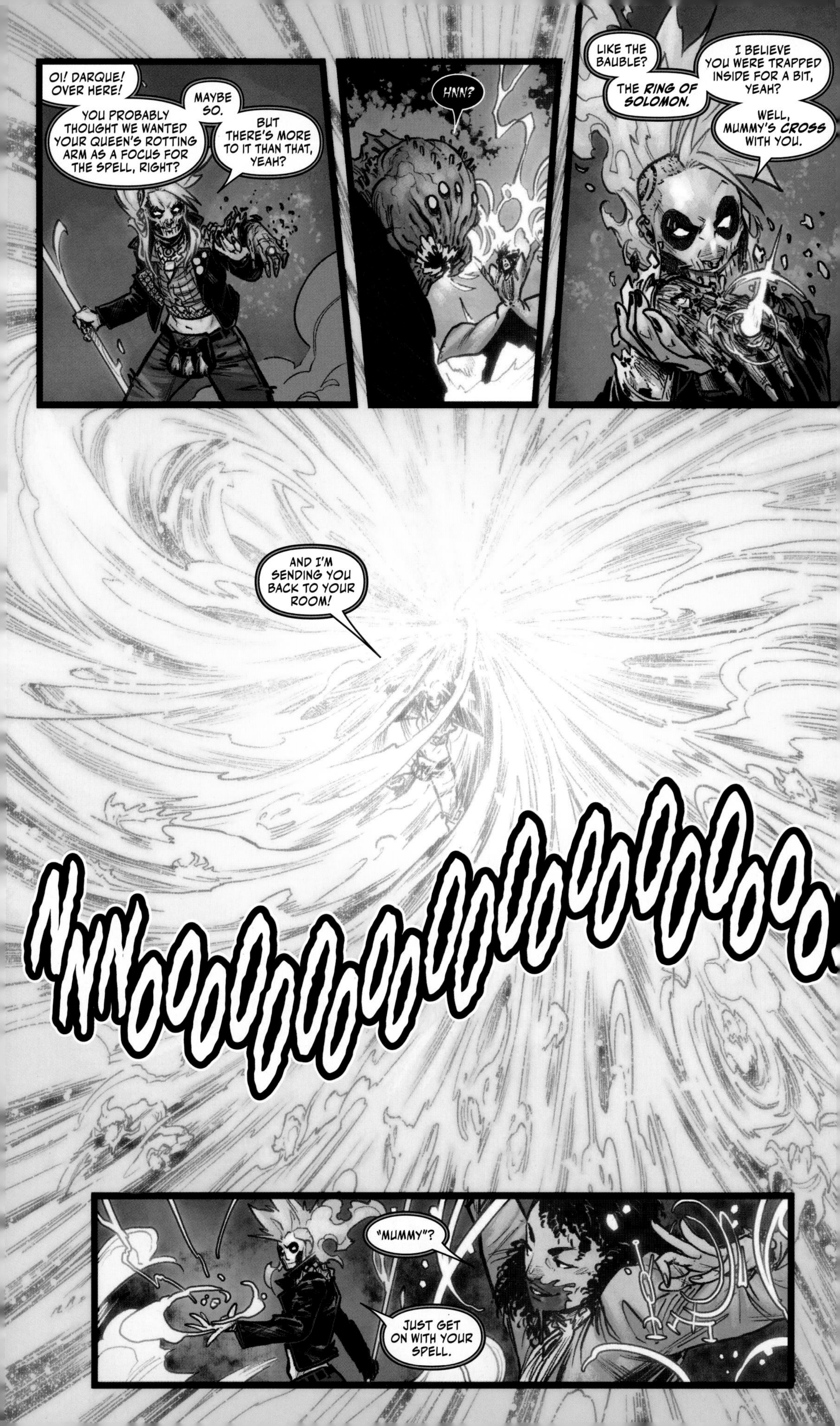
OI! DARQUE! OVER HERE!
YOU PROBABLY THOUGHT WE WANTED YOUR QUEEN'S ROTTING ARM AS A FOCUS FOR THE SPELL, RIGHT?
MAYBE SO.
BUT THERE'S MORE TO IT THAN THAT, YEAH?
HNN?
LIKE THE BAUBLE?
THE RING OF SOLOMON.
I BELIEVE YOU WERE TRAPPED INSIDE FOR A BIT, YEAH?
WELL, MUMMY'S CROSS WITH YOU.
AND I'M SENDING YOU BACK TO YOUR ROOM!
NNNooooooooooooooooooo...
"MUMMY"?
JUST GET ON WITH YOUR SPELL.

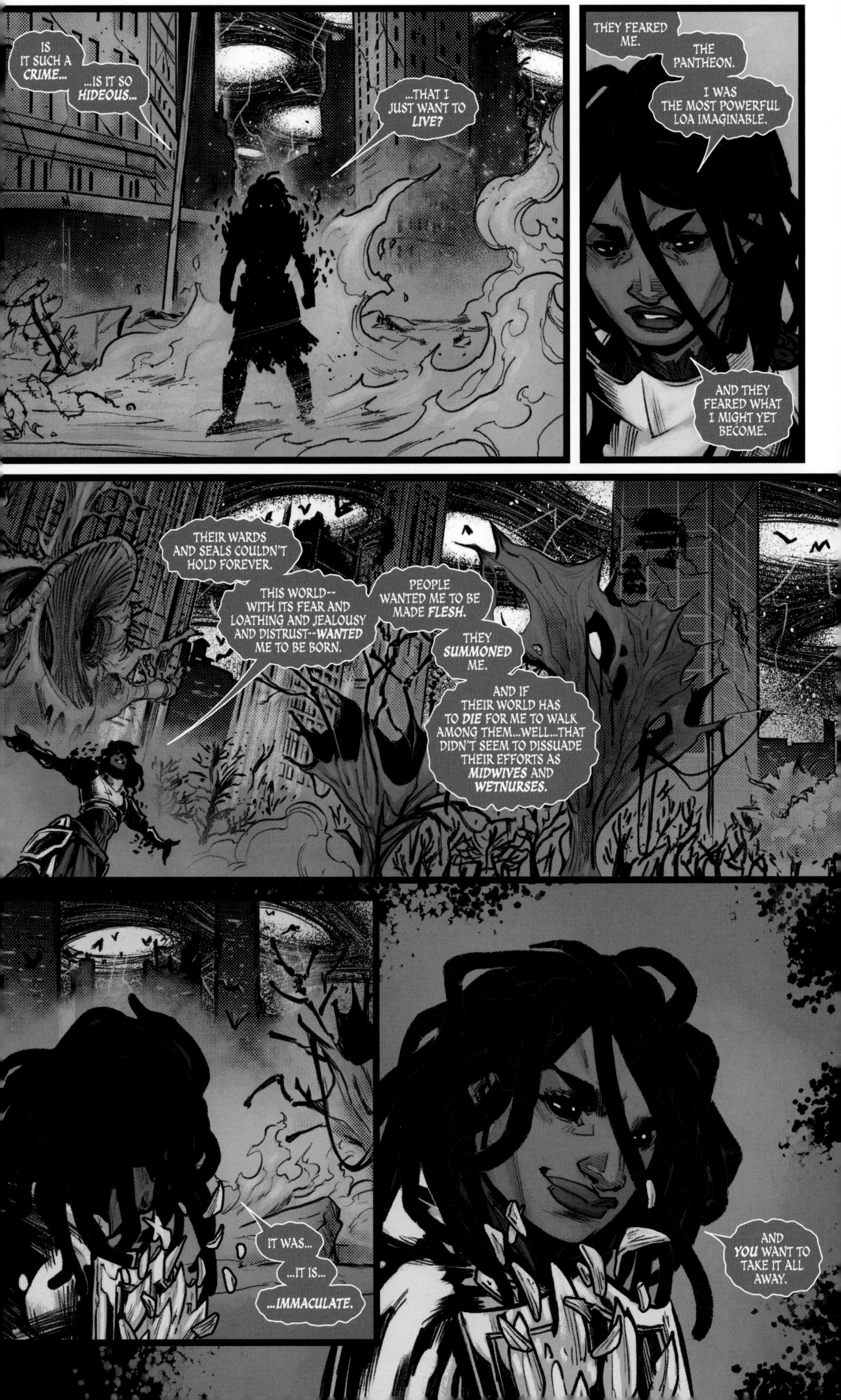

IS IT SUCH A *CRIME...*
...IS IT SO *HIDEOUS...*
...THAT I JUST WANT TO *LIVE?*
THEY FEARED ME.
THE PANTHEON.
I WAS THE MOST POWERFUL LOA IMAGINABLE.
AND THEY FEARED WHAT I MIGHT YET BECOME.
THEIR WARDS AND SEALS COULDN'T HOLD FOREVER.
THIS WORLD-- WITH ITS FEAR AND LOATHING AND JEALOUSY AND DISTRUST--*WANTED* ME TO BE BORN.
PEOPLE WANTED ME TO BE MADE *FLESH.*
THEY *SUMMONED* ME.
AND IF THEIR WORLD HAS TO *DIE* FOR ME TO WALK AMONG THEM...WELL...THAT DIDN'T SEEM TO DISSUADE THEIR EFFORTS AS *MIDWIVES* AND *WETNURSES.*
IT WAS...
...IT IS...
...IMMACULATE.
AND *YOU* WANT TO TAKE IT ALL AWAY.

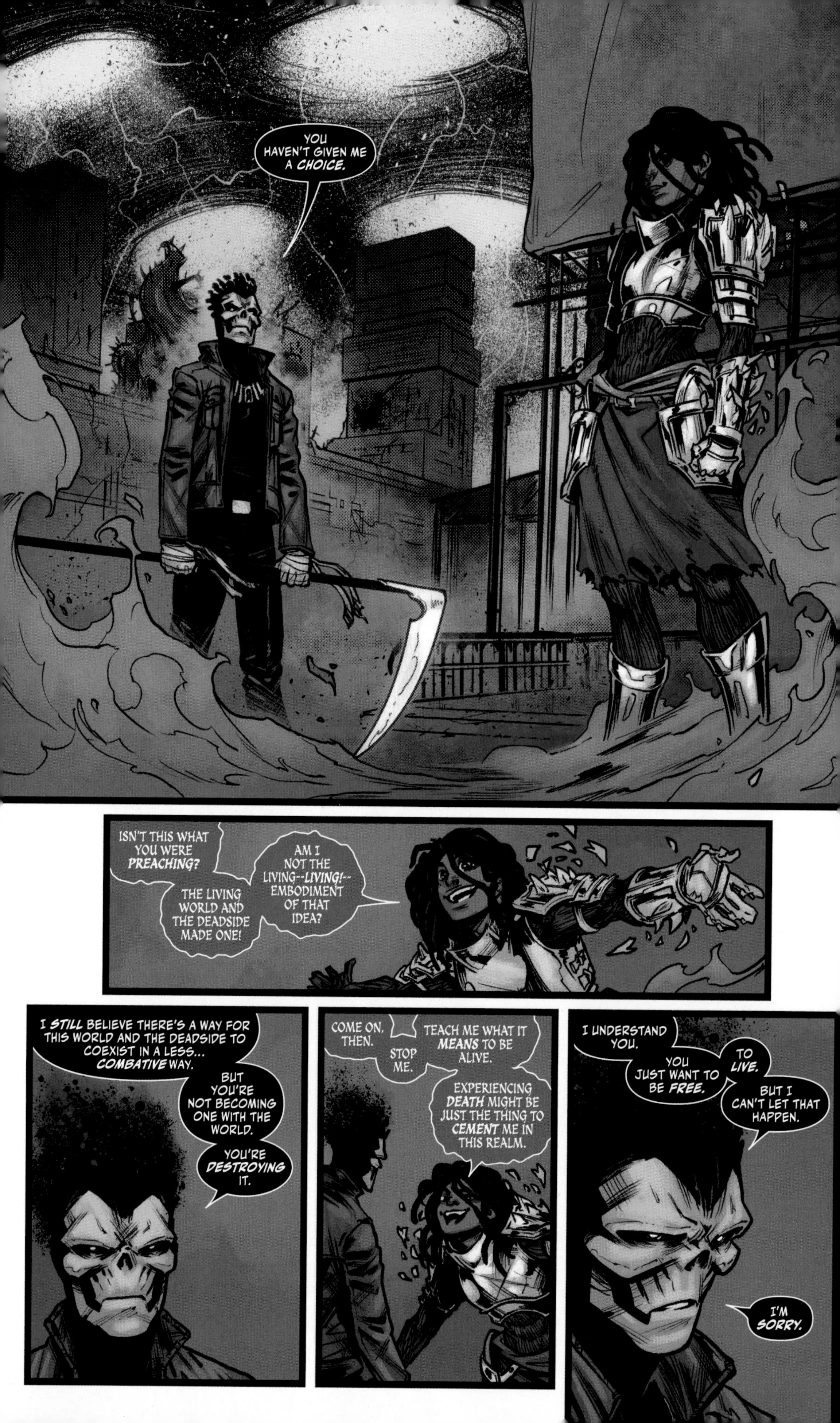
YOU HAVEN'T GIVEN ME A CHOICE.
ISN'T THIS WHAT YOU WERE PREACHING?
THE LIVING WORLD AND THE DEADSIDE MADE ONE!
AM I NOT THE LIVING--LIVING!--EMBODIMENT OF THAT IDEA?
I STILL BELIEVE THERE'S A WAY FOR THIS WORLD AND THE DEADSIDE TO COEXIST IN A LESS... COMBATIVE WAY.
BUT YOU'RE NOT BECOMING ONE WITH THE WORLD.
YOU'RE DESTROYING IT.
COME ON, THEN.
STOP ME.
TEACH ME WHAT IT MEANS TO BE ALIVE.
EXPERIENCING DEATH MIGHT BE JUST THE THING TO CEMENT ME IN THIS REALM.
I UNDERSTAND YOU.
YOU JUST WANT TO BE FREE.
TO LIVE.
BUT I CAN'T LET THAT HAPPEN.
I'M SORRY.

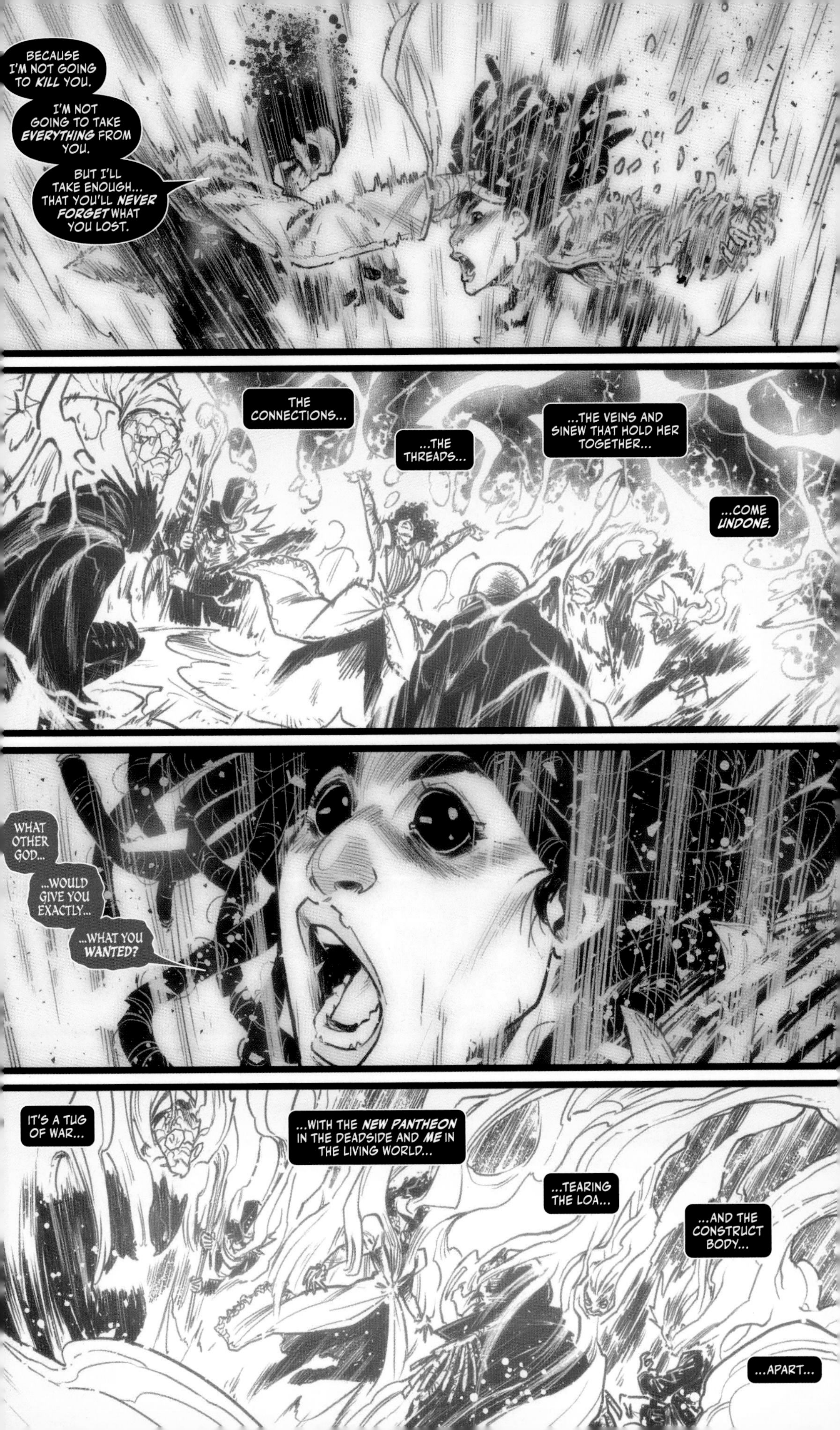
BECAUSE I'M NOT GOING TO KILL YOU.
I'M NOT GOING TO TAKE EVERYTHING FROM YOU.
BUT I'LL TAKE ENOUGH... THAT YOU'LL NEVER FORGET WHAT YOU LOST.
THE CONNECTIONS...
...THE THREADS...
...THE VEINS AND SINEW THAT HOLD HER TOGETHER...
...COME UNDONE.
WHAT OTHER GOD...
...WOULD GIVE YOU EXACTLY...
...WHAT YOU WANTED?
IT'S A TUG OF WAR...
...WITH THE NEW PANTHEON IN THE DEADSIDE AND ME IN THE LIVING WORLD...
...TEARING THE LOA...
...AND THE CONSTRUCT BODY...
...APART...

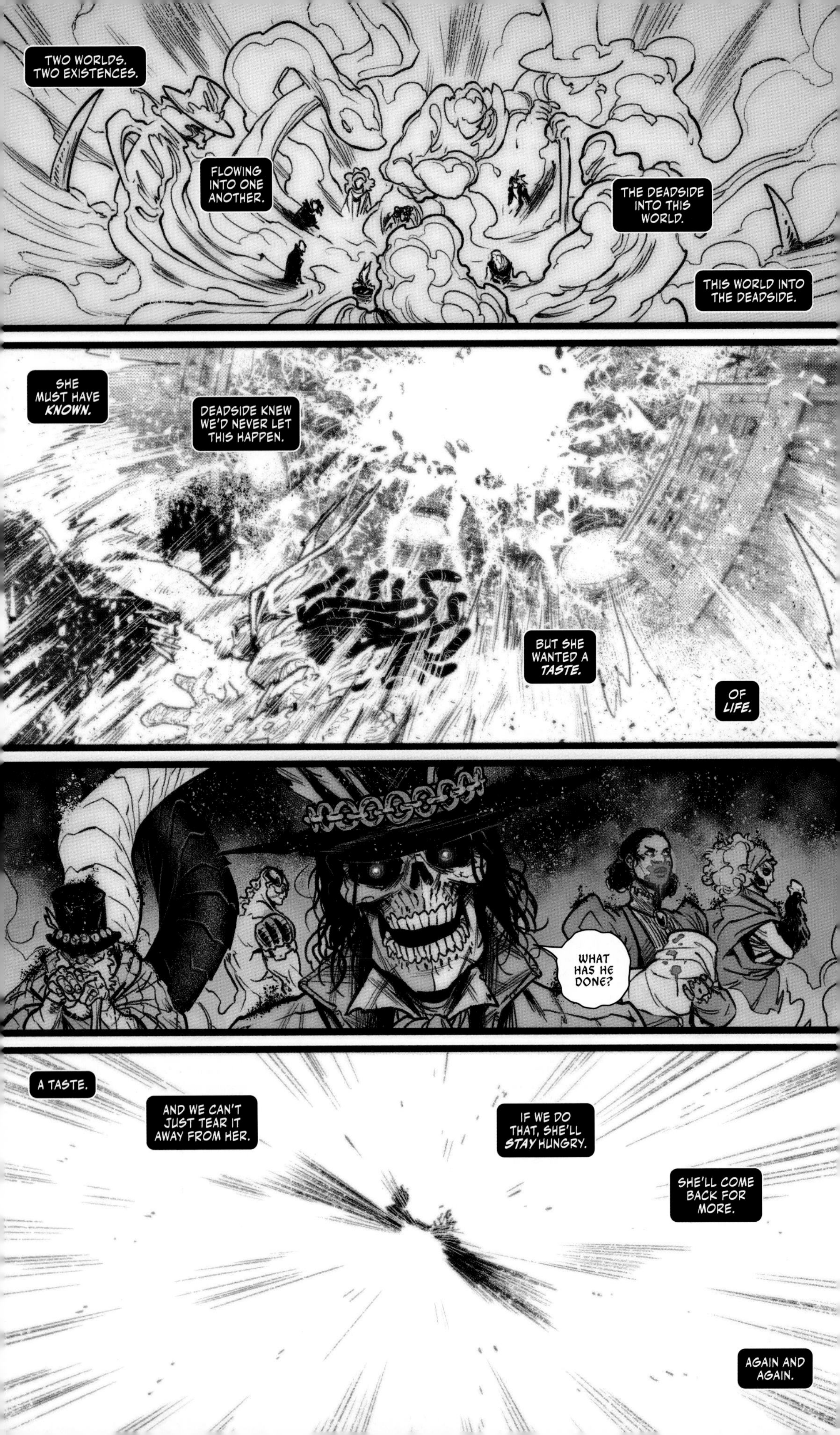

TWO WORLDS. TWO EXISTENCES.
FLOWING INTO ONE ANOTHER.
THE DEADSIDE INTO THIS WORLD.
THIS WORLD INTO THE DEADSIDE.
SHE MUST HAVE *KNOWN.*
DEADSIDE KNEW WE'D NEVER LET THIS HAPPEN.
BUT SHE WANTED A *TASTE.*
OF *LIFE.*
WHAT HAS HE DONE?
A TASTE.
AND WE CAN'T JUST TEAR IT AWAY FROM HER.
IF WE DO THAT, SHE'LL *STAY* HUNGRY.
SHE'LL COME BACK FOR MORE.
AGAIN AND AGAIN.

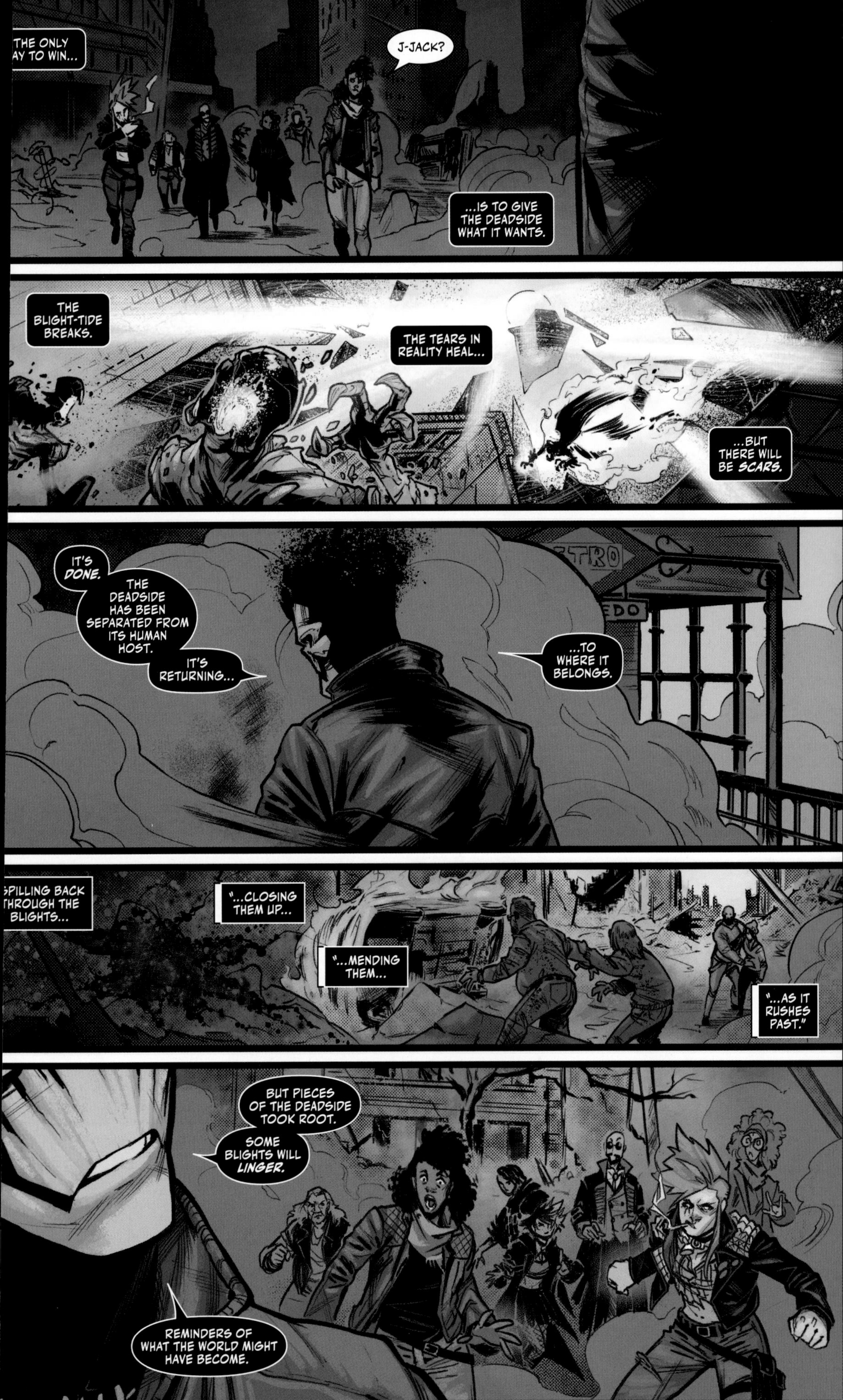
THE ONLY
AY TO WIN...
J-JACK?
...IS TO GIVE THE DEADSIDE WHAT IT WANTS.
THE BLIGHT-TIDE BREAKS.
THE TEARS IN REALITY HEAL...
...BUT THERE WILL BE SCARS.
IT'S DONE.
THE DEADSIDE HAS BEEN SEPARATED FROM ITS HUMAN HOST.
IT'S RETURNING...
...TO WHERE IT BELONGS.
ETRO
EDO
SPILLING BACK THROUGH THE BLIGHTS...
"...CLOSING THEM UP...
"...MENDING THEM...
"...AS IT RUSHES PAST."
BUT PIECES OF THE DEADSIDE TOOK ROOT.
SOME BLIGHTS WILL LINGER.
REMINDERS OF WHAT THE WORLD MIGHT HAVE BECOME.

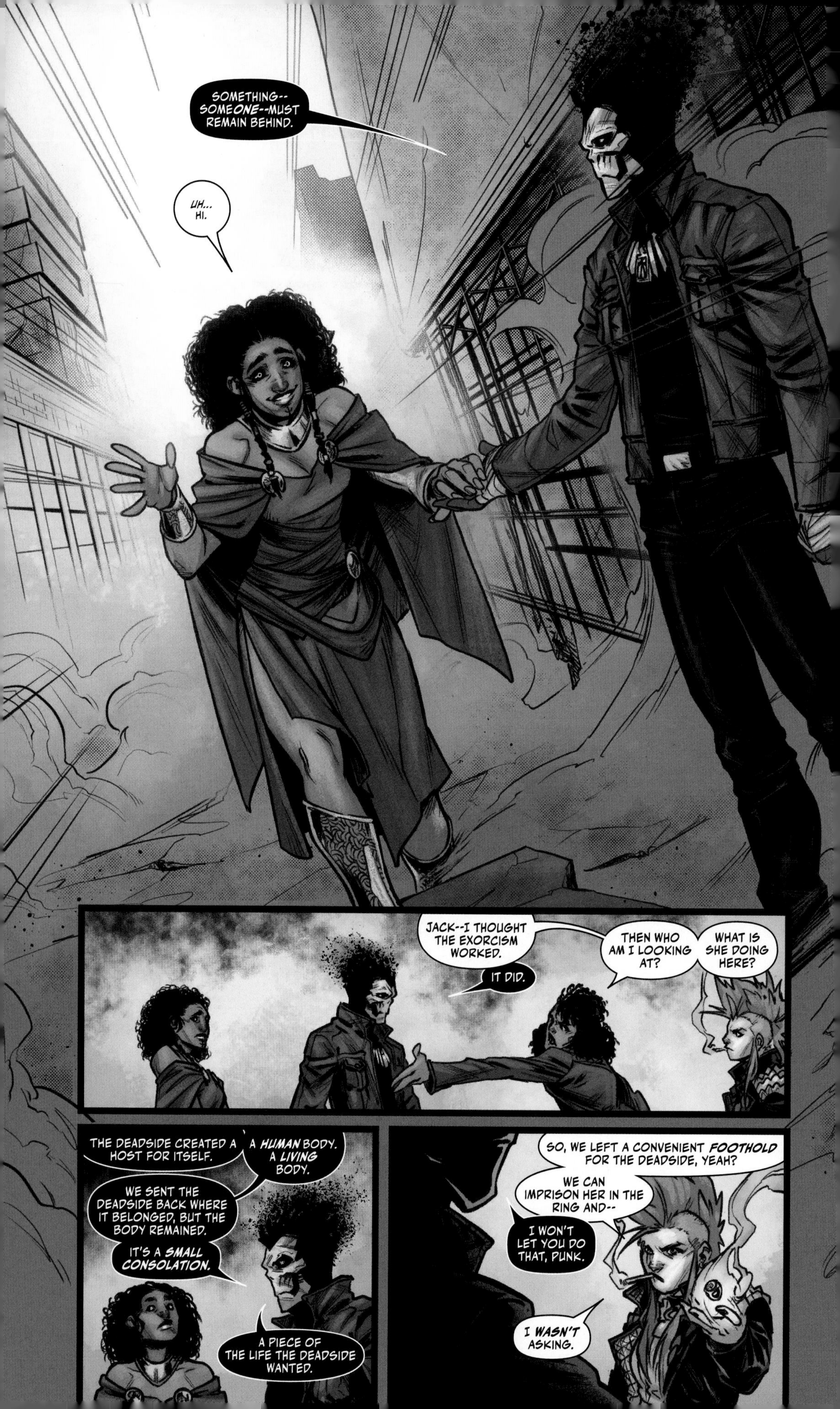
SOMETHING--
SOMEONE--MUST REMAIN BEHIND.
UH... HI.
JACK--I THOUGHT THE EXORCISM WORKED.
IT DID.
THEN WHO AM I LOOKING AT?
WHAT IS SHE DOING HERE?
THE DEADSIDE CREATED A HOST FOR ITSELF.
A HUMAN BODY. A LIVING BODY.
WE SENT THE DEADSIDE BACK WHERE IT BELONGED, BUT THE BODY REMAINED.
IT'S A SMALL CONSOLATION.
A PIECE OF THE LIFE THE DEADSIDE WANTED.
SO, WE LEFT A CONVENIENT FOOTHOLD FOR THE DEADSIDE, YEAH?
WE CAN IMPRISON HER IN THE RING AND--
I WON'T LET YOU DO THAT, PUNK.
I WASN'T ASKING.

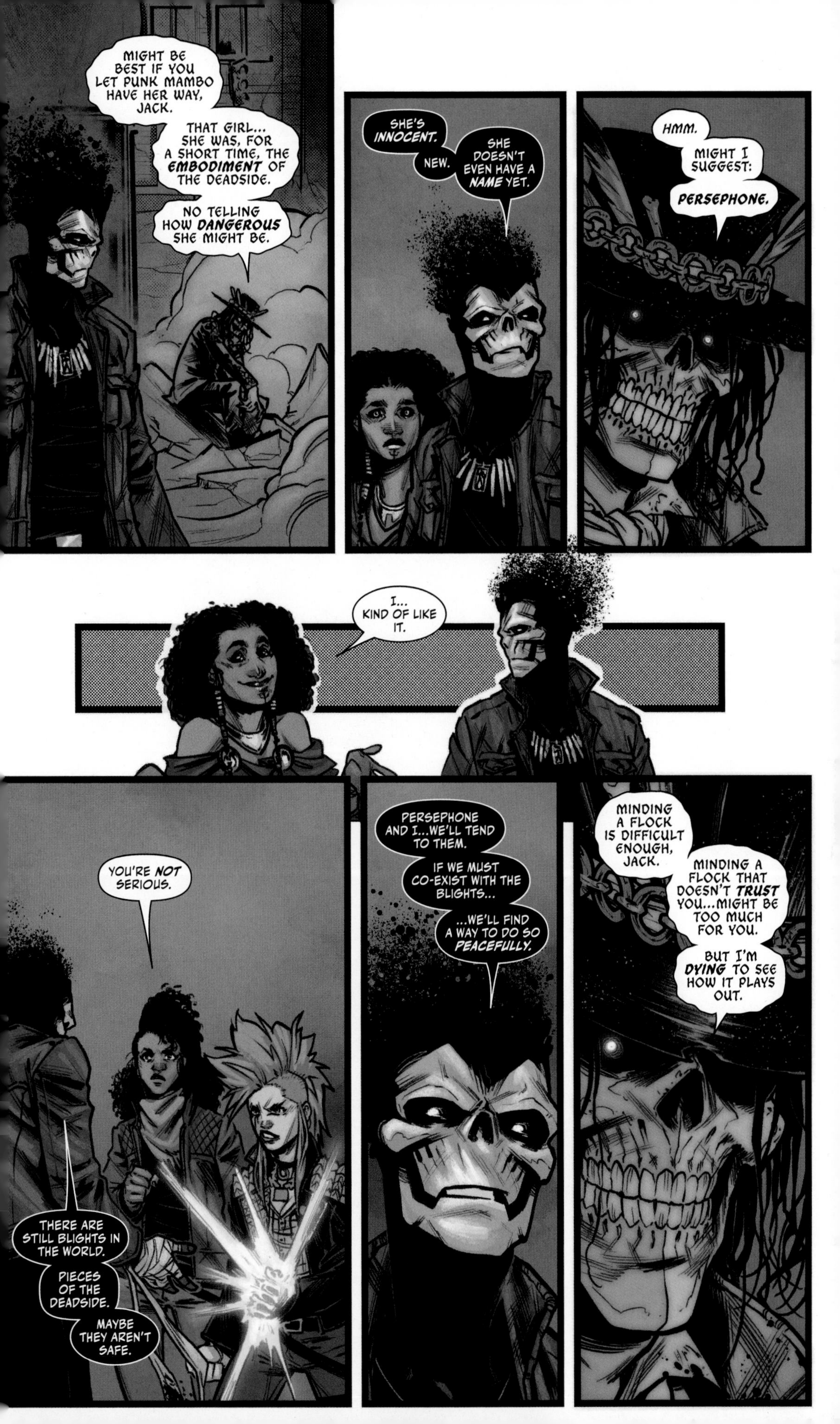
MIGHT BE BEST IF YOU LET PUNK MAMBO HAVE HER WAY, JACK.
THAT GIRL... SHE WAS, FOR A SHORT TIME, THE EMBODIMENT OF THE DEADSIDE.
NO TELLING HOW DANGEROUS SHE MIGHT BE.
SHE'S INNOCENT.
NEW.
SHE DOESN'T EVEN HAVE A NAME YET.
HMM.
MIGHT I SUGGEST:
PERSEPHONE.
I... KIND OF LIKE IT.
YOU'RE NOT SERIOUS.
THERE ARE STILL BLIGHTS IN THE WORLD.
PIECES OF THE DEADSIDE.
MAYBE THEY AREN'T SAFE.
PERSEPHONE AND I...WE'LL TEND TO THEM.
IF WE MUST CO-EXIST WITH THE BLIGHTS...
...WE'LL FIND A WAY TO DO SO PEACEFULLY.
MINDING A FLOCK IS DIFFICULT ENOUGH, JACK.
MINDING A FLOCK THAT DOESN'T TRUST YOU...MIGHT BE TOO MUCH FOR YOU.
BUT I'M DYING TO SEE HOW IT PLAYS OUT.

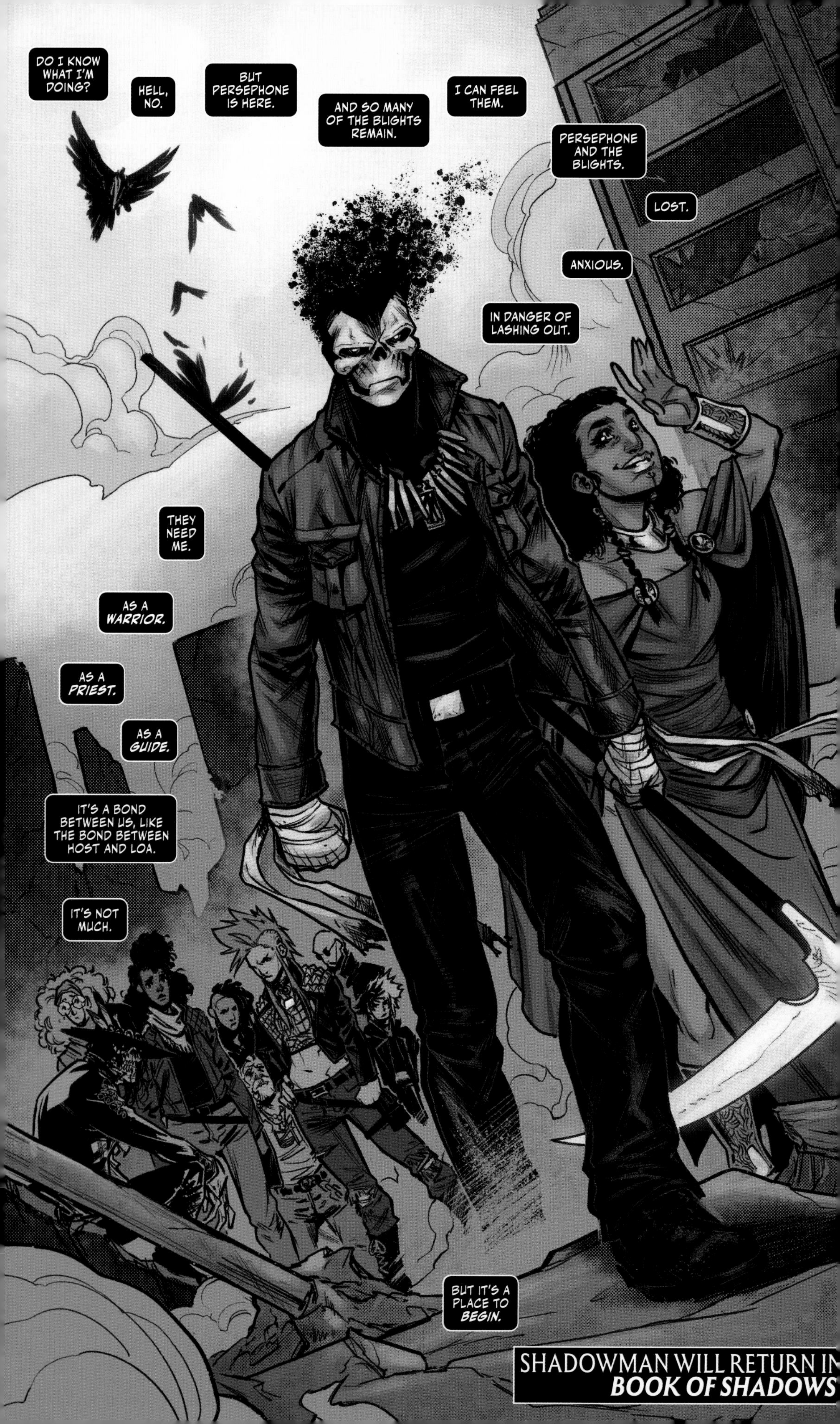
DO I KNOW WHAT I'M DOING?
HELL, NO.
BUT PERSEPHONE IS HERE.
AND SO MANY OF THE BLIGHTS REMAIN.
I CAN FEEL THEM.
PERSEPHONE AND THE BLIGHTS.
LOST.
ANXIOUS.
IN DANGER OF LASHING OUT.
THEY NEED ME.
AS A *WARRIOR.*
AS A *PRIEST.*
AS A *GUIDE.*
IT'S A BOND BETWEEN US, LIKE THE BOND BETWEEN HOST AND LOA.
IT'S NOT MUCH.
BUT IT'S A PLACE TO *BEGIN.*
SHADOWMAN WILL RETURN IN
BOOK OF SHADOWS

GALLERY

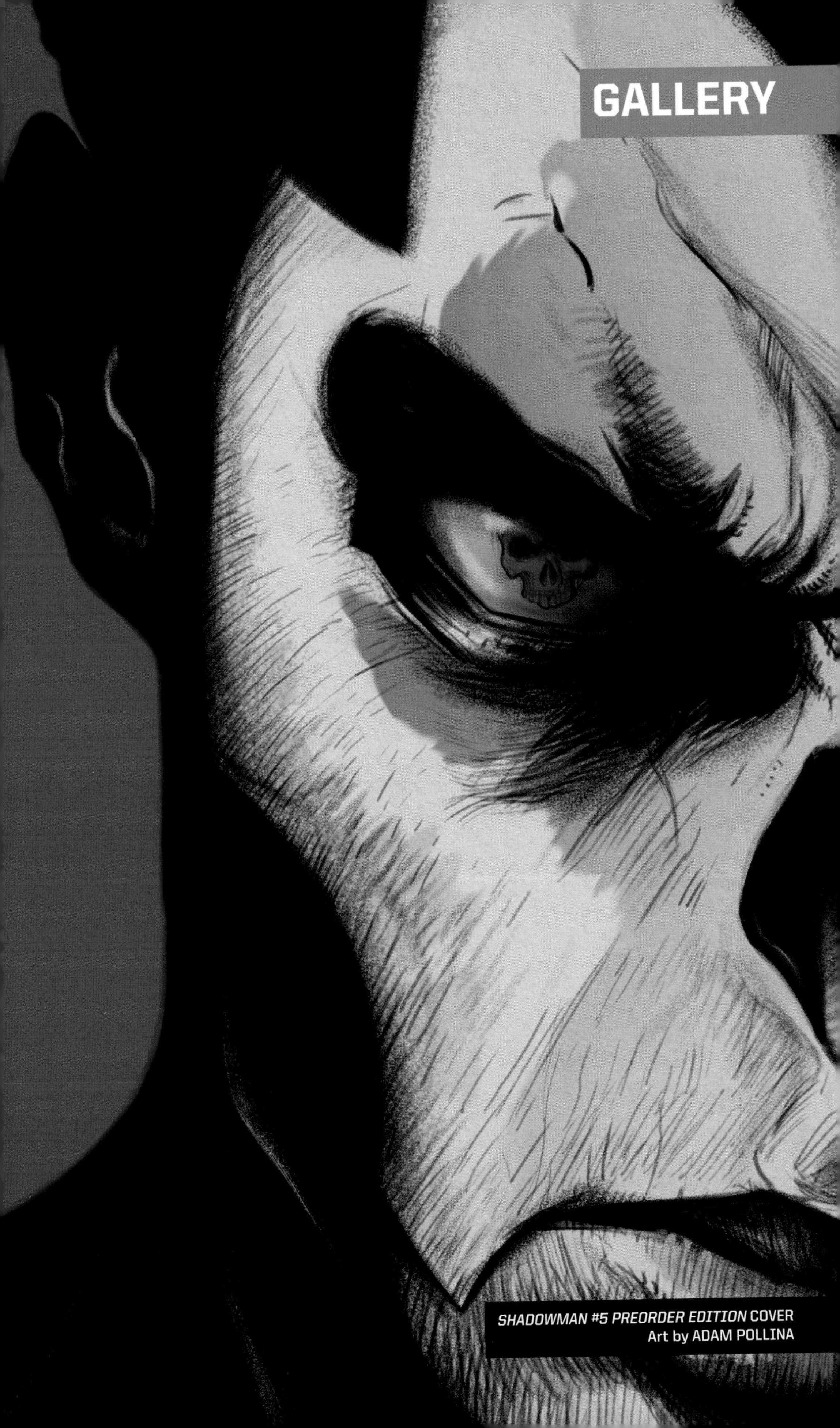

SHADOWMAN #5 PREORDER EDITION COVER
Art by ADAM POLLINA

SHADOWMAN #6 HORROR MOVIE
VARIANT COVER
Art by ADAM GORHAM

There are some very good reasons
to be afraid of the Deadside.
SHADOWMAN
VALIANT ENTERTAINMENT PRODUCTION JACK BONIFACE SHADOWMAN
CULLEN BUNN PEDRO ANDREO JORDIE BELLAIRE CLAYTON COWLES ADAM GORHAM
JACK BONIFACE ALYSSA MYLES THE NEW ABETTORS PUNK MAMBO SHADOWMAN
SHADOWMAN ISSUE #6 FEBRUARY 2022
VALIANT
VALIANTENTERTAINMENT.COM

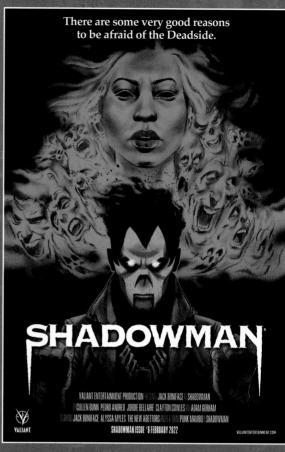

SHADOWMAN #6 PREORDER EDITION COVER
Art by PEDRO ANDREO with ANDREW DALHOUSE

SHADOWMAN #5 HORROR MOVIE
VARIANT COVER (facing)
Art by JONATHAN MARKS BARRAVECCHIA

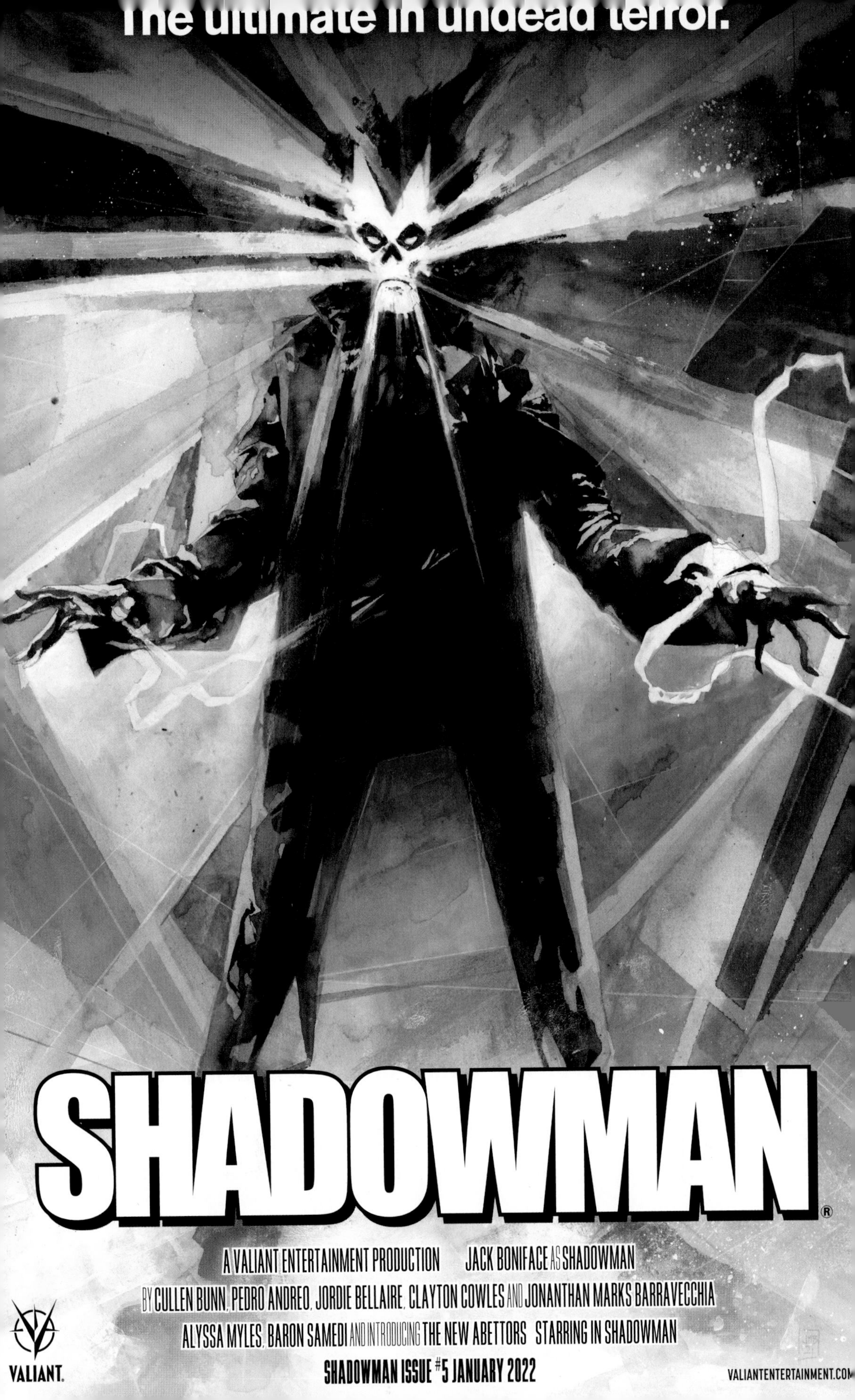
The ultimate in undead terror.
SHADOWMAN®
A VALIANT ENTERTAINMENT PRODUCTION
JACK BONIFACE AS SHADOWMAN
BY CULLEN BUNN, PEDRO ANDREO, JORDIE BELLAIRE, CLAYTON COWLES AND JONANTHAN MARKS BARRAVECCHIA
ALYSSA MYLES, BARON SAMEDI AND INTRODUCING THE NEW ABETTORS STARRING IN SHADOWMAN
SHADOWMAN ISSUE #5 JANUARY 2022
VALIANT.
VALIANTENTERTAINMENT.COM

SHADOWMAN #7 HORROR MOVIE
VARIANT COVER
Art by DAN BRERETON

The tide of terror that swept across the world is here.

THE SHADOWMAN®

VALIANT ENTERTAINMENT PRODUCTION PRESENTS JACK BONIFACE AS SHADOWMAN

BY CULLEN BUNN, PEDRO ANDREO, JORDIE BELLAIRE, CLAYTON COWLES AND DAN BRERETON

STARRING JACK BONIFACE, ALYSSA MYLES, THE NEW ABETTORS WITH SPECIAL GUEST APPEARANCE BY PUNK MAMBO

SHADOWMAN ISSUE #7 MARCH 2022

VALIANT.

VALIANTENTERTAINMENT.CO

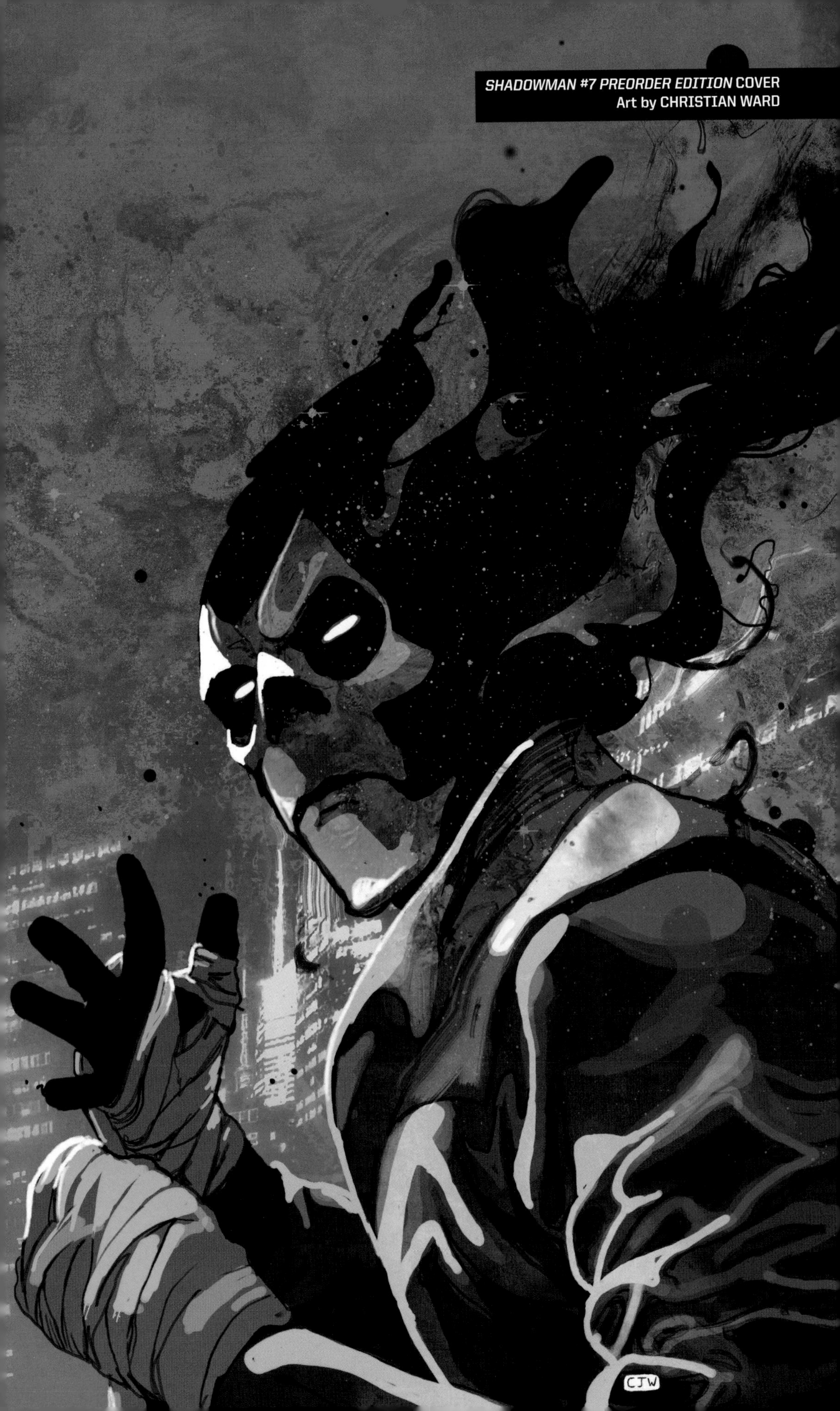
CJW

SHADOWMAN #7 PREORDER EDITION COVER
Art by CHRISTIAN WARD

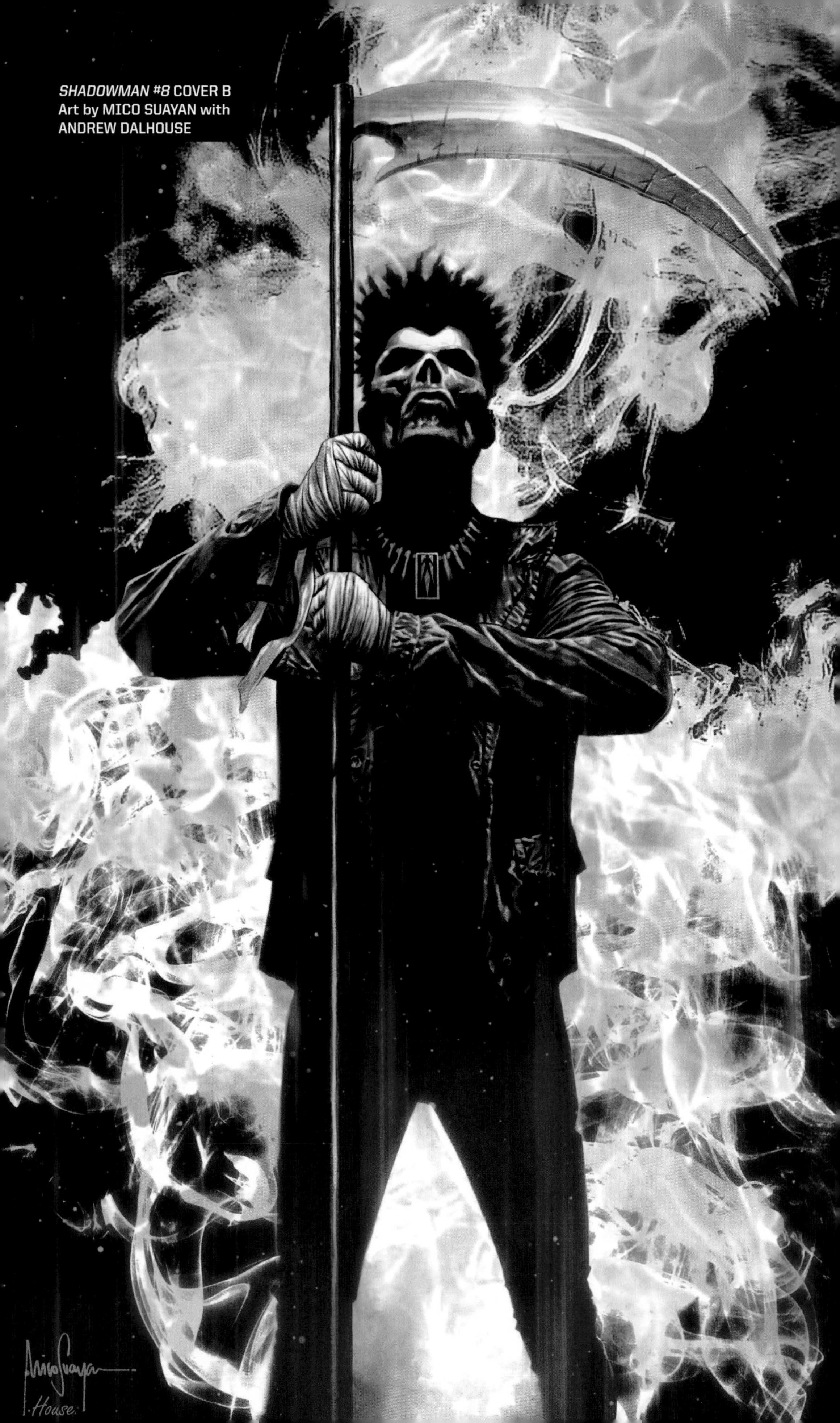

SHADOWMAN #8 COVER B
Art by MICO SUAYAN with
ANDREW DALHOUSE

THE FIGHT TO SAVE THE LIVESIDE:

Several different Valiant heroes fight against the forces of the Deadside. Although they are putting up a good fight, they do not fully grasp the powers they are up against. These heroes are:

NINJAK: a former special agent of MI6's Ninja Programme. He is the greatest mercenary in the Valiant Universe and an expert in many different types of combat.

THE ETERNAL WARRIOR: an immortal champion in the fight of good against evil. Millennia of training has allowed him to become an expert in most forms of combat.

BLOODSHOT: a super-soldier project created by the secret government organization Project Rising Spirit. Special nanites in his bloodstream give him a variety of powers, including the ability to recover from almost any trauma by consuming protein.

DOCTOR MIRAGE: a former TV personality, paranormal investigator, and scientist. She inherited the alias Doctor Mirage from her deceased husband, Li Hwen Mirage. She can communicate with the dead.

ROKU: a martial artist assassin and adversary to Ninjak. She is employed by the Weaponeer organization and is a member of the mysterious Shadow Seven.

X-O MANOWAR: a 5th Century Visigoth warrior, Aric of Dacia was abducted and enslaved by a race of aliens known as The Vine. Bonding with the sentient armor Shanhara, he managed to escape and found himself in the modern day. Together, they protect the Earth as X-O Manowar.

COPY BY **CULLEN BUNN**, ARTWORK BY **PEDRO ANDREO** WITH **JORDIE BELLAIRE**

ORIGINALLY PRESENTED IN **SHADOWMAN #7 PREORDER EDITION**

THE HOWARD STREET CEMETERY

In the heart of Salem, Massachusetts, lays the Howard Street Cemetery. This cemetery was the center of the 1692 witch hysteria that plagued Salem, and contains the bodies of its many early settlers. Although many innocents died at the hands of superstitious townsfolk, there was one man, named Giles Corey, that was deemed to be incomparably guilty.

Born in England around 1611, Corey emigrated to Salem and remained there until 1659. He owned an extensive plot of farmland, which bolstered his appearance of being a prosperous farmer. However, Corey's reputation, personality, and relationships damaged that persona. Although he had become a full member of the village's church and had close ties with the Porter faction, his reputation of selfishness toward others and his scandalous lifestyle made him a prime target to be accused of witchcraft. Corey's previous encounters with the law further supported his guilt during the witch trials. In 1675, Corey pummeled and killed a farm worker named Jacob Goodale. He was found guilty of the murder and ordered to pay a substantial fine.

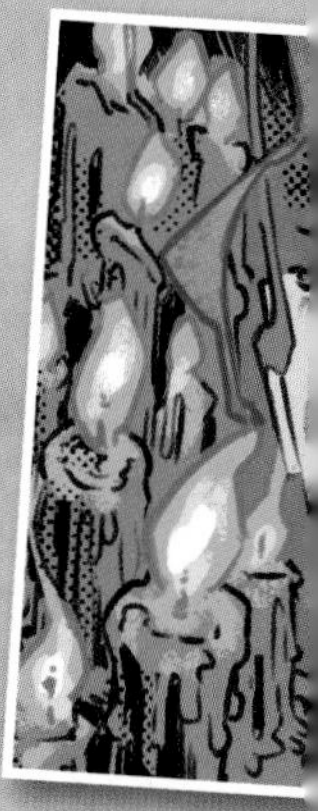

Giles Corey was one of the six men to be executed during the

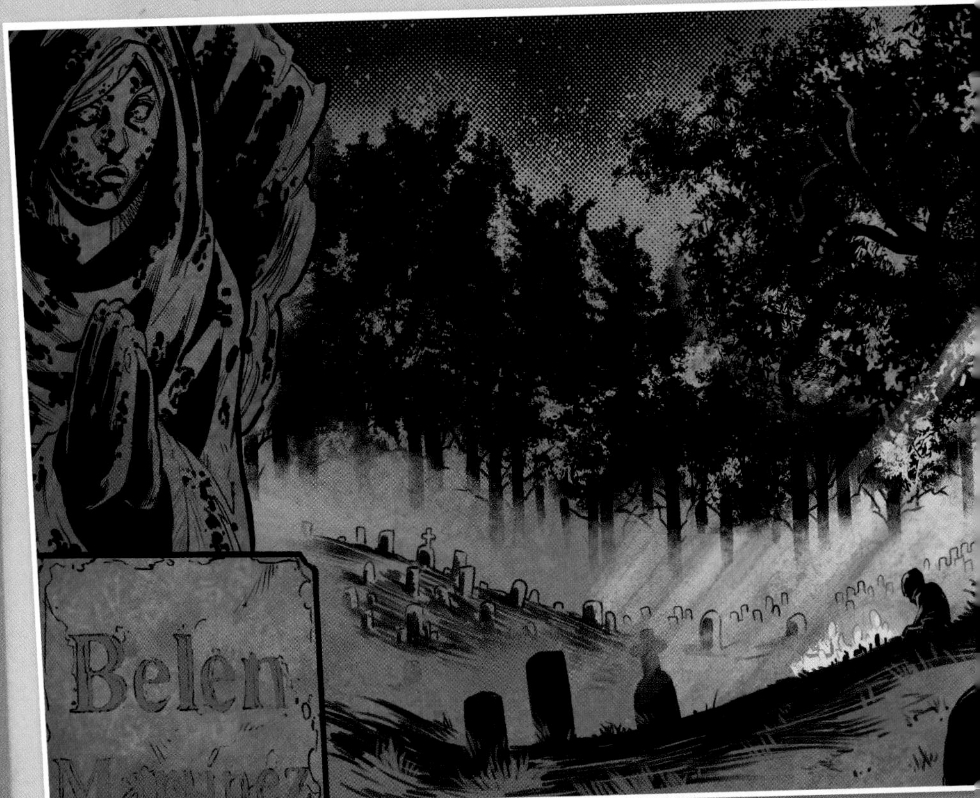
Belen

ORIGINALLY PRESENTED IN ***SHADOWMAN #5 PREORDER EDITION***

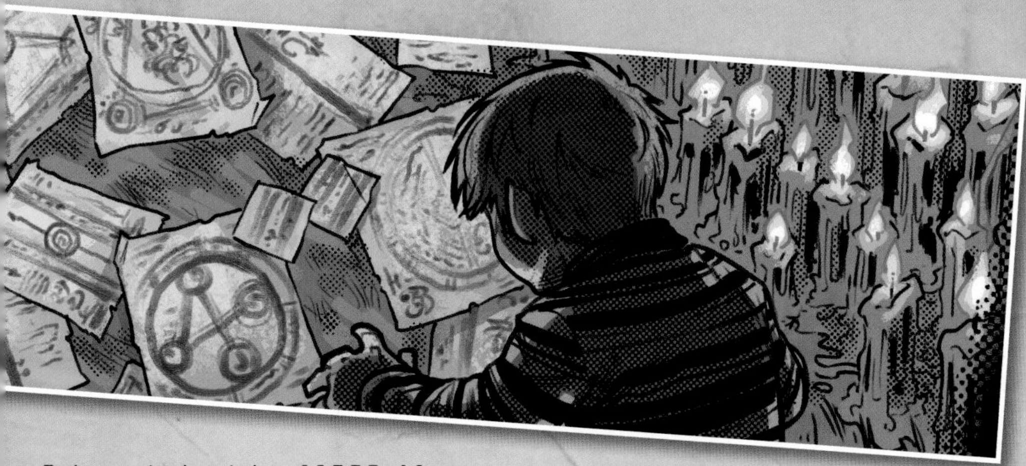

Salem witch trials of 1692. After being convicted, John Proctor, George Burroughs, George Jacobs Sr., John Willard, and Samuel Wardwell were all hanged. Corey, on the other hand, was pressed to death with stones because he refused to stand trial for crimes he did not commit. Giles Corey was slowly, tortuously, pressed to death in the field next to the jail. Rocks were piled onto his chest in an attempt to make him confess. With every denial, more rocks were added. His famous last words were "more weight," which were uttered as a final attempt to expedite his death while also showing that not even imminent death could convince him to stand trial. It is even told that the Sheriff took his cane and pressed Giles' tongue back into his mouth before he died after two days of being slowly crushed. Giles never admitted to being a witch, and with his last breath put a curse on the town.

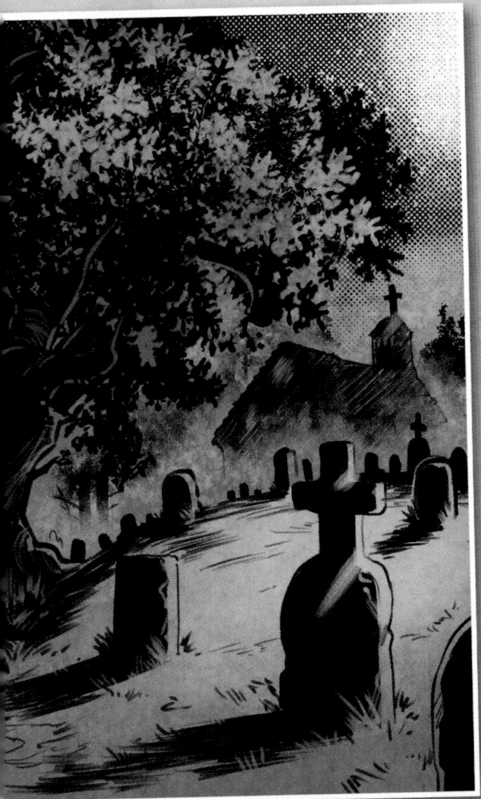

The Howard Street Cemetery was then established in 1801. The cemetery is reportedly haunted by Corey and some have claimed to feel his icy touch while walking through it. It is also rumored that his ghost appears in the cemetery shortly before a tragic event takes place in the town. Although he hasn't proved to be extraordinarily malicious, it's encouraged to use caution while traveling through the Howard Street Cemetery at night. ■

ARTWORK BY **PEDRO ANDREO** WITH **JORDIE BELLAIRE**

THE BLIGHTS OF WAVERLY HILL SANATORIUM

This story begins in 1883 when Major Thomas H. Hays bought the land known today as "Waverly Hill." On this plot of land, he constructed his family's home. Because their home was too far from any established schools, Hays decided to open a local school for his daughters to attend. This structure started as one-room schoolhouse, and he hired Lizzie Lee Harris as the teacher. Miss Harris had a fondness for Walter Scott's *Waverley* novels, so she named the schoolhouse Waverley School. Hays thought that the name sounded peaceful, and subsequently decided to name his property Waverley Hill to match.

Eventually, the Board of Tuberculosis Hospital bought the land from Hays and opened a sanatorium. In the early 1900s, Jefferson County was severely stricken with an outbreak of tuberculosis, and had the highest case rates in the whole country. The sickness skyrocketed at time because of all the wetlands along the Ohio River, which were perfect for the tuberculosis bacteria. To try to contain the disease, a two-story wooden sanatorium was opened, which consisted of an administrative building and two open air pavilions, each housing wenty patients, for the treatment of "early cases."

They decided to keep the name as Waverly Hills Sanatorium as a nod to the previous schoolhouse. On August 31, 1912, all tuberculosis patients from the Louisville City Hospital were relocated to temporary quarters in tents on the grounds of Waverly Hills pending the completion of a hospital for the "advanced cases."

In December 1912, this hospital was finally opened, but the delay lost many more lives for those that needed more stable quarters to heal. The medical staff was desperate. Patients at Waverly could expect treatments that varied from balloons implanted

in their lungs to the removal of ribs and chest muscle to allow for lung expansion—all without painkillers. And since antibiotics did not exist in the time that the sanatorium was active, other more subtle forms of aid were used to treat tuberculosis patients. For example, heat lamps, fresh air, and positive talk and reassurance helped to keep patients alive, since the death rate of tuberculosis patients at the time was one death per day. However, at the peak of the disease, the sight of the dead being carried away in full view of the patients lowered the patient morale. Therefore, the sanatorium tried transporting the dead bodies as secretively as possible to increase the morale and lower the death rates. To do this, they used a feature of the sanatorium called the tunnel.

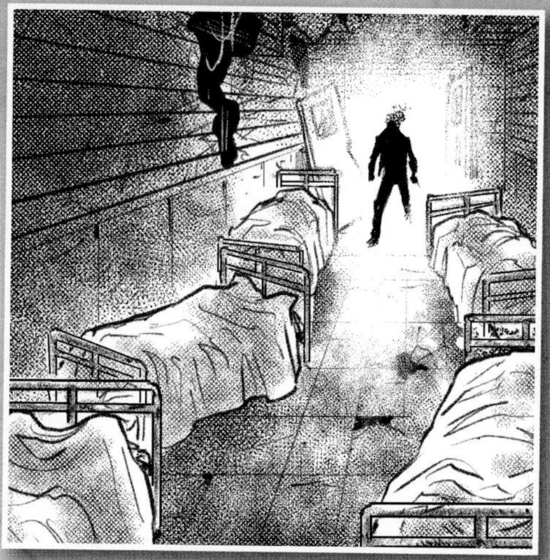

The tunnel was an entrance and exit for the workers of the sanatorium. It was built on the first floor with the rest of the building. The corridor is 500 feet to the bottom of the hill and has a set of stairs on one side, which were the stairs used for the workers. On the other side, there was a cart that moved up and down the staircase which transported supplies and other necessities. The doctors and workers of this time also believed that this would help to lower the disease's spreading rate.

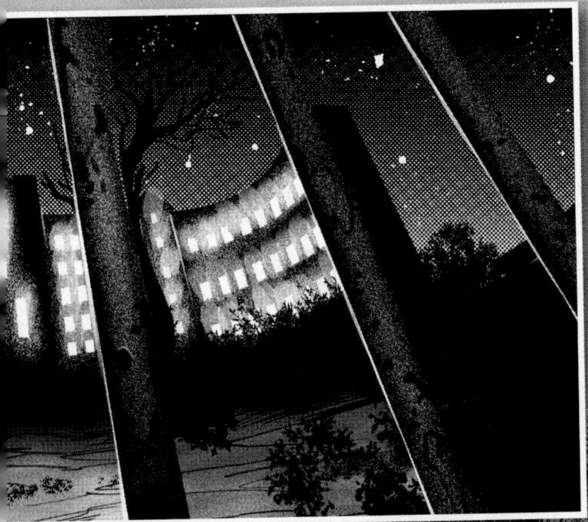

Amongst the many tales of hauntings at the Waverly Hill Sanatorium, two are the most common. There are reports of a nurse that could not handle the pressure of caring for so many sicks souls, and because of this, she hung herself. Her spirit still roams the abandoned halls. Another is that a little boy named Timmy had his life cut short. He spends his days looking for someone to play with—and they say if you roll a ball down an empty hall, it will often be returned. ■

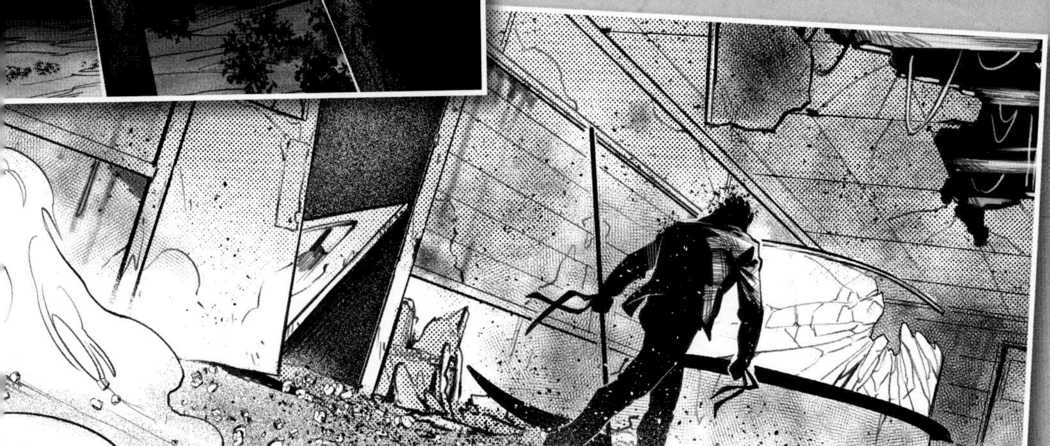

ARTWORK BY **PEDRO ANDREO** WITH **JORDIE BELLAIRE**

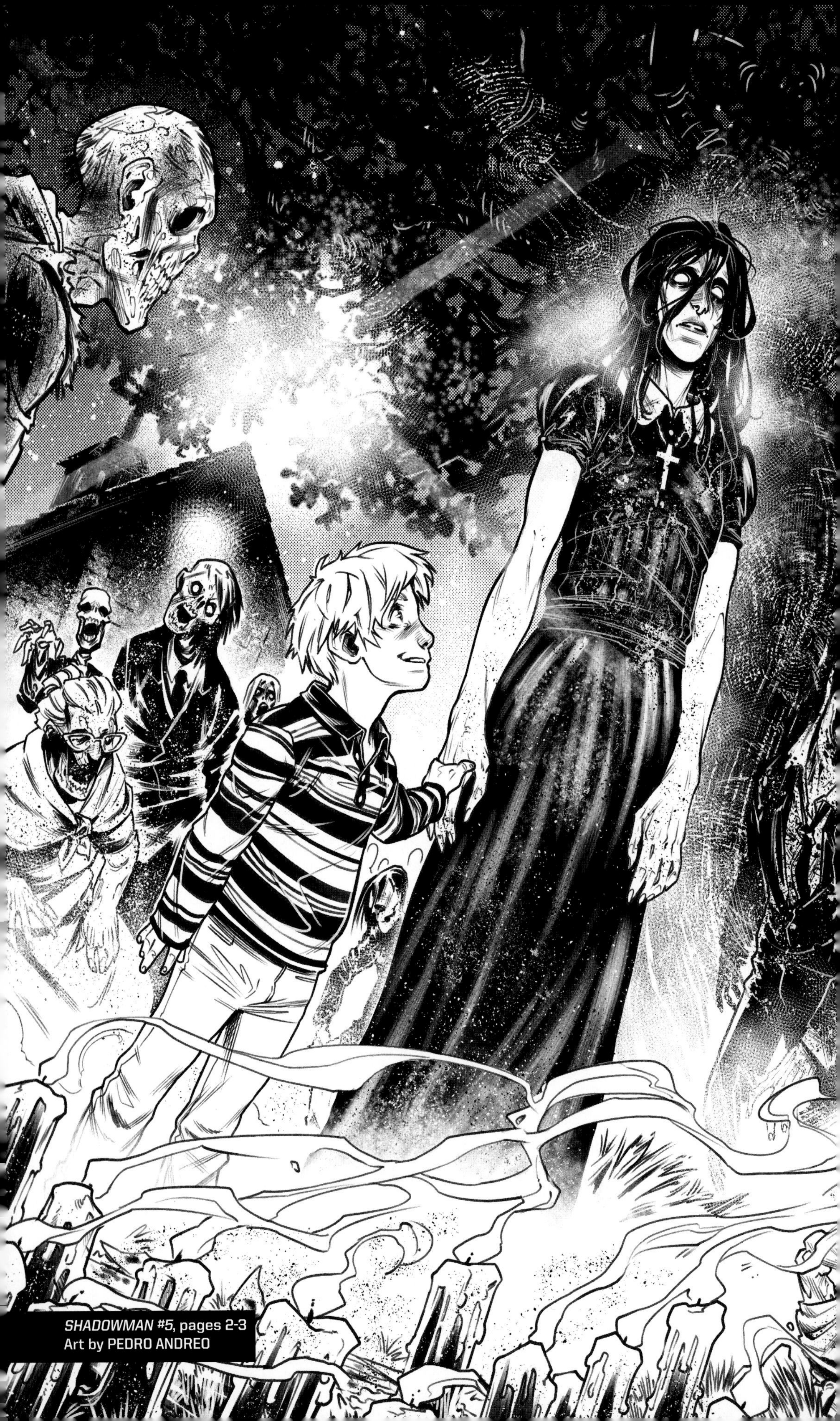

SHADOWMAN #5, pages 2-3
Art by PEDRO ANDREO

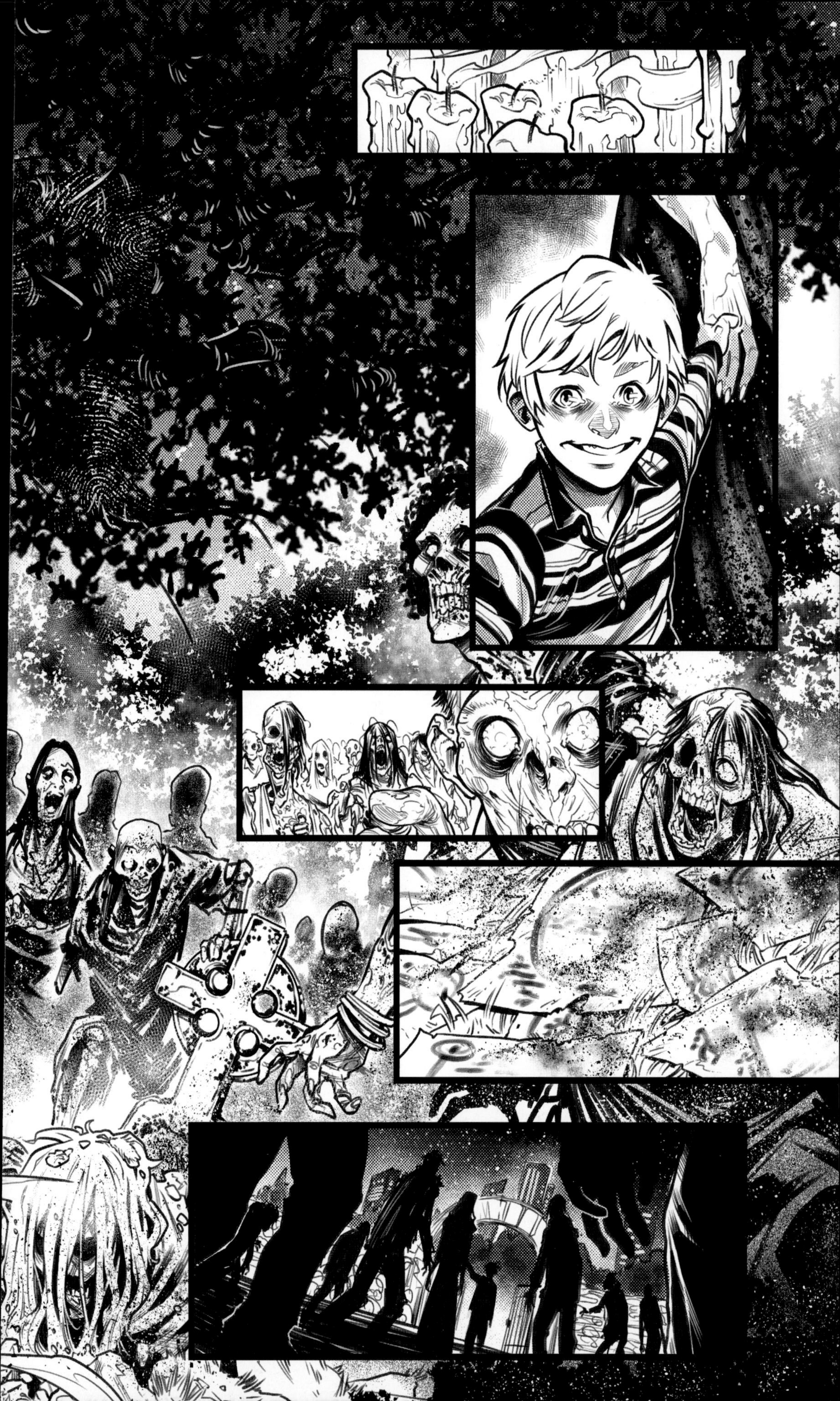

SHADOWMAN #5, pages 8, 9, and (facing) 10
Art by PEDRO ANDREO

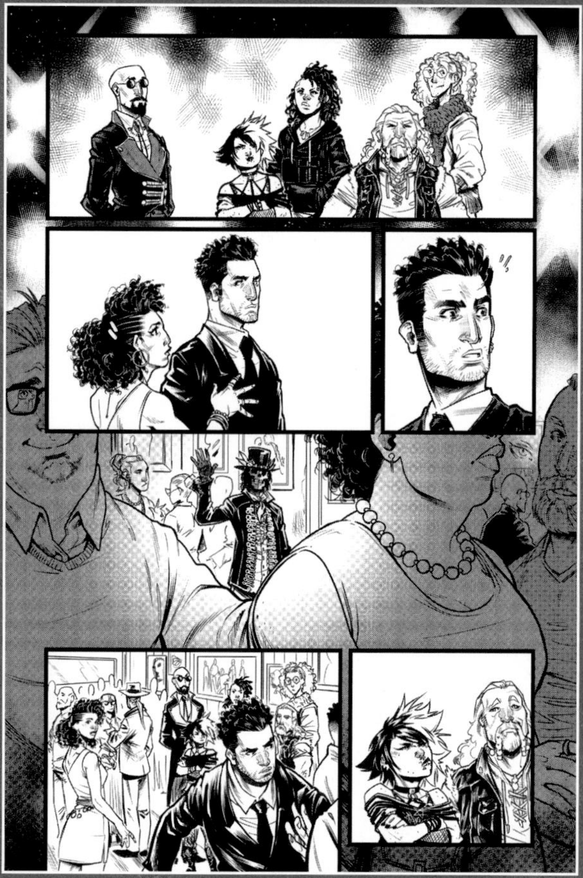

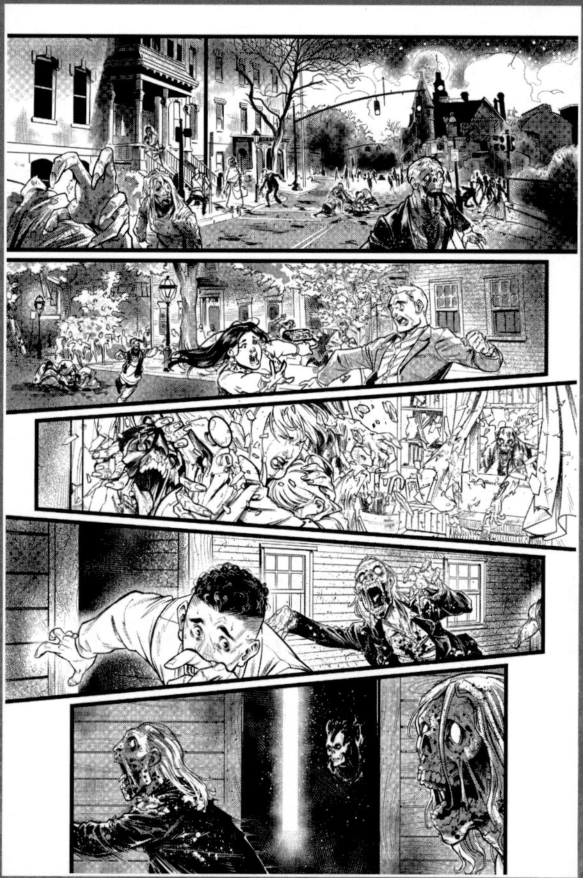

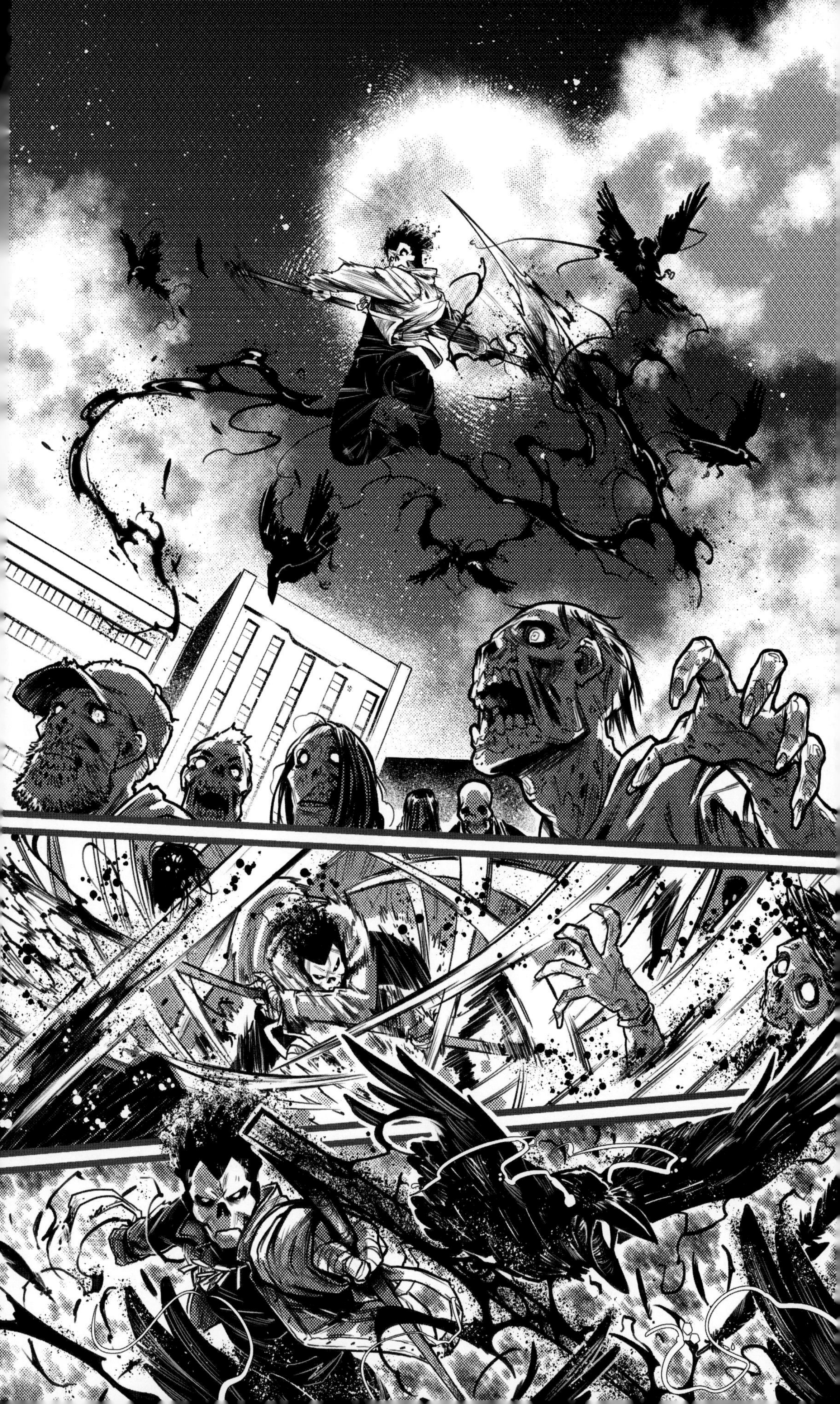

SHADOWMAN #6, pages 9, 10, and (facing) 11
Art by PEDRO ANDREO

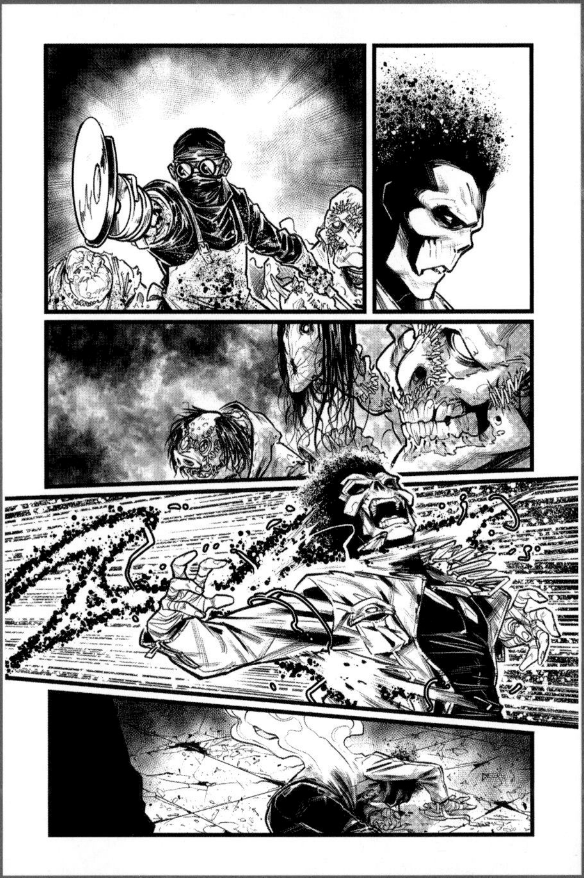

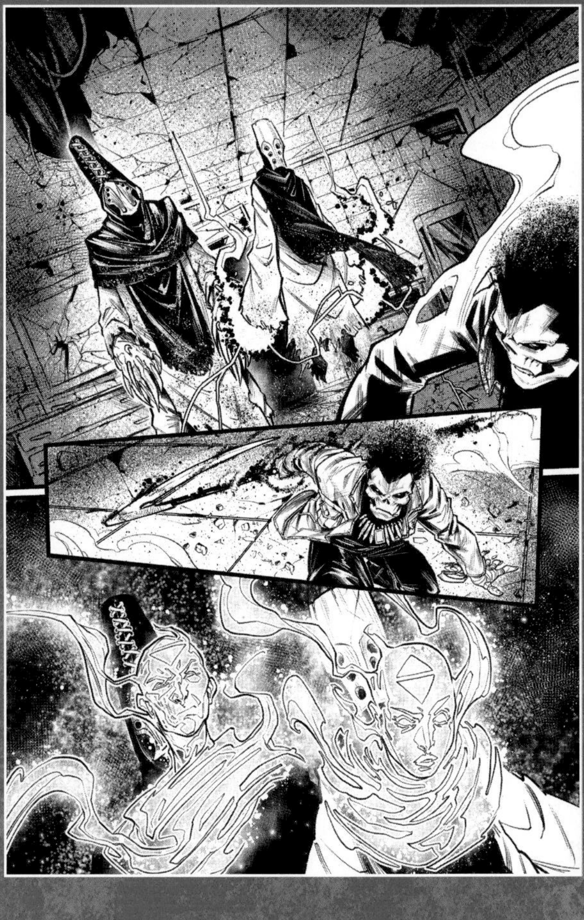

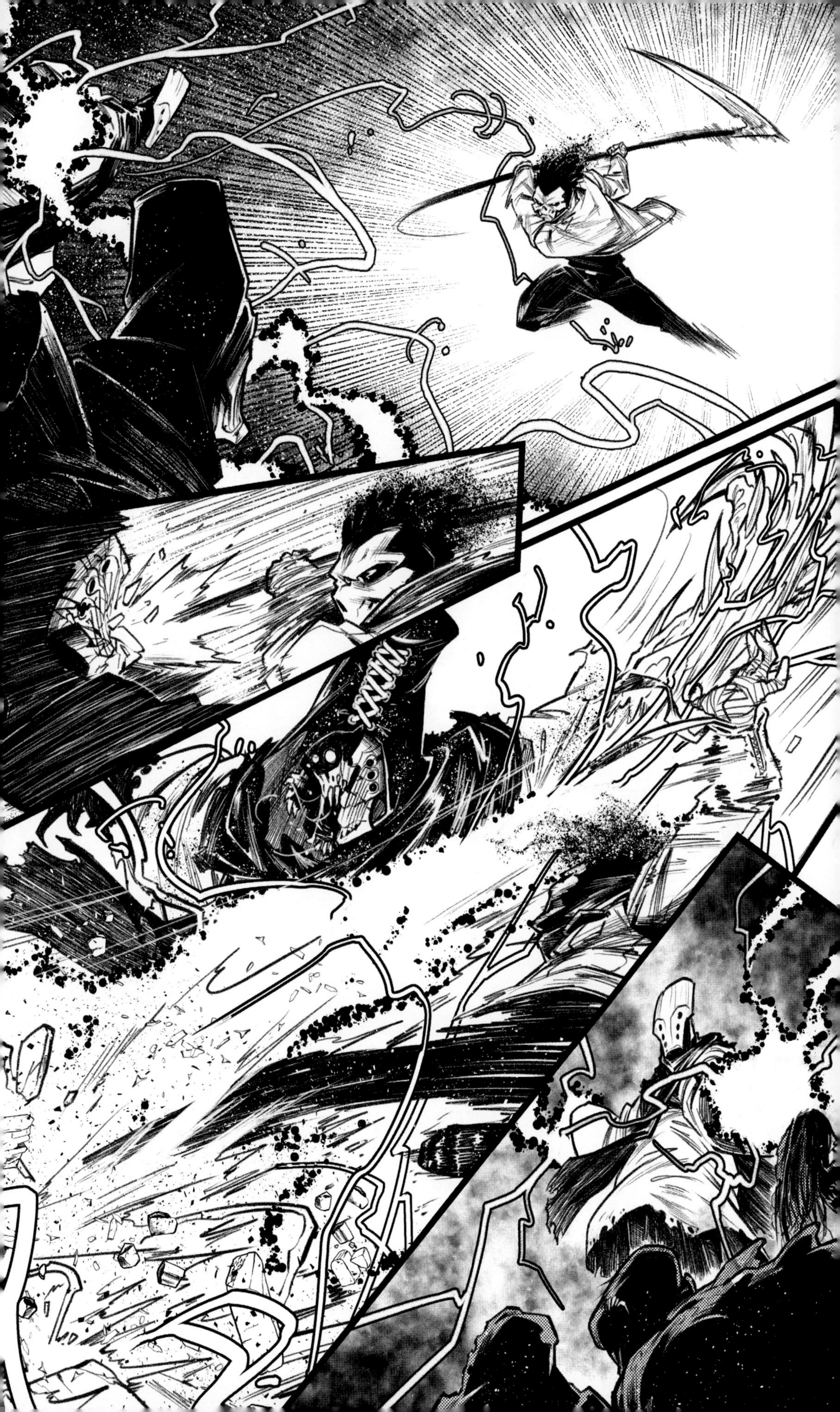

EXPLORE THE VALIANT U

ACTION & ADVENTURE

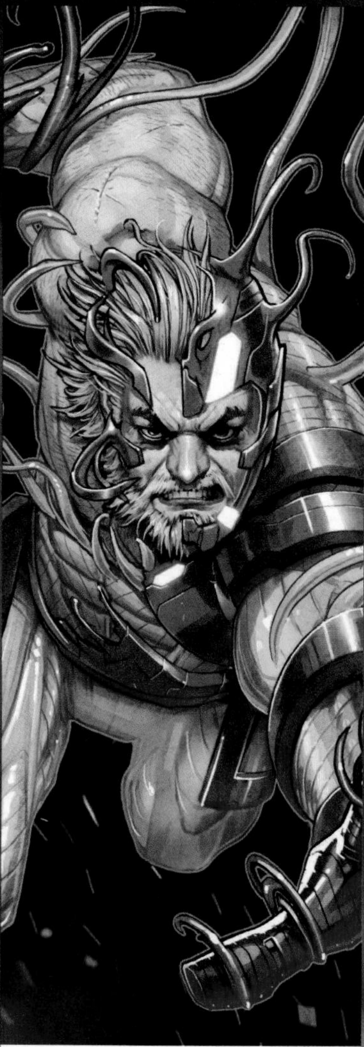

BLOODSHOT BOOK ONE
ISBN: 978-1-68215-255-3
NINJAK BOOK ONE
ISBN: 978-168215-410-6
SAVAGE
ISBN: 978-1-68215-189-1
WRATH OF THE ETERNAL WARRIOR VOL. 1: RISEN
ISBN: 978-1-68215-123-5
X-O MANOWAR (2019) BOOK ONE
ISBN: 978-1-68215-368-0

BLOCKBUSTER ADVENTURE

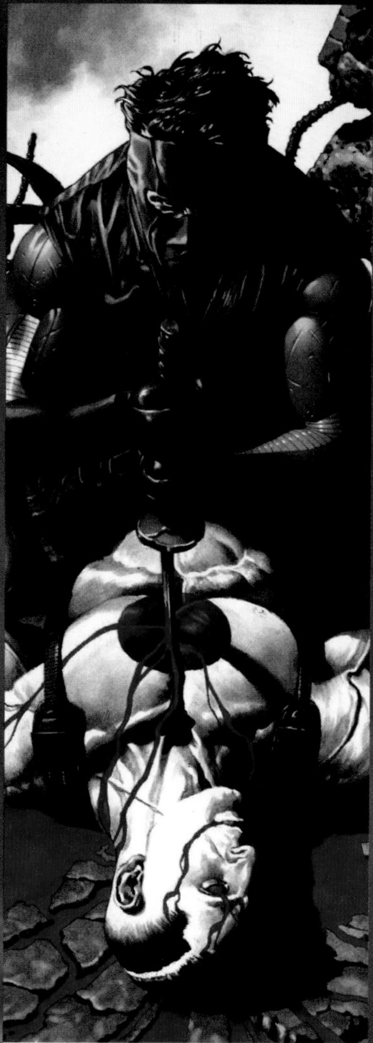

4001 A.D.
ISBN: 978-1-68215-143-3
ARMOR HUNTERS
ISBN: 978-1-939346-45-2
BOOK OF DEATH
ISBN: 978-1-939346-97-1
FALLEN WORLD
ISBN: 978-1-68215-331-4
HARBINGER WARS
ISBN: 978-1-939346-09-4
HARBINGER WARS 2
ISBN: 978-1-68215-289-8
INCURSION
ISBN: 978-1-68215-303-1
THE VALIANT
ISBN: 978-168215-364-2

COMEDY

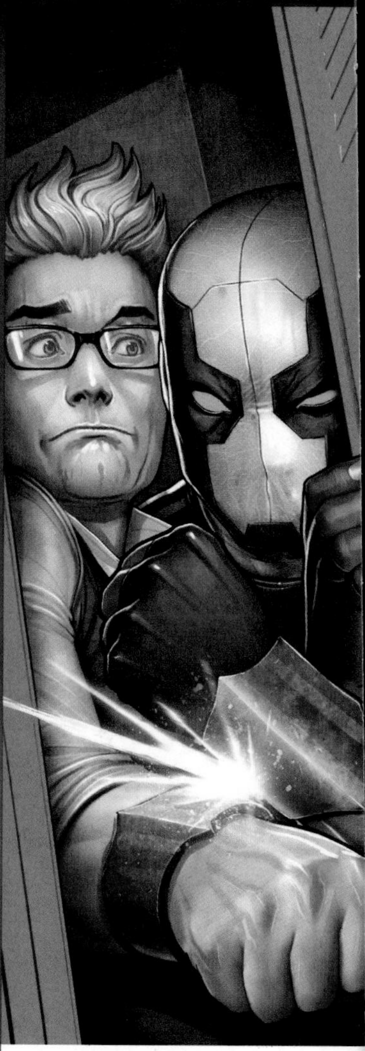

A&A: THE ADVENTURES OF ARCHER & ARMSTRONG VOL. 1: IN THE BAG
ISBN: 978-1-68215-149-5
THE DELINQUENTS
ISBN: 978-1-939346-51-3
QUANTUM AND WOODY! (2020): EARTH'S LAST CHOICE
ISBN: 978-1-68215-362-8

VERSE STARTING AT $9.99

HORROR & MYSTERY

SCIENCE FICTION & FANTASY

TEEN ADVENTURE

~BOOK OF~ SHADOWS

VALIANT

A SHADOW. A PUNK. A WARRIOR. A GHOST. A MYSTERY.

Master of horror Cullen Bunn (*Venom*) and bone-chilling artist Vicente Cifuentes (*Justice League Dark*) present BOOK OF SHADOWS, a supernatural event that forms a brand-new team in the Valiant Universe... but will they be enough to stop the wrath of Exarch Fane?

Collecting BOOK OF SHADOWS #1–4.

TRADE PAPERBACK
ISBN: 978-1-68215-436-6